Voices of the Civil War

Voices of the Civil War · Shenandoah 1864

By the Editors of Time-Life Books, Alexandria, Virginia

Contents

THE SHENANDOAH VALLEY

War returned to the Shenandoah Valley of Virginia in 1864, as the opposing armies fought their way up and down the length of this vital region. This artist's rendering shows the setting for a six-month-long campaign that featured a succession of clashes large and small and ended with Federal control of the Valley.

Tom's Brook

Valley Turnpike

MASSANUTTEN MOUNTAIN

New Market

Harrisonburg

Luray

South Fork of the Shenandoah River

Thornton's Gap

To Lexington

Staunton

Port Republic

Fisher's Gap

Piedmont

Swift Run Gap

BLUE RIDGE MOUNTAINS

Waynesboro

Brown's Gap

Rockfish Gap

Stanardsville

Culpeper

Charlottesville

To Lynchburg

Hagerstown

Martinsburg

Winchester　Stephenson's Depot

Shepherdstown

trasburg　Kernstown

SOUTH MOUNTAIN

Charles Town

Berryville

Harpers Ferry

Middletown

Frederick

Shenandoah River

Monocacy Junction

Front Royal

Snicker's Gap

Leesburg

Ashby's Gap

Manassas Gap

Purcellville

Chester Gap

Potomac River

Rockville

Warrenton

Manassas Junction

Washington, D.C.

Alexandria

Potomac River

7

Return to the Valley

On the night of May 10, 1864, the cadets of the Virginia Military Institute in Lexington were abruptly roused from their bunks by the rattling of drums calling them to muster. It had been a day of light duty for the young men, with ceremonies marking the first anniversary of the death of General Thomas Jonathan "Stonewall" Jackson, who had been a professor at VMI before gaining immortality on the battlefield.

For three years these cadets had devoured the news of the war and longed to be of service to the cause for which their fallen hero, Jackson, had given his all. But so far the conflict had not intruded on their quiet campus in the Shenandoah Valley. That was soon to change.

After the more than 200 cadets found their places in formation, their adjutant stepped foward and delivered an electrifying message. On the orders of Major General John C.

Residents go about their business on Lexington's main street after the departure of General David Hunter's Federals. In the distance stand the burned-out ruins of VMI, a target of the destructive three-day Yankee visit in June 1864.

Breckinridge, commander of the Department of Western Virginia, the young men were to march at dawn. The Yankees were threatening again in the Valley, and this time the cadets were joining the ranks to resist them.

Committing these boy soldiers to combat duty was an extreme measure that reflected the Confederacy's dire situation. VMI was the West Point of the South, and its cadets represented the cream of the Confederacy's young manhood. They were being groomed to take their place in the next generation of Southern military leaders.

But Breckinridge was woefully short of manpower and needed every able-bodied infantryman he could find to confront the latest Yankee threat. He could expect no reinforcements from General Robert E. Lee, who was being pressed by the Federals to the east as never before. Lee's Army of Northern Virginia, itself outnumbered, was grudgingly giving ground in Virginia's Wilderness, hounded by Lieutenant General Ulysses S. Grant's Army of the Potomac.

Lee depended on the Shenandoah Valley to provision his army. This lush, productive region along Virginia's western border was one of the Confederacy's cornucopia. Unlike the war-scarred terrain of eastern Virginia, the Valley's land, protected by the barrier of the Blue Ridge Mountains, had not been much trampled by passing armies. The battles fought in the Valley—notably those of Stonewall Jackson's 1862 campaign—had been few and relatively small.

Having thus remained in Confederate hands for the past three years, the Valley continued to produce the food supplies that helped sustain the Rebel fighting men. To lose its bounty now would be a disaster. Losing the Valley would also mean cutting vital lines of communication —the Virginia Central Railroad, with its main station at Staunton, and the Virginia & Tennessee Railroad, which wound its way to Richmond through the Blue Ridge and Lynchburg. Even worse, from the Rebel point of view, a Federal force in the Valley would be in a position to strike a blow—perhaps a decisive one— against Lee's left flank.

The Confederate forces available to defend the Valley were small and scattered. Brigadier General John D. Imboden had 1,000 cavalrymen and 600 raw militia around his Valley District headquarters at Staunton. About 150 miles to the southwest, at Dublin, Breckinridge could muster 6,500 men.

Breckinridge was a seasoned leader. In 1856, at age 35, he had become the youngest man ever elected vice president of the United States. He was representing his home state of Kentucky in the U.S. Senate when the war broke out; after some soul-searching he joined the Confederate army.

As a brigadier general, he had led troops at Shiloh, Corinth, Vicksburg, and Chattanooga. Major General John B. Gordon, who would soon serve with Breckinridge in the Valley, admired him greatly. "Tall, erect and commanding in physique," Gordon later wrote, "he would have been selected in any martial group as a typ-

ical leader. Under fire and in extreme peril he was strikingly courageous, alert and self-poised."

Now, in May 1864, Breckinridge faced Federal threats coming from two directions. On May 2 Union brigadier general George Crook marched out of the Kanawha Valley of West Virginia with 6,000 infantrymen, heading southeast toward Dublin. His orders were to cut the Virginia & Tennessee Railroad at the New River Bridge and then advance on Staunton and sever the Virginia Central. At the same time, Breckinridge learned of the approach of a Yankee army of 8,500 men under Major General Franz Sigel, which was advancing south up the Valley from Martinsburg.

The Rebel commander moved swiftly, sending about half his force on a rigorous march to Staunton while he raced ahead on horseback with his staff. The other half of his army was to stay put and meet Crook's attack.

Although the outnumbered Rebels left behind at Dublin were well deployed for the defense, Crook's Federals, at a cost of almost 700 men, overpowered them in a brief but fierce clash known as the Battle of Cloyd's Mountain. The Confederates suffered 530 casualties, including their commander, Brigadier General Albert G. Jenkins, who was mortally wounded. Outside town the next morning, Crook's men burned the New River Bridge while a Federal band played martial airs.

Having accomplished the first part of his mission, Crook now suffered a curious collapse of will. Instead of advancing on Staunton to link up with Sigel, he withdrew 50 miles west into the Alleghenies—later claiming that he feared being cut off by forces detached from Lee's army. His timidity would prove costly— now Breckinridge had only Sigel to deal with.

German-born Franz Sigel was a political general—a prime example of that breed of

Civil War commander who, without having shown any evidence of military competence, was awarded high rank because of his influential position in civilian life. The leader of St. Louis' large German community when the war broke out, Sigel received a commission and rapid promotion to major general, primarily to encourage enlistment among the 1.25 million German-Americans in the North.

Grant expected nothing of Sigel in the Valley; in his mind it was Crook who would do the important work. But Sigel could at least meet Crook in Staunton with reinforcements and supplies. "If Sigel can't skin, himself," Grant said in a Lincolnesque bit of homespun philosophy, "he can hold a leg whilst someone else skins."

Sigel interrupted his march frequently, jittery over rumors of the enemy lurking on all sides. He lingered in Winchester for days, drilling his men—he and his staff shouting orders in German to perplexed officers who understood not a word. On May 5 he staged a mock battle in which an entire regiment, obeying orders, marched away and, having been forgotten, kept marching for the entire day. The

On May 15, 1864, John C. Breckinridge's Rebels defeated Franz Sigel at New Market, Virginia. On May 19 a new Federal commander, David Hunter, ordered farms and other property burnt, and Lee dispatched a force under Jubal Early to oppose him. After defeating Hunter at Lynchburg on June 18, Early invaded Maryland, advancing to Washington, D.C., before turning back. Philip Sheridan was then ordered to head a unified Federal command and take the Valley. In the fall, Sheridan won battles at Winchester, Fisher's Hill, and Cedar Creek, achieving Federal control of the region.

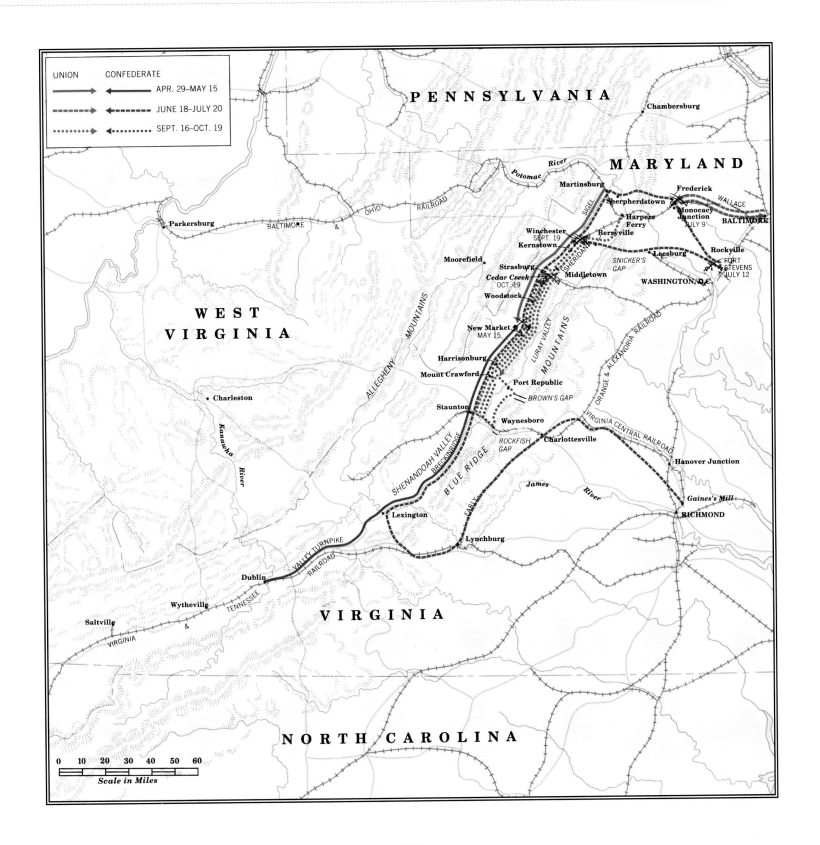

UNION   CONFEDERATE

APR. 29–MAY 15

JUNE 18–JULY 20

SEPT. 16–OCT. 19

PENNSYLVANIA

Chambersburg

MARYLAND

Potomac   River

Parkersburg

BALTIMORE   &   OHIO   RAILROAD

Martinsburg

Sherpherdstown

Harpers
Ferry

Frederick

Monocacy
Junction
JULY 9

WALLACE

BALTIMORE

SIGEL

Winchester
SEPT. 19

Kernstown

Bernyville

SHERIDAN

SNICKER'S
GAP

Leesburg

Rockville

FORT
STEVENS
JULY 12

Moorefield

Strasburg

Cedar Creek
OCT. 19

Middletown

WASHINGTON, D.C.

Woodstock

WEST
VIRGINIA

ALLEGHENY   MOUNTAINS

LURAY VALLEY

MOUNTAINS

New Market
MAY 15.

ORANGE & ALEXANDRIA RAILROAD

Harrisonburg

Mount Crawford

Port Republic

BROWN'S GAP

Charleston

Staunton

Waynesboro

VIRGINIA CENTRAL RAILROAD

Kanawha

River

SHENANDOAH VALLEY

BRECKINRIDGE

BLUE RIDGE

ROCKFISH
GAP

Charlottesville

Hanover Junction

James   River

Gaines's Mill

Lexington

EARLY

Lynchburg

RICHMOND

Dublin

VALLEY TURNPIKE   RAILROAD

Wytheville

TENNESSEE

VIRGINIA

Saltville

&

VIRGINIA

NORTH   CAROLINA

0   10   20   30   40   50   60

Scale in Miles

debacle, said a Federal officer, "bred in everyone the most supreme contempt for General Sigel and his crowd of foreign adventurers."

While Sigel was playing at war, Imboden's Confederate cavalry was bedeviling his advance. On May 5 a company of rangers under Captain John H. "Hanse" McNeill emerged from hideouts and destroyed a Baltimore & Ohio Railroad repair shop and storage yard. When Sigel sent 500 of his troopers after McNeill, Imboden staged an ambush that routed the Yankee pursuers. A few days later Imboden surprised the 1st New York Cavalry outside New Market, putting those Yankees to desperate flight, mostly on foot, into the nearby mountains.

Breckinridge, meanwhile, led his troops— the VMI cadets included—north out of Staunton at dawn on May 13. Early on the morning of the 15th, in a steady downpour, he intercepted Sigel on the outskirts of New Market. Breckinridge deployed his forces astride the Valley Turnpike and moved foward. Supported by artillery, the Confederates climbed steadily up Manor's Hill and brushed aside Sigel's first line of defense.

Sigel organized a new line farther north, on Bushong's Hill. Breckinridge brought his artillery up, rode along his line to steady his men, and gave the order to charge. But just as the Rebels came within musket shot of Sigel's main line, their advance stalled and a barrage of Federal artillery abruptly blew open a gap in their line.

A Yankee countercharge through that gap might cost the battle. Breckinridge was forced to make a difficult decision. "Put in the cadets," an officer urged.

"They are only children," anguished Breckinridge. "Will they stand?" A few moments later, however, he gave the command: "Put the boys in, and may God forgive me for the order."

The cadets rose with a cheer and surged foward into a storm of Federal shot and shell. A number of them went down, but the rest resolutely charged into the gap. The inspirited Rebel line resumed its surge foward, swarming over Bushong's Hill and putting Sigel's army to flight northward.

When Breckinridge realized that the victory was his, he rode over to the cadets. "Well done, Virginians," he said to them proudly. "Well done, men." But the boy soldiers had paid a high price for their moment of glory— 10 killed and 47 wounded, almost one fourth of their number.

In the wake of the battle at New Market, both high commands made changes. Now that the threat to the Valley had been averted—perhaps for months, the Confederates hoped—Robert E. Lee recalled Breckinridge to join him at New Hanover in the fight against Grant's Army of the Potomac. And Washington replaced the incompetent Sigel with an exceedingly aggressive officer who determined to give the Valley no respite.

Major General David Hunter, the new commander, was a tense, scowling officer who frequently boiled over with rage. More than anything else, he despised slavery and eagerly sought opportunities to punish anyone connected with that institution—including civilians.

Grant instructed Hunter to join Crook and destroy rail hubs, first at Charlottesville, then at Lynchburg. But Hunter began a campaign of destruction before he ever reached a railroad. On May 24, south of Winchester, he burned a house merely on the suspicion that it harbored a sniper.

As his army of 8,500 moved south, the burning continued. Hunter wrought havoc with an enthusiasm that sometimes disturbed even his own men. Every day, whether or not shots had been fired, columns of smoke from burning houses and barns marked the army's course up the Valley. His nickname, Black Dave, given to him years earlier because of his dark hair and swarthy face, now took on a new, more sinister meaning.

Confederate forces in the Shenandoah, meanwhile, had now come under the command of Brigadier General William E. "Grumble" Jones, a cantankerous disciplinarian who swore at his men and drilled them endlessly but nevertheless earned their respect. Under orders from Richmond to stop the new Federal threat, Jones gathered all available forces— 5,600 men—and maneuvered them into a blocking position at the village of Piedmont, eight miles south of Port Republic.

On the morning of June 5, the Federals repeatedly attacked Jones' Rebels but were unable to dislodge them from their breastworks. By the afternoon, Hunter was discouraged and ready to withdraw but decided on a last assault. This time the Yankees managed to break part of the enemy line, and fortunes turned in an instant. Jones, trying to rally his men, was shot dead from his horse, and the demoralized Rebels fell back in disorder.

At a cost of 830 casualties, Hunter had dealt the Confederate force a smashing blow, killing or wounding 600 and taking more than 1,000 prisoners. For the first time in the war, a Federal army was now loose in the Valley.

On the day after the battle, Hunter descended on Staunton to impose a harsh lesson on the defenseless town. Although he had instructed his troops to concentrate on wrecking property of military significance, individual Federal soldiers joined with "riffraff of the town" in looting Staunton.

On June 8 Crook and the Army of the Kanawha arrived, swelling Hunter's force to 18,000 men. Hunter intended to take them eastward across the Blue Ridge to seize Lynchburg and its huge rail hub and supply depot.

Responding to this danger, Robert E. Lee sent for one of his best subordinates, Lieutenant General Jubal A. Early, and ordered him to take the Army of Northern Virginia's Second Corps west. He was to save Lynchburg and drive Hunter from the Valley. Then, if Early deemed it feasible, he should go farther—strike north into Maryland and all the way to Washington, D.C., forcing Grant to loosen his grip on Richmond and Petersburg.

Early was a profane, tobacco-chewing curmudgeon known to his men as Old Jube. He was indifferent to his own appearance, dismissive of advice, and quick to blame his subordinates when something went wrong. Major Henry Kyd Douglas, formerly of his staff, candidly cataloged Early's complexities: "Arbitrary, cynical, with strong prejudices, he was personally disagreeable; he made few admirers or friends either by his manners or his habits." But as Lee well knew, he was a fighter.

As Early hastily got under way, Hunter's Federals paused at Lexington on their march to Lynchburg and stayed long enough to burn the Virginia Military Institute, having deemed it both an enemy military installation and a breeding ground of treason. Then the Federals set out again, crossing the Blue Ridge. On June 17, as Hunter approached Lynchburg, delaying actions by Rebel cavalry slowed his advance to a crawl. That afternoon Early raced into the town with the vanguard of his three divisions.

The next morning, while Hunter was deploying his army and probing toward the city, Early lashed out at the Federals. Stunned by this sudden escalation of enemy resistance, Hunter concluded, incorrectly, that he faced

impossible odds—"a force at least double the numerical strength of mine." He abandoned the attack and withdrew during the night, not stopping until he had fled through the Alleghenies and into the Kanawha Valley. Early now had a wide-open path to Washington.

Early's army of 10,000 infantrymen, many marching in worn-out shoes or barefoot, started north down the Valley pike. Although the general and his men had grown hardened to the havoc of war, they were shocked by the ravages of "Black Dave" Hunter in the Shenandoah. "Houses had been burned, and helpless women and children left without shelter," Early wrote later. "The country had been stripped of provisions and many families left without a morsel to eat."

On July 5 Early's troops crossed the Potomac River at Shepherdstown, entering Union territory. The next day, as the Rebel columns marched eastward through Maryland, Brigadier General John McCausland took his brigade of cavalry north to Hagerstown and threatened to burn the place unless paid a ransom—reparation for Hunter's destruction of civilian property in the Valley. He collected $20,000 from the city fathers.

As word of the Rebel invasion spread, Federal authorities scrambled to throw a roadblock across Early's path. While Grant sent a division northward from the Army of the Potomac, Major General Lewis Wallace, responsible for the western approaches to Washington and Baltimore, assembled a patchwork force of militiamen and home guards at Monocacy Junction, through which the road to the capital passed.

On the morning of July 9, Early found Wallace's little force—now augmented by two brigades from the Army of the Potomac's VI Corps—in position on high ground behind the Monocacy River, guarding the B&O Railroad

bridge and a smaller wooden span nearby. Early sent one of his divisions directly against the Federals at the railroad bridge and dispatched another to ford the river and assail the position from below, on the Yankee left.

Wallace's troops put up a surprisingly effective defense, but Early's larger force attacked repeatedly and gradually wore the Federals down. Late in the afternoon, the Rebels finally broke Wallace's line, cleared the railroad bridge, and sent the Yankees retreating.

As Early's columns drew closer to Washington, government agencies in the capital flew into a frenzy. Officials combed the hospitals for walking wounded and dragooned government employees, and marched these conscripts to the city's defenses. At the same time they prepared the Potomac bridges for demolition.

Despite this alarm, there was little real threat to the capital. The city was surrounded by a formidable ring of forts bristling with cannon and mortars. About 10,000 troops could be assembled to defend Washington, and 15,000 more were on their way from the Army of the Potomac.

At midday on July 11 Early drew up before Fort Stevens, the northernmost of Washington's fortresses, beyond which he could see the dome of the U.S. Capitol five miles away. He thought the fort "feebly manned" and ordered an immediate attack.

But the effort was more than Early's men were up to. Exhausted from marching, fighting, and extreme summer heat, they were too weak to do more than spar with the fort's skirmishers. That night, Early learned that massive reinforcements were streaming into Washington from Virginia and realized that he would soon have to withdraw.

The next day, as Early's troops peppered the fort with musket fire, President Abraham

Lincoln arrived in a carriage to view the action. To the horror of those present, the president stood on the parapet, exposed to Rebel fire, and descended only with reluctance.

That evening Early gave his army the command to turn around and head back to Virginia. "He seemed in a droll humor, perhaps one of relief," Henry Kyd Douglas remembered. "For he said to me in his falsetto drawl: 'Major, we haven't taken Washington, but we've scared Abe Lincoln like hell!'" Early marched almost due west, through Leesburg and across the Blue Ridge to Berryville, pursued ineffectually by Federal troops. By July 22 he had reconcentrated his army at Strasburg.

To his north, at Kernstown, Crook had amassed a Federal force of 12,000 infantrymen with orders to hound the retreating Early out of the Valley. But suddenly Early was no longer retreating. On the morning of July 24, he doubled back on the Valley pike and launched a surprise attack at Kernstown that slammed into the unsuspecting Federals. Their lines disintegrating, Crook's troops fled northward across the Potomac into Maryland.

Once more the Yankees had been humiliated and the Valley saved for the Confederacy. In hot pursuit of the fleeing enemy, Early tore up some B&O tracks at Martinsburg and sent his cavalry on raiding forays. On July 30 Rebel troopers under General McCausland occupied Chambersburg, Pennsylvania, and demanded $100,000 in gold as further reparation for Hunter's destruction in the Shenandoah. When the money was not forthcoming, McCausland burned the town.

But Early's threat against Washington would turn out to be the Confederacy's high-water mark in the campaign. Soon Ulysses S. Grant, frustrated by Federal reverses in the Valley, would pick a worthy adversary for "Old Jube."

CHRONOLOGY

1864

May 9	*Battle of Cloyd's Mountain*
May 15	*Battle of New Market*
May 19	*Breckinridge leaves the Valley to join Lee*
May 21	*Hunter replaces Sigel*
May 26	*Hunter begins march up the Valley*
June 5	*Battle of Piedmont*
June 6	*Federals occupy Staunton*
June 7	*Lee returns Breckinridge to the Valley*
June 11	*Hunter sacks Lexington*
June 17	*Early reaches Lynchburg*
June 18	*Hunter repulsed at Lynchburg and retreats*
June 23-July 2	*Early advances from Lynchburg to Winchester*
July 5-6	*Confederates cross the Potomac into Maryland*
July 9	*Battle of Monocacy*
July 11-12	*Skirmishes along Washington's defenses*
July 14	*Early recrosses the Potomac back to Virginia*
July 18	*Engagement at Snicker's Gap*
July 20	*Engagement at Stephenson's Depot*
July 24	*Second Battle of Kernstown*
July 30	*Burning of Chambersburg*
August 6	*Sheridan assumes Federal command*
August 7	*Engagement at Moorefield*
August 16-22	*Anderson reinforces Early; Federals withdraw northward*
August 21	*Engagement at Charles Town*
September 3	*Engagement at Berryville*
September 15	*Anderson leaves the Valley*
September 19	*Battle of Winchester*
September 22	*Battle of Fisher's Hill*
October 9	*Engagement at Tom's Brook*
October 19	*Battle of Cedar Creek*

ORDER OF BATTLE

CONFEDERATE

May-June 1864

Department of Western Virginia Breckinridge/W. E. Jones

(to May 19)	(from June 2)
Wharton's Brigade	*B. H. Jones' Brigade*
Echols' Brigade	*Browne's Brigade*
	Vaughn's Brigade
Cavalry Brigade Imboden	*Harper's Valley Reserves*
	Cavalry Brigade Imboden

July 1864

Army of the Valley District Early

Breckinridge's Corps		Second Corps	
Echols'/Wharton's	Gordon's Division	Ramseur's Division	Rodes' Division
Division	*Evans' Brigade*	*Lilley's Brigade*	*Battle's Brigade*
Wharton's/Forsberg's	*Terry's Brigade*	*Lewis' Brigade*	*Cook's Brigade*
Brigade	*York's Brigade*	*Johnston's Brigade*	*Cox's Brigade*
Patton's Brigade			*Grimes' Brigade*
Forsberg's/Smith's			
Brigade			
Vaughn's Brigade			

Cavalry Ransom
Imboden's Brigade
McCausland's Brigade
Johnson's Brigade
Jackson's Brigade

FEDERAL

May-June 1864

Department of West Virginia Sigel/Hunter

1st Division Sullivan	2d Division Crook	1st Cavalry Division	2d Cavalry Division
Moor's/Wells' Brigade	(after June 8)	Stahel/Duffié	Averell (after June 8)
Thoburn's Brigade	*Hayes' Brigade*	*Tibbits'/McReynolds'/*	*Schoonmaker's Brigade*
	White's Brigade	*Taylor's Brigade*	*Powell's Brigade*
	Campbell's Brigade	*Wynkoop's Brigade*	

July 1864

Department of West Virginia Hunter

Army of West Virginia Crook

1st Division Sullivan/Thoburn	2d Division Crook/Duval	3d Division Mulligan
Wells' Brigade	*Hayes' Brigade*	*Harris' Brigade*
Thoburn's/Ely's Brigade	*White's/Johnson's Brigade*	*Linton's Brigade*
Campbell's Brigade		

1st Cavalry Division Duffié	2d Cavalry Division Averell
Tibbits' Brigade	*Schoonmaker's Brigade*
Wynkoop's/Higgins' Brigade	*Powell's Brigade*

Reserve Division Sigel/Howe
(numerous unbrigaded units
defending Harpers Ferry and
surrounding area)

Middle Department (VIII Corps) Wallace

Tyler's Brigade
Morris' Brigade
Kenly's/Lockwood's Brigade
Cavalry Clendenin

Army of the Potomac (part)

Bulk of VI and XIX Corps present
by mid-July, but only Wheaton's
and Ricketts' divisions of the VI Corps
significantly engaged

Department of Washington Augur

Artillery and garrison units manning
the defenses of Washington

LIEUTENANT THOMAS B. GATCH

DAVIS' MARYLAND (C.S.) BATTALION, IMBODEN'S BRIGADE

The scion of an old Baltimore family, Gatch went south to serve the Confederacy. He was wounded at Gettysburg but recovered by the spring of 1864 and fought in the Valley until captured near Harrisonburg on September 24. He spent the rest of the war as a prisoner at Fort Delaware, not taking the oath of allegiance until June 1865. After the war, he represented Baltimore County in the Maryland state legislature and served as clerk of the courts.

About the 1st of May, 1864, we received information that a force was assembling in the lower Valley, of which we notified General Imboden, who came down to our post and ordered us to send three or four of the most reliable and best mounted men down the Valley as far as we could safely get and find out what forces were there and where located, the armament and strength as far as possible, and to get back as soon as possible. I concluded to go myself, and took with me Lieutenant Riley, who knew every foot of the ground, First Sergeant Lon Cross, and Dick Gilmore. We got near Kernstown that day and learned from an intimate friend of Lieutenant Riley, whose son was a lieutenant in the Stonewall Brigade, that a considerable force was assembling on the Berryville Road, near Winchester, and had come principally from Harper's Ferry. We concluded that the only way to get accurate information was to get behind them, so we started for Gun-

Major General John C. Breckinridge came to Virginia from the ill-fated Army of Tennessee after the Confederate defeat at Chattanooga. He received this sword and scabbard from the Floridians and Tennesseans of Finley's and Bates' brigades in early 1864 when he left to command the Department of Southwestern Virginia.

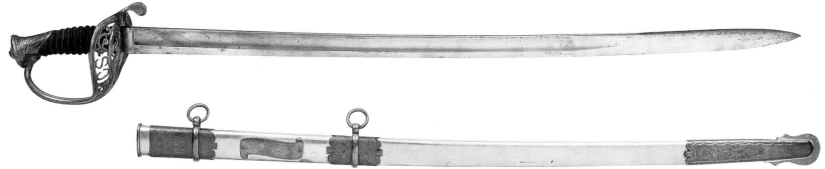

swamp Hollow, a favorite rendezvous for our scouts. We found that they had passed the day before, and were commanded by General [Sigel], and that there were two batteries of artillery, two brigades of infantry, one commanded by [Colonel Moor], almost entirely composed of Germans; two regiments of Pennsylvania infantry, and two companies of cavalry, four mule teams and four ambulances. This information was obtained from a friend of Lieutenant Riley who had seen them pass, confirmed by a friend of his with whom some of the officers had lunched. They said they were going up the Valley to clean it up. . . . We concluded that this information was as accurate as we could get, and we started back and got to our post about midnight. The next morning we wrote up our report, all four of us signed it, and we then started for General Imboden's headquarters to report, when we were surprised to receive an order to report to General Breckinridge, the first intimation to us that he was in command of the Valley forces. We found him at New Market and delivered our report, which he carefully examined and then questioned us minutely as to how we obtained our information. After seemingly being satisfied of its accuracy, he directed us to watch them as they got farther up the Valley and report again. After they had passed Middletown, we got a report verifying our first, which we reported. They made very slow progress, stopped at Strasburg two or three days, and made an attempt to capture our picket post at Tom's Brook, but failed.

LIEUTENANT WILLIAM HEWITT

12TH WEST VIRGINIA INFANTRY, THOBURN'S BRIGADE

Many of General Franz Sigel's men had fought before in the Shenandoah Valley, and some had endured the humiliation of General Robert H. Milroy's defeat at Winchester in June 1863, acquiring the derisive label "Milroy's boys." Returning to the Valley in 1864, these Federals passed over the scene of their earlier failure. Hewitt's luck this time was no better. Captured while helping a wounded comrade from the field at New Market, he was sent to the infamous Andersonville prison camp.

All along the pike from Martinsburg to Winchester on the march between the two towns, could be seen the graves of soldiers of the one or the other side who had fallen as victims of the cruel, bloody, wicked war. There was perhaps not a mile of the whole route over which we passed along which there could not be seen a soldier's grave, and at Winchester there were thousands buried. Everywhere could be seen the destructiveness and paralyzing effects of the war. Fences were torn down, farms were stripped of live stock, high grass was growing up to the edge of the towns, and it seemed as if the country was deserted by its inhabitants. Everything and the condition of things generally were object lessons teaching of the baleful effects of war.

On this day we passed through the historic and memorable old town of Winchester and camped about two miles beyond the town. The next day we had brigade drill under the supervision of Gen. Sigel. We remained here about a week during which time the organization of the army was completed. Our stay here afforded the boys of the Twelfth an opportunity to walk over the old battle ground of the Winchester battle fought on our side under Gen. Milroy. The boys examined the scene of the battle with considerable eager curious interest.

While we were at this point, there were extra precautions taken against a surprise. Strong picket forces were kept out, five companies being sent out on some of the roads, at least, and orders were given to keep one-third of the men up at night all the time, showing that Gen. Sigel was a vigilant careful commander. This alertness and these precautions indicated that we were drawing near the enemy, and gave a hint of coming clash of arms, which indeed was not far in the future.

The command of the 9th, moved up the Valley, our brigade in advance under Col. Thoburn. We marched 13 miles on this day and camped in the evening at Cedar Creek. . . .

. . . When the command reached Fisher's Hill after leaving Cedar Creek, it was halted and the men were ordered to load. Those who had been under fire before, felt the gravity of the outlook, and it was noticeable that more than one brave man looked very serious as he tore the paper from his cartridge. We remained at our camp near Woodstock one day with nothing unusual occurring, when on the next day our regiment with two pieces of artillery was ordered up the Valley about seven miles, one mile south of Edinburgh, as an advance picket. Some Rebel cavalry were seen here at a distance. . . . There was a pouring rain that night and the soldiers got a taste of the beauties of soldier life, getting thoroughly soaked with rain. Some tried to sleep; others preferred to stand or sit around roaring fires. In some cases those who tried to sleep found the water collecting in pools around their bodies. . . .

. . . All was quiet at the picket post in the night and in the morning John W. Crow and another soldier asked Capt. Bartlett of the company, if they might go to a house several hundred yards distant to get some bread. He said that they might go, but told them to not go any farther. It was a spider-and-the-fly-case—they did not come back again. At all events we did not see them for several months afterward, when they came back as exchanged prisoners. They then told that when they went to the house mentioned, the mistress said that she had no bread, but she thought they could get it at a house a little farther off, probably knowing what would happen if they went there. They went and were captured. . . .

. . . The Twelfth was relieved from picket in the morning . . . and we returned to our camp near Edinburgh, the rain still falling. On our way we met the First Virginia and the Thirty-fourth Massachusetts going up the pike. It began to look as though things were approaching a crisis.

Although General Sigel (above), the loser at New Market, had "manifested perfect coolness and personal courage," according to one account, he was scourged after the battle for the inept handling of his troops and relieved of command.

CADET JOHN S. WISE
VIRGINIA MILITARY INSTITUTE

The son of Virginia's former governor, Wise was assigned, with three schoolmates, to guard the cadets' baggage wagon at the Battle of New Market. They abandoned this post to get into the fight. Of the four, Wise and a comrade were wounded and another cadet was killed. Wise is seen here later in 1864, shortly after receiving his commission.

Long roll had been beaten several times of late, sometimes to catch absentees, and once for a fire in the town. Grumblingly the cadets hurried down to their places in the ranks, expecting to be soon dismissed and to return to their beds. A group of officers, intently scanning by the light of a lantern a paper held by the adjutant, stood near the statue of George Washington, opposite the arch. The companies were marched together. The adjutant commanded attention, and proceeded to read the orders in his hands.

They announced that the enemy in heavy force was advancing up the Shenandoah valley; that General Lee could not spare any forces to meet him; that General Breckinridge had been ordered to assemble troops from southwestern Virginia and elsewhere at Staunton; and that the cadets should join him there at the earliest practicable moment. The corps was ordered to march, with four companies of infantry and a section of artillery, by the Staunton pike, at break of day.

First sergeants were ordered to detail eight artillerists from each of the four companies, to report for duty immediately, and man a section of artillery.

As these orders were announced, not a sound was heard from the boys who stood there, with beating hearts, in the military posture of parade rest.

"Parade's dismissed," piped the adjutant. The sergeants side-stepped us to our respective company parades. . . .

. . . Sergeants detail[ed] their artillery and ammunition squads, and order[ed] us to appear with canteens, haversacks, and blankets at four A.M. Still silence reigned. Then, as company after company broke ranks, the air was rent with wild cheering at the thought that our hour was come at last.

Elsewhere in the Confederacy, death, disaster, disappointment may have by this time chilled the ardor of our people, but here, in this little band of fledgelings, the hope of battle flamed as brightly as on the morning of Manassas.

We breakfasted by candle-light, and filled our haversacks from the mess-hall tables. In the gray of morning, we wound down the hill to the river, tramped heavily across the bridge, ascended the pike beyond, cheered the fading turrets of the school; and sunrise found us going at a four-mile gait to Staunton, our gallant little battery rumbling behind.

We were every way fitted for this kind of work by our hard drilling, and marched into Staunton in the afternoon of the second day, showing little ill effects of travel. . . .

We found a pleasant camping ground on the outskirts of the town, and thither the whole population flocked for inspection of the corps, and to witness dress parade, for our fame was widespread. The attention bestowed upon the cadets was enough to turn the heads of much humbler persons than ourselves. We were asked to visit nearly every house in town. . . .

At night, the town was hilarious. Several dances were arranged, and, as dancing was a cadet accomplishment, we were in our element.

The adoration bestowed upon us by young girls disgusted the regular officers. Before our coming, they had had things all their own way. Now, they found that fierce mustaches and heavy cavalry boots must give place to the downy cheeks and merry, twinkling feet we brought from Lexington. A big blonde captain, who was wearing a stunning bunch of gilt aiguillettes, looked as if he would snap my head off when I trotted up and whisked his partner away from him. They could not and would not understand why girls preferred these little, untitled whippersnappers to officers of distinction. Veterans forgot that youth loves youth.

Doubtless some feeling of this sort prompted the band of a regiment of grimy veterans to strike up "Rock-a-bye, Baby," when the cadets marched by them. Quick as soldiers' love of fun, the men took up the air, accompanying it by rocking their guns in their arms as if putting them to sleep. It produced a perfect roar of amusement with everybody but ourselves. We were furious.

All this on the eve of a battle? Yes, of course. Why not? To be sure, everybody knew there was going to be a fight. That was what we came for. But nobody among us knew or cared just when or where it was coming off. Life is too full of trouble for petty officers or privates, or young girls, to bother themselves hunting up such disagreeable details in advance. That was the business of generals. They were to have all the glory; and so we were willing they should have all the solicitude, anxiety, and preoccupation.

At dress parade, May 12, orders were read for the movement of the army down the valley the following morning. We always moved on time. Now, who would have believed that a number of girls were up to see us off, or that two or three were crying? Yet it was so. And quick work of the naked boy with the cross-bow I call that.

As we passed some slaughter-pens on the outskirts, an old Irish butcher, in his shirt sleeves, hung over his gate, pipe in mouth. With a twinkle in his eye he watched the corps go by, at last exclaiming, "Begorra, an' it's no purtier dhrove av pigs hev passed this gate since this hog-killing began."

We made a good day's march, and camped that night near Harrisonburg. During the day, we met several couriers bearing dispatches; they reported the enemy advancing in heavy force.

A native of Warrenton, Virginia, Scott Shipp graduated from VMI in 1859 and stayed on as a mathematics and Latin professor. When war came, he served briefly in the army but was appointed commandant of cadets on January 1, 1862. At New Market, a shell fragment struck his left shoulder, knocking him down, but he escaped with only a slight wound. Shipp spent a total of 61 years with VMI, becoming superintendent in 1890.

New Market

Although Sigel had been in no hurry to come to grips with Breckinridge, he felt compelled to assert himself after learning of the rout of the Federal cavalry rear guard by Imboden's horsemen. On May 14 he ordered Colonel Augustus Moor southward up the Valley Turnpike toward New Market. Moor reached the town with nearly 2,400 men—three infantry regiments, 900 cavalrymen, and artillery.

That evening the Federals skirmished with some of Imboden's brigade, primarily Colonel George H. Smith's 62d Virginia Mounted Infantry. The action ended with Smith holding a line just south of New Market. Some of Moor's troops camped on Bushong's Hill, less than two miles to the north, while others took up positions closer to the enemy on Manor's Hill, and one regiment even pushed forward into the town.

Early next morning Breckinridge marched his small Confederate army north toward New Market. Confederate cavalry tested the Federal line just after sunrise, and Rebel artillery on Shirley's Hill was soon dueling with Yankee guns on Manor's Hill. Breckinridge had planned initially to lure the enemy into an attack, but he decided that the open terrain favored an offensive maneuver. The North Fork of the Shenandoah and Smith's Creek protected his flanks, freeing the bulk of his infantry for a northward advance west of the Valley pike.

The Confederate line had Brigadier General Gabriel C. Wharton's brigade on the left, Brigadier General John Echols' brigade to the right rear, and the 26th Virginia and the VMI cadets in reserve. Rebel cavalry stood watch east of the pike. On Manor's Hill, Colonel John E. Wynkoop's Federal cavalry and some horse artillery held Moor's right, with the 18th Connecticut, the 123d Ohio, and the 1st West Virginia aligned eastward.

The battle opened under a pouring rain. For about an hour, starting at 11:30 a.m., the Confederates applied heavy pressure. Breckinridge shifted the 26th Virginia to the left of his front line—leaving the VMI cadets as his only reserve—and placed artillery along the pike.

Union commander Sigel arrived on the field about noon and decided that he could not reinforce Moor's line effectively. He ordered a retreat, and over the next two hours Moor conducted a fighting withdrawal toward Bushong's Hill—although many men of the 123d Ohio and the 18th Connecticut kept right on retreating past the hill and down the pike. East of the road Brigadier General Julius Stahel's cavalry division covered the Federal left until Imboden positioned troopers and artillery on its flank. Cannon fire then compelled Stahel to pull back.

Shortly before 2:30 p.m. Sigel had established his final line on Bushong's Hill. Three batteries of artillery crowned the ridge on the right, followed in order by the 34th Massachusetts, the 1st West Virginia, and the 54th Pennsylvania of Colonel Joseph Thoburn's brigade. The 12th West Virginia served as a reserve, and Stahel's cavalry held the left.

Wharton's brigade was taking heavy losses as it pushed through Moor's position and neared Bushong's Hill. A gap developed between its right and the 62d Virginia, advancing alongside that flank. The Federals moved to exploit the opening, and Breckinridge, his line about to be broken, reluctantly turned to the only reserves he had left—the cadets. The ardent youngsters entered the breach against punishing fire, taking many casualties, but they steadied the line.

With Wharton's brigade at a standstill and Echols' men lagging slightly behind east of the pike, Sigel sensed an opportunity to counterattack. At about 2:45 p.m., he sent Stahel's cavalry on an assault along the pike, but it retired quickly in the face of artillery fire and musketry. Then the infantry tried. The 34th Massachusetts and 54th Pennsylvania gained ground near the Bushong house, but a poor effort by the 1st West Virginia doomed them. "As we neared the crest of the hill," wrote a Massachusetts man, the West Virginians "turned and went back, leaving the 34th rushing alone into the enemy's line." Meanwhile, Confederate infantry took a heavy toll of gunners and horses among the batteries near the North Fork. Sigel ordered some of the batteries to retire.

The slackening Federal artillery fire gave Breckinridge the opportunity to renew his assault. Just after 3:00 p.m. his entire force, the cadets included, charged. Colonel George D. Wells of the 34th Massachusetts wrote, "The Rebels were coming on at the double quick, and concentrating their whole fire upon us. I told the men to run, and get out of fire as quickly as possible, and rally behind the first cavalry we found in the rear." The Federal line soon collapsed, and Sigel's army broke into an all-out retreat.

Sigel had put about 6,300 of his 8,940 men into the battle, suffering casualties of 97 killed, 520 wounded, and 225 missing. Nearly 4,900 of Breckinridge's 5,325 men had fought, among whom 43 were killed, at least 474 wounded, and three missing.

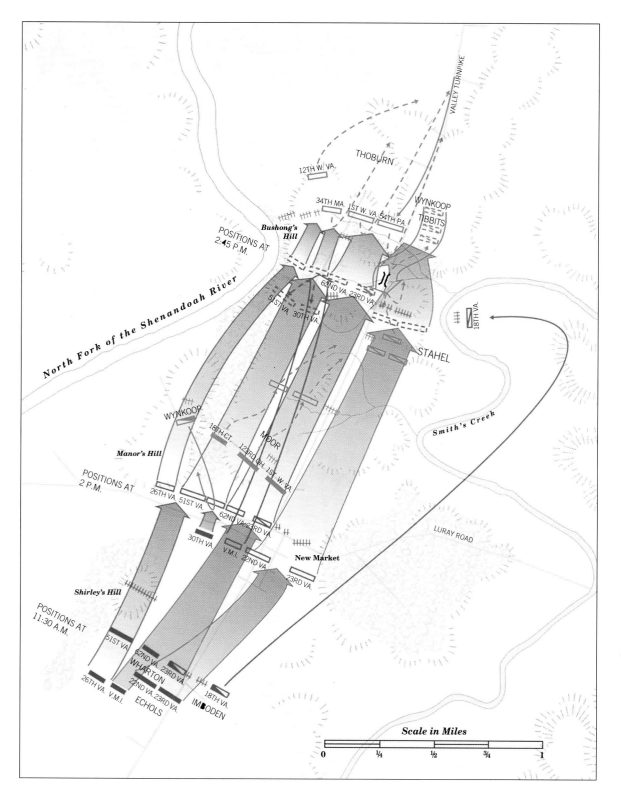

POSITIONS AT
2:45 P.M.

**Bushong's
Hill**

North Fork of the Shenandoah River

VALLEY TURNPIKE

THOBURN

12TH W. VA.

34TH MA. 1ST W. VA. 54TH PA.

WYNKOOP
TIBBITS

18TH VA.

63RD VA. 23RD VA.

51ST VA. 30TH VA.

STAHEL

Smith's Creek

WYNKOOP

18TH CT.

MOOR

123RD OH. 1ST W. VA.

Manor's Hill

POSITIONS AT
2 P.M.

26TH VA. 51ST VA.

62ND VA. 23RD VA.

30TH VA.

V.M.I. 22ND VA.

LURAY ROAD

New Market

23RD VA.

Shirley's Hill

POSITIONS AT
11:30 A.M.

51ST VA.

62ND VA. 23RD VA.

WHARTON

26TH VA. V.M.I.

22ND VA. 23RD VA.

ECHOLS

18TH VA.

IMBODEN

Scale in Miles

0   ¼   ½   ¾   1

After waiting through most of the
morning of May 15 for Sigel to attack,
Breckinridge took the initiative shortly
before noon. He first pitched into Moor's
Federals, who were deployed from
Manor's Hill to the north end of the
town. Sigel, meanwhile, formed a
new line with the rest of his troops on
Bushong's Hill, while Moor's regiments
fell back toward this second position.
The Confederates pressed ahead under
heavy fire, repulsing a pair of Yankee
counterattacks as they closed in on Sigel's
line. Finally around 3:00 p.m., a climactic Rebel surge routed the Yankees
and ended Sigel's career in the Valley.

LIEUTENANT CHARLES M. KEYES

123D OHIO INFANTRY, MOOR'S BRIGADE

In June 1863 Keyes and most of his regiment were surrendered at the Second Battle of Winchester. Although the enlisted men were exchanged in August, most of the officers were held much longer, seriously impairing the unit's efficiency. Confederate cavalry captured the regiment again near Farmville in 1865.

The next morning our brigade was manuevred around in various directions, the artillery placed in position, and things began to look as though a battle was imminent, but for some unknown reason, the remainder of our little army was not brought up; about noon the enemy opened upon us with artillery, to which our batteries rapidly replied, and soon their lines could be seen coming across the fields, two deep, one directly behind the other, with a heavy line of skirmishers in advance, and nothing but our brigade to receive them. We were in a good position, and with the artillery on either flank, awaited their approach. Soon our cannons opened on their rapidly advancing lines, dealing death and destruction, but not checking them for an instant; on they came, sweeping like an avalanche upon our little band. We held our fire until they were almost within pistol shot, when we poured in our volleys, with terrific effect; rapidly were our well directed volleys given, doubling their first line back upon their second, that still came unfalteringly on, lapping by our little line, both on the right flank and

This view of the battlefield, seen from the position of the leftmost regiment of Moor's Federal line, just north of New Market, shows the open ground across which the Yankees faced Breckinridge's Rebel infantry on May 15. The Rebels descended Shirley's Hill, in the background, advanced over this field, and swept Moor's men back.

the left, rapidly firing as they advanced until our little band could no longer withstand their overwhelming numbers, and slowly we began to retire—taking our cannon back through a cedar thicket, our pathway marked with the blood of our braves. As they appeared over the eminence we had lately occupied, they poured in upon us such a storm of shot and shell, so thick that the very air seemed alive with bullets.

CADET JOHN CLARKE HOWARD
VIRGINIA MILITARY INSTITUTE

Howard and his comrades had followed behind the main line during the initial attack that drove Moor's brigade from the field. Breckinridge's men then encountered heavy resistance from Colonel Joseph Thoburn's brigade, and their advance ground to a halt, compelling Breckinridge to make his fateful decision to "put the boys in." The cadets joined the already bloodied Virginia regiments to make one climactic charge that sealed the Rebel victory.

Next came the order for the second line of battle to advance, and we marched with it. Having seen the experience of the first line, I knew it was practically certain it would be repeated in the case of the second. As we were nearing the summit of the ridge, I wondered—for boys, and men, too, sometimes, will have very absurd thoughts—I wondered if, from my position on the almost extreme right, I looked down the battalion I was any more likely to get hit than if I looked in front. Anyhow, I looked; and while looking, the first shell exploded just in front. Subprofessor A. G. Hill, in command of Company C, was about the center of the battalion. I think I must have been looking at him at the instant; at any rate, I saw him fall, and also saw that two other men had been knocked down. I did not know at the time who those two were, but heard afterwards that they were Wise and Crank. Captain Hill fell like a log, apparently just as stiffly as a log would have fallen. I thought he was killed, but I have since heard that no man killed outright ever falls that way—that they crumple and come down, all stiffness of the joints being lost.

We now marched on down the hill in front, which was a right steep one. There was a road at the bottom, and just beyond the road a fence. Crossing this fence we were halted and ordered to take off blankets and everything else, except gun and equipment. This looked like business, stripping for the fight, and we began to think our work was really

cut out for us. "Attention, Battalion! Forward!" This was the beginning of that long-ascending field, the main theater of the fight. The ascent at first was steeper than it afterwards became, but in a very little while we were within range of the Federal infantry as well as artillery as they directed their fire against the line. I heard the hiss of the bullets and saw where they had struck the ground in different directions, right, left, and in front, but I was a green hand, and didn't know that this meant we were among the Minie balls. A few minutes after being under fire we were halted, and the corps commenced marking time; but as we lay

Cadet Francis L. Smith of Alexandria, Virginia, wore this shell jacket at New Market, where he received two wounds. One bullet shattered his jawbone. The second bullet, which he later incorporated into the watch fob shown here, broke his collarbone. Smith survived and went on to become an attorney and state senator.

down almost instantly for a few seconds, a cadet near me remarked: "What damn fool gave the order to mark time under this fire." We were up again almost instantly, and then forward. We could clearly hear the firing of the Southern artillery over our heads, and hoped it would silence some of the hostile guns in front—which, in a measure, it did. . . .

My position was within two or three files of the first Sergeant, E. M. Ross, and all through the fight I was within a few feet of him and the Captain, Henry Wise. I shall never forget Ross's face. This was not his first battle. For a time he had been with the regular Confederate army, the "Regulars," as at that time they were called. His face expressed anxiety; I can see it as plainly in memory to-day as I did then. He had ignored himself entirely. I didn't think a thought of what might happen to him crossed his mind, but he was thinking of the battalion, not merely his own company, but the entire battalion, believing and hoping, but with that touch of anxiety, that his brother cadets would do their duty. He must have been reassured by our bearing; however scared within, we contrived not to show it without. We felt that we were indeed "in the fight" and with a good many preconceived ideas much shaken up. This was really the beginning to us of that hot advance over that muddy field. I lost both of my shoe strings, and wonder that I did not lose my shoes. However, I was too busy then to investigate the cause. Hissing Minies and the hoarse shriek of the shells demanded too painfully much attention, and I was engaged in recalling some of my many derelictions of duty and forming good resolutions for the future. Matters were already serious, and were becoming more so every minute, as we neared the hostile antagonism in front. Men were falling, but, "each stepping where his comrade stood," the integrity of the corps was kept. I was nearly at the extreme right and could see the entire length of the battalion, and again and again I wondered how it was able to keep its formation so well. I know now, though I did not then, how much drill and the habit of obedience had to do with that parade ground line. Once, owing to some mistake, we were advancing in column, but the mistake was quickly rectified, and we swept left into line with the swing of a gate on its hinges. . . .

. . . Fifty yards or so to our right was a Confederate officer who had been wounded and was lying nearly prostrate on the ground. Not quite, however; he was resting on his left elbow, and, forgetful of self, apparently oblivious of his wounds, his handsome young face shone brightly and his sword waved from side to side in sympathetic encouragement of his comrades. Another shell exploded and he was cut down for the second time. Prostrate now, and with the "Last Roll Call" sounding in his ears, the heroic soul still waved back and forth under the self-renunciatory impulse of the life leaving the earth and to its acclaim in heaven. . . .

What effect that waving sword may have had as a cheering incentive on anyone else—for many beside myself must have witnessed the incident—I do not know, but I know there was no giving back as we pressed forward through the storm. We were in the culminating struggle for victory or defeat. Men were falling in no infrequency. . . . We were halted in an inclosure surrounding a dwelling, and ordered to lie down just in front of the house. It would have been more satisfactory to my inner feelings had we been behind the house. I look back upon that orchard as the most awful spot on the battle field, and, as the shot and shell tore over and around us, I was reminded by their malignant shriek of the driving snowstorm, whose flakes I could see, and marveled not at the number hit, but that all were not killed. . . . A crisis had been reached: the fire was too hot for irresponsive action, and retreat or advance was the alternative. We considered a retreat no part of the game, and "forward" was the order. We were halted for some reason before climbing the fence of the inclosure. I saw a cedar tree a yard high or thereabout, with a trunk as big as my thumb. Not a very effective defensive, but, no matter, anything from a white oak to a wheat straw was better than nothing, and I threw myself down behind it. One of the company, Ashleigh, apparently concluded that if a tree of that dimension could protect one person it might perhaps be stretched to protect two, and threw himself down full length on my body. A bullet tried to find us, but fortunately failed, cutting the trousers of both without touching the leg of either. . . .

And now once more forward. The first thing to do was climb the fence, which impressed itself on me so indelibly as never to have been forgotten. It was an ordinary rail fence, probably about four feet high, but as I surmounted the topmost rail I felt at least ten feet up in the air and the special object of hostile aim. . . . Captain Wise was leading and giving necessary orders, his face bright and fearless as though enjoying himself. . . . Ross, on the right, was himself again. He had witnessed the bearing of the battalion from the first and its bearing now, and every trace of anxiety had left his face, driven out by exultant pride. . . . The shot-torn standard of the Corps floated triumphantly.

> "The cadets, gallant little boys, were sent up to reënforce us, and no veterans ever behaved better than those brave little fellows (the flower of the South), and I remember how I thought it shameful to subject such youths to such a fire."

SERGEANT THOMAS H. NEILSON
62D VIRGINIA INFANTRY, IMBODEN'S BRIGADE

Neilson's unit normally fought as mounted infantry, but Breckinridge, short on foot soldiers, dismounted it for this battle. The 62d suffered severely at New Market, losing 92 men killed or wounded—20 percent of its original combat strength. Attached to the 62d at New Market was Captain Charles H. Woodson's company of the 1st Missouri Cavalry, which lost 40 of 62 men engaged. Breckinridge, impressed with the 62d, refused to return it to Imboden after the battle.

Our colonel, George H. Smith . . . , came before the regiment and said simply: "Boys, our duty to-day is to take that hill. Forward, guide center, charge!" Our batteries, which were vainly trying to shell the hill to cover our advance, had to be silenced, as the shells were falling in our rear. We started to charge, but had advanced only a short distance when the battery limbered up and retreated, making several stops to shell us as we advanced, until they finally made a stand in an apple orchard on a hill just below the town. The 62d Virginia was thrown forward in advance of the main line, and received the concentrated fire of the artillery, belching double-shotted canister into us, as well as the fire of a brigade on the crest of the hill in the rear of and supporting the battery. . . .

. . . There was a steep declivity at the foot of the hill which partly shielded us from the battery's fire; and as we had charged about a mile and three-fourths over muddy plowed fields (it was raining), we halted a moment to get our breath and close up ranks for the final assault. The cadets, gallant little boys, were sent up to reënforce us, and no veterans ever behaved better than those brave little fellows (the flower of the South), and I remember how I thought it shameful to subject such youths to such a fire.

COLONEL GEORGE D. WELLS
34TH MASSACHUSETTS INFANTRY, THOBURN'S BRIGADE

While the 34th was spending much of its early service on garrison duty, Wells, a Boston attorney, read up on the military arts and drilled the regiment into a highly disciplined unit. This training paid off in the Valley. At New Market, the 34th was the last Federal unit to withdraw. Wells was killed on a reconnaissance near Cedar Creek on October 13.

The fight beat anything I ever dreamed of in the way of fire. For a while our regiments took it all alone, and I began to think I should never get the rascals off the field. On the way back to our second line, after getting well out of reach I had to go back into fire six times to bring the colors off. The bearer would halt wherever anybody told him, but he would not move back except at my direct order. Nothing could have been better than the way in which the command was extricated finally. Lots of amusing incidents of course. I heard one fellow say in utter disgust at hearing my order to run—"My God! This to the 34th in their first fight!"

All the regimental dogs but one were killed. One big black bob-tail,

In May 1862 VMI cadet Benjamin A. Colonna (left) and his schoolmates accompanied Stonewall Jackson into the Alleghenies but remained in reserve at the Battle of McDowell. Two years later, under Breckinridge, Cadet Captain Colonna led VMI Company D into battle at New Market. After the war Colonna worked for the U.S. Coast and Geodetic Survey. In 1884 he was injured in an avalanche in Washington State and never fully recovered. He later extensively mapped the New Market battlefield and played a principal role in the initial preservation of the Bushong house and outbuildings, pictured above, over whose grounds the cadets had charged in their advance on the Federal position.

who used to distinguish himself by catching jigs, and running at my grey horse on brigade drill to my great discomfiture, started ahead of us on our charge in great glee, but was on his back kicking at empty air with all four feet before he had gone ten paces. My beautiful bay horse . . . got three balls in him, and was left dead on the field. The old grey as usual got off without a scratch. "The bullet is not moulded etc." as Cowdin pertinently remarked, which can hit him.

COLONEL DAVID H. STROTHER
STAFF, MAJOR GENERAL FRANZ SIGEL

A Valley native, Strother gained prewar fame as a writer and an artist. When Confederate conscription officers knocked on his door in 1861, Strother turned them away with a loaded revolver. Spurred to action by his father's last words, Strother joined the Union army in 1862. His knowledge of the Valley proved invaluable.

Sigel seemed in a state of excitement and rode here and there with Stahel and Moor, all jabbering in German. In his excitement he seemed to forget his English entirely, and the purely American portion of his staff were totally useless to him. I followed him up and down until I got tired, and, finding a group of his staff officers together near a battery, I stopped and got a drink of whiskey and a cracker which an artillery man gave me. These officers said the General had ordered them to remain there, but seeing him riding rapidly to the artillery position on our right, we started to join him. Just then the enemy appeared, advancing in two lines of battle extending unbroken along our whole front, while along the front of the cavalry a line of skirmishers was seen pushing forward. Our artillery immediately opened, all the guns firing with great rapidity. The enemy's artillery played chiefly on our cavalry which after making a few futile movements was totally withdrawn to the rear. The Rebel infantry continued to move in advance; in spite of our

furious artillery fire their lines were steady and clean, no officers either mounted or on foot appearing among them. When within three hundred yards they began to yell as usual, and the musketry from both lines opened with great fury. Our men began to break immediately, running to the rear by ones, twos, and finally by streams.

Seeing this demoralization beginning, I drew my sword and attempted to rally the fugitives. The example was followed by many other officers of the staff. Lieutenant Meigs was especially excited, and I saw him cut down a straggler with his sabre. Our position was becoming very hot. Our lines were falling back and were rapidly disintegrating and becoming a rout. As they retired, the Rebel yells approached rapidly and their fire both of musketry and artillery now concentrated on the crumbling lines. The staff officers gradually retreated, exposed to a hail of balls and shells. As I was about to sabre a fugitive, he fell struck by a ball in the side and cried to his comrades to carry him away. Colonel Starr's horse received a severe wound from a shell which he died of that night. While we stood together trying to form a line of the rallied men, a cannon shot ploughed the ground just at our horses' feet, not twelve inches from their hoofs. A moment later a spent musket ball struck me plump in the breast and bounded off without hurting me. Seeing that our attempts to rally the infantry were futile and that the artillery were retiring as fast as possible, I also retired, hoping to be able to rally the men on Rude's Hill when we could get out of range of the Rebel fire.

Ranked first in West Point's Class of 1863, Lieutenant John R. Meigs served as a staff engineer in the Valley campaign. He played a critical role in the Federal victory at Piedmont, locating a gap in the Confederate lines that was exploited decisively. His controversial death on October 7 at the hands of Rebel horsemen provoked Yankee reprisals against the nearby village of Dayton.

ELIZA CLINEDINST
RESIDENT OF NEW MARKET

Clinedinst, later a beloved figure to VMI veterans, was one of many townswomen who served as nurses after the Battle of New Market, when every large building in town was put into service as a hospital. The local Baptist church was converted into an operating room, and town doctors and Confederate surgeons worked throughout the dark, rainy night administering care to friend and foe alike.

They commenced carrying the dead from the field as the cadets passed on down the road. They carried some of them by our door, and the red blood dripped and dripped on the pavement. I could not stay in after I saw this. I ran on down to the battle field to help with the wounded. I was the first woman to go there. Some came afterwards and did noble work. O, what a sickening sight after the battle. I stayed up all night to help the wounded. A cold rain was falling and so many shivered with such severe chills. We helped to carry the wounded into the old Rice home. We made a fire and gave them warm drinks; but many died that night. Our poor soldiers, how they suffered and died that day! . . .

I left the field to come home to make tea for the wounded. On my way up I met the poor little boy soldiers of the Virginia Military Institute. One cadet wanted to borrow an ax to cut wood to make a fire and get supper. They were too proud to beg. I took them in and gave them their supper. One said he was fifteen years old. He wanted his bread spread with preserves. He sat down just like a little child to eat from mother's hand. I returned to the battle field with the hot tea, and on my way down I met many cadets coming into town. Nearly all were barefooted. They lost their shoes in the mud as they ran through a plowed field, and all were so hungry and tired.

They told me about a poor little cadet lying down at the Lightfoot farm, badly wounded. I told them to bring him up to my home, where he would be more comfortable. He laid there all night, but in the morning after the battle . . . Moses Ezekiel . . . brought him to my home in an ambulance and carried him in. My good old mother put him in her own bed, as it was the only bed we had downstairs. When we laid him down he looked up at me, and said: "Sister, what a good, soft bed." Mother had an old-time feather bed, and it must have felt soft to him after lying on the hard ground. This sweet little cadet was from Amelia County, Va. His name was Thomas Garland Jefferson. He was about sixteen years of age, was blue-eyed, and had golden hair. I will never forget him and his sweet, boyish face. He was shot in the breast, and the bullet was cut out of his back. His sufferings were intense, but he bore up so well and never complained. Cadet Ezekiel nursed him very tenderly. His own mother could not have done more for him. . . . When Cadet Jefferson fell, two of his comrades hastened to his aid. Indifferent to his own comfort, with outstretched hand he pointed to the front, saying: "That is the place for you; you can do me no good." He urged them to

Cadet Thomas Garland Jefferson (above) was shot in the chest at New Market and died three days later. Cadet Moses Ezekiel cut a lock of Jefferson's hair and later delivered it to the fallen youth's grieving mother in Richmond.

Moses J. Ezekiel of Richmond considered the title VMI cadet "the proudest and most honored . . . I can ever possess." After the war Ezekiel went on to gain fame throughout the United States and Europe as an award-winning artist and sculptor. His works adorned such notable venues as London's Westminster Abbey and the Corcoran Gallery of Art, in Washington, D.C. He is buried beneath one of his own creations, the Confederate Memorial at Arlington National Cemetery.

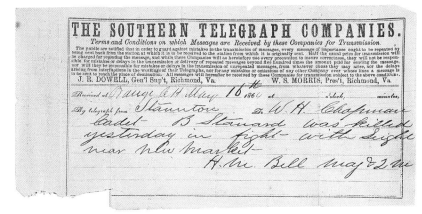

This telegram informed the family of Cadet Jaqueline B. "Jack" Stanard of his death. Cadet Corporal John S. Wise, who had taken Stanard from guard duty into battle, later lamented, "My heart half-reproached me for ordering him into the fight."

LIEUTENANT COLONEL WILLIAM S. LINCOLN

34TH MASSACHUSETTS INFANTRY, THOBURN'S BRIGADE

Wounded at New Market, Lincoln spent the next two months in captivity. After the battle he and other wounded Federals were sent to Harrisonburg, where they were treated kindly by local families. In July, just before he was to be sent to Richmond, Lincoln escaped to West Virginia with a small group of fellow prisoners.

the front, saying words which should be immortal. The evening before he died, he called Cadet Ezekiel to read for him. He read the fourteenth chapter of St. John: "Let not your heart be troubled. Ye believe in God, believe also in me. In my Father's house are many mansions. I go to prepare a place for you." What a deathbed scene, the little Jew cadet reading the New Testament to his Christian comrade in his last hours. Could anything be more touching? I went to smooth his pillow, and he said: "Sister, what beautiful hands." He called: "Duncan, come and light a candle; it is growing dark." The blindness of death came over him. He died about midnight in Moses Ezekiel's arms. He was buried in the old churchyard where they fought so bravely.

The close of the 15th of May, 1864, left me, with many of my companions in arms, wounded and in the hands of the enemy. . . . As the day closed, some sixty of us found ourselves stretched in and around an old barn, near the battlefield, closely guarded by Rebel soldiers. During the early hours of the evening, and well into the night,

Captain Patrick Graham was among the 180 men of the 54th Pennsylvania who were wounded at New Market. Graham remained in the Confederate hospital at Harrisonburg until September, when he was transferred to Richmond. He ended up at Camp Asylum, a prison for sick and wounded captives in Columbia, South Carolina. He was finally exchanged on March 1, 1865, still suffering from his wound.

With the morning light we were able to recognize, and enquire as to each other's condition. Another night passed, with the addition of a few more to our number, among whom was Capt. Fox of ours, from whom we learned of the death of Capt. Bacon, of our color company.

Late in the afternoon of this day (Tuesday), with an armed Rebel on each side of us, Capt. Fox and myself made a slow march into town, and to the office of the Provost Marshal. Here our names and ranks were registered, and we were directed to report ourselves at the hospital. At this place our wounds were examined and partially dressed; a thick slice of bread (the only food which either of us had had since Sunday morning) was given to each, and we were told that we might "look out for ourselves" till we were wanted. We procured lodgings at the Village hotel, where we staid till Thursday, when we were informed that we were wanted again at the hospital. Reporting, we found drawn up before the door of the building a long wagon, without cover, without springs, with no seat, and not even straw upon which to sit or lie, into which we were directed to get, as we were to be sent, in this way, to Harrisonburg, some twenty miles away. . . . Our journey was a sad and tiresome one.

our party received accessions from such wounded Union soldiers as were able to make their way unaided; or too severely wounded to walk, were brought in by the enemy. Occasionally, by the light of a lantern, some Rebel officer would examine us. "Are there any Confederate wounded here?" was asked by Major Meem, Medical Director on the staff of Gen. Breckenbridge, as he stood at the head of a goodly sized party of Rebel surgeons. No answer was returned by any of us, as the question was addressed to no one in particular. "I say, you d——d Yankee sons of b——s, are there any Confederate wounded here?" "No, sir!" was the reply. "Then this is no place for us, gentlemen!" said the Major; and he turned away. Among the wounded was Capt. Graham of the 54th Pennsylvania. He had been shot directly through the right lung, and each breath he drew sent the air *whistling* through the wound, disturbing the dying, who laid near. "I wish, Major," said I to Meem, "you would give a look to this officer, before you go." "We've got enough to do to attend to the confederate wounded," said he; but spite of the remark turned to comply with the request. As he drew the shirt from the wound in the Captain's breast, he broke out with "All he wants is a *d——d good horn of whiskey*," and walked off. All his companions followed, save one (I wish I knew and could give his name), who lingering behind, closed the wound with a piece of plaster, and gave him to drink from a jug in the hands of an Orderly.

SERGEANT WILLIAM A. MCILHENNY
1ST MARYLAND (U.S.) POTOMAC HOME BRIGADE

Serving primarily in the Valley, the 1st Maryland—or Cole's cavalry, as it was more commonly known—had successfully attacked Mosby's camp earlier in the war, initiating a series of clashes between the two units. On June 5, 1864, the Marylanders helped rout Imboden's cavalry at Piedmont. McIlhenny then convinced an elderly Valley woman that they had driven off the "Yankees." She rewarded her supposed deliverers with breakfast.

May 16, 1864

These last few days have been disasterous for the Union Army in Virginia! Early yesterday morning we were ordered to march from Cedar Springs to New Market. Our cavalry battalion was in the advance with the infantry away behind us. Even before we got to New Market we heard the sounds of battle. When we got in sight of the town our battalion was immediately thrown out on the skirmish line on the north side of the town. The rebel line of battle under General Breckenridge was drawn up just south of the town. They were ready for us.

Our battalion marched directly into their artillery fire. Shells were dropping all around us and musket balls were whistling. The rebels were so close that we could see their long grey line of infantrymen advancing. Where were our regiments of infantry? The rebel infantry was nearing gunshot range. Just as they started firing a regiment of our men arrived. We fell back for them to form in line. But it was too late! The rebels were upon us, firing at close range. They mowed our men down like grass. Our cavalry tried to keep together, but were impeded by the retreating infantry men escaping from the hot fire of Breckenridge's pursuing men. Many of them didn't escape. All the way to the Shenandoah River they were hot on our heels.

Our cavalry had been the first to cross the river in the morning, and now we formed a rear guard under [Colonel] Taylor and were the last to re-cross it. Then, with musket balls still whistling around us we had the job of setting fire to the bridge which our engineers had built just six days before.

We rode all night and passed through the gap in the mountains at Mt. Jackson. From there on we retreated to Cedar Springs in good order. The rebels didn't follow us. We are dead tired and the taste of defeat is bitter in our mouths.

COLONEL JOSEPH THOBURN
Brigade Commander, Army of the Shenandoah

Soon after his birth Thoburn and his family left Ireland and immigrated to St. Clairsville, Ohio. The outbreak of the war found him practicing medicine in Wheeling, Virginia, where he enlisted in the 1st Virginia (U.S.) as a surgeon and was elected colonel when the unit reorganized for three years' service. He served extensively in the Valley, was seriously wounded at Kernstown in 1862, and rose to division command before he was killed at Cedar Creek.

*M*ay 22, 1864: Maj. Gen'l Sigel was relieved yesterday by Maj. Gen'l Hunter. I rejoice at the change. Hunter will be a very poor Gen'l indeed if he is not better than Sigel. The latter is a well informed military man, honest and devoted to our cause. But he lacks the practical common sense that enables a man to adapt himself to circumstances. He has courage; still he becomes flurried when in action and his orders are not clear and prompt. I feel kindly towards the Gen'l—yet I would rather he would never have another command. Gen'l Hunter has some reputation as a military man. He appears to be very energetic and active. Yet I would rather have seen him made a better start. To begin with, his first Gen'l order promising the men

half rations and mule meat was not wise. Men can endure a great deal but they should not be promised the worst until we get to the worst. He required the command to move this morning, every man carrying an extra pair of shoes, and many of the men are without any shoes at all and none to be had. He ordered one hundred rounds of ammunition to be carried in the knapsack when there is not a knapsack in the command, all having been left at Martinsburg. And there is not one hundred rounds of ammunition to the man to be had. All this only proves that he has spoken too fast. He begins to work before he knows the material he has to work with. Still I like his energy and if he has some military judgment on the field we may do very well. Our movement into the interior with a small force is hazardous, and requires a very discreet as well as bold commander.

Major General David Hunter was 61 when he took over Sigel's command. At First Manassas, Hunter had led a division into the battle but was wounded shortly after the fighting began. He later commanded the area encompassing the coasts of the Carolinas and Georgia, where he created controversy by freeing the slaves in his department and recruiting the first black regiment. Although the administration rebuked Hunter, it adopted both practices a few months later when President Lincoln issued the Emancipation Proclamation.

LIEUTENANT COLONEL CHARLES HALPINE

STAFF, MAJOR GENERAL DAVID HUNTER

Halpine gained fame during the war writing under the pen name "Miles O'Reilly." Although a staunch Democrat, he became close friends with Hunter, a radical Republican. Halpine believed that Hunter possessed "a heart over-flowing with kindness, though liable to sudden fits of rage."

Up the Shenandoah to Harrisonburgh, the country had been traversed and desolated in repeated campaigns—fields without fences, showing where armies had encamped; desolate and fire-blackened stone chimneys, standing up like pillars to mark where happy homes had ceased to be; long grave-trenches of red earth, recalling the legend that here Stonewall Jackson had whipped Banks, or Milroy, or given rude check to Fremont, or held his own and accomplished his purpose of retreat, despite the headlong fury of General Shields's attack. Martinsburgh was a desolate and forsaken town, which had changed masters half a dozen times under the fluctuating fortunes of

battle—soon to have two changes more. Winchester was much the same—aristocratic and bitterly rebellious—with vast earthworks and forts on the hills surrounding it, but utterly indefensible from the nature of the country in which it lay. At Strasburg and Woodstock the people were sullenly silent as we passed through the streets—only some shrill-tongued females having the boldness to cry:

"We've seen men with your colored clothes go up this valley afore; and we've seen 'em come back this way a mighty sight faster than they went up."

All the bridges from Cedar Creek to Newmarket had been broken down by General Sigel, about ten or twelve days before our advance, in his headlong retreat from the latter place, fancying himself pursued all the way by the victorious forces of General Breckinridge, who had really only followed him in force as far as Edinburgh—also a bitterly rebellious and much-scourged town, famous in the South for its manufacture of patent medicines. At Newmarket, or rather at Rood's Hill, on this side of it, we came on the shocking *débris* of the recent battle, many scores of our men being so imperfectly buried that their blackened and wormy limbs protruded through the earth, while the air was horribly impregnated with the *Bouquet de Rottenhoss*—as "Porte Crayon" used to call the dead remains of our cavalry and artillery animals.

This game box was made by Port Republic resident I. B. Sheets while he was incarcerated at Fort Delaware prison. Sheets had taken potshots at Union soldiers during fighting near his home in June 1862. When some of these same soldiers returned to Port Republic with Hunter's command, they saw to it that Sheets was arrested and held as a military prisoner for the rest of the war.

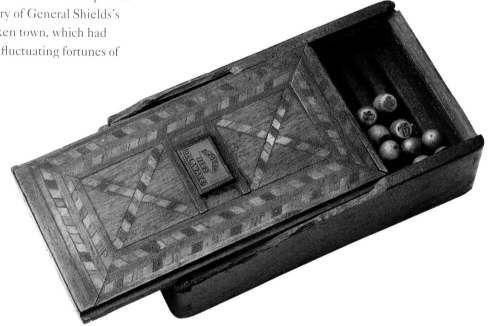

BRIGADIER GENERAL JOHN D. IMBODEN

BRIGADE COMMANDER, ARMY OF THE VALLEY

Born and reared in the Valley, Imboden spent most of the war defending his native soil. Three of his brothers served in his brigade's 18th Virginia Cavalry; one, Captain Frank Imboden, was captured in the opening action of the Battle of Piedmont. A fourth brother had fought with the VMI cadets at New Market.

During the night about two thousand men, sent forward by General Jones, joined me. To my dismay I found they were not generally organized in bodies larger than battalions, and in companies and fragments of companies hastily collected from Southwestern Virginia, between Lynchburg and Tennessee, and in large part indifferently armed. Indeed, many of the men were convalescents taken from the hospitals, and furloughed dismounted cavalrymen who had gone home for a remount, and were taken possession of by General Jones wherever he could find them, and hurried by rail through Lynchburg and Staunton to the front. I spent the entire night of the 3d in obtaining a list of all these small bodies of men, out of which by daybreak on the 4th I had composed, on paper, two brigades and assigned officers to their command. . . . During the day General Vaughan, of Tennessee, with from six hundred to eight hundred of his greatly reduced brigade, also joined us. We now had a force of something over four thousand men, including one regular and excellent six-gun battery, and one extemporized artillery company of "reserves," from Staunton, with five guns. Hunter, with eleven thousand superbly-appointed troops of all arms, was only eight miles distant in our front, and Crook and Averill, with seven thousand more, only two days' march in our rear; the two bodies rapidly approaching each other, and we between them in the condition I have just described, and with no hope of further assistance. Obviously our policy was to fight Hunter at the earliest moment, and possibly defeat him, and then turn upon Crook and Averill and do the best we could. . . . Jones, of course, assumed the command. He was an old army officer, brave as a lion, and had seen much service, and was known as a hard fighter. He was a man, however, of high temper, morose and fretful to such a degree that he was known by the soubriquet of "Grumble Jones." He held the fighting qualities of the enemy in great contempt, and never would admit the possibility of defeat where the odds against him were not much over two to one. So that when he took command of our little army . . . he was entirely confident that he could whip Hunter.

Confederate commander Brigadier General William E. "Grumble" Jones, although an able cavalry officer, could not get along with General "Jeb" Stuart and transferred to East Tennessee in 1863. He scored a series of impressive victories there, and the Richmond papers dubbed him "the Stonewall Jackson of East Tennessee."

LIEUTENANT CARTER F. BERKELEY
McClanahan's (Virginia) Battery, Imboden's Brigade

Valley native Berkeley led a two-gun section of artillery throughout the campaign. Serving under Captain John C. McClanahan, these Augusta County gunners played a key role in the Confederate victory at New Market. When Breckinridge left the Valley afterward, McClanahan stayed behind with Imboden. His four 3-inch ordnance rifles and two howitzers formed the nucleus of the Rebels' artillery but were outgunned by Captain Henry A. DuPont's Federal artillerists at Piedmont.

I shall never forget the scene, as we passed through the village, our horses on the run, and our boys yelling enthusiastically as they always did when going to the front. My boys were inspired by the glory of battle, and when that feeling takes possession of men, all fear vanishes. . . .

We all had that feeling that day, and were inspired by one still stronger, for behind us were our mothers, wives, sisters and sweethearts. "At home bright eyes were sparkling for us, and we would defend them to the last."

There were some ladies standing in a porch waving their handkerchiefs and cheering as we passed, as was usual with the noble women of the valley, when they saw our men going into battle. One of them cried out, "Lieutenant, don't let your men make so much noise, they will scare all the Yankees away before you can get a shot at them." We passed through the village a few hours later; the dear women were gone, and the house they had left was riddled with shot and shell and filled with dead and wounded soldiers.

We soon came up to Imboden, retiring before an overwhelming body of cavalry, supported by infantry and artillery, and beyond the hill on which we took our position, the whole country looked blue, and behind them was the smoke of burning barns.

SERGEANT GEORGE C. SETCHELL
18th Connecticut Infantry, Moor's Brigade

Setchell, shown here in 1860, was 26 in the spring of 1864. His regiment had seen hard service in the Valley, but before Piedmont Hunter derided the 18th for its performance at New Market. The enraged New Englanders resolved that if they met any "Rebs that day some of them would get hurt."

This kepi belonged to Lieutenant George J. Pratt of the 18th Virginia Cavalry, which successfully attacked Hunter's advance guard on June 5 but soon found itself overwhelmed by Major General Julius Stahel's Yankee horsemen. Imboden had to bring up the rest of his brigade to rescue the 18th from disaster.

We kept on advancing and did not fire a shot in return. When we got within one half to three quarters of a mile from the Rebs, the right of our line came alongside the banks of the same stream we had crossed lower down.

It was a warm day, and as I was very dry, I thought I would run down to the stream to get a drink, and to fill my canteen. I told Sgt. Charles Carroll, of Company F, and he handed me his canteen, also. The bank was 12 to 15 feet high, but the other bank was about on a level with the stream, and beyond were trees and underbrush.

I dipped up my quart coffee cup full and tipped back my head to drink. But I took only a swallow, for some 60 feet from me, partly be-

Colonel William G. Ely, the highly respected commander of the 18th Connecticut Infantry, was captured at Winchester in 1863 and missed the Battle of New Market. He was exchanged in time for Piedmont, where his return lifted the New Englanders' sagging morale and rejuvenated the regiment's fighting spirit. He boldly led the 18th in several charges against the Confederate breastworks at Piedmont.

"It is so blamed aggravating to stand up and be shot at, and not be able to return fire."

But I knew better, and insisted that it was so.

As luck would have it we were just entering a fringe of woods on the side of the hill and a bullet cut a twig from one of the limbs. It fell in such a way that the colonel saw that the bullet must have come from the right, and it was very nearly a line shot for him as he sat on his horse. He acknowledged the truth at once by exclaiming in his usual tone, but a bit more quickly, "I believe you are right, Sergeant." . . .

We had now got pretty near the Rebs' first line of works. This was a stone wall about a foot and a half high, with a few rails on top of it. We were ordered to charge, and went over it with a rush, driving the Rebs ahead of us like a flock of sheep. Where I went over the wall, a Reb had left his gun leaning up against the rails, and about a dozen cartridges lay on the stone wall. These I put in my blouse pocket, and grabbing the gun, I started on a run to catch up.

I thought at last I was to have a chance to shoot back a few times, at least. It is so blamed aggravating to stand up and be shot at, and not be able to return fire. But I was destined to be disappointed. I had gone but a short distance when the colonel spied me with the gun. Again his sonorous voice rang out, "Throw away the gun, Sergeant, stick to your flag."

Well! You bet I was mad. I took the thing by the muzzle, and wound it around a tree in good shape. I made a pair of twins of it in about two seconds. As I turned around from the tree, I spied a Rebel lieutenant skulking off behind a rock. In our rush we had run right past him, and he was now trying to get off among the trees to our right.

I could run like a deer in those days, and had lots of practice. We had been licked in every fight we had had up to that time, and we all had to run. . . . So I went for the lieutenant like a western cyclone, and had nearly reached him, when again my beloved colonel's voice rang out: "Come back, Sergeant! Let somebody that's got a gun go after him!" And there I had just smashed a gun, and by his orders too. But I came back, like the cat, and Charlie Thurber had the honor of capturing the blooming Reb, and he had a real live sword and a pistol hung to him, too!

hind a tree, was a Johnnie Reb loading his gun, and partly hidden were a good many more. I looked around to sing out to some of our boys, but the bank hid them and hid me from them. I don't believe the Rebs could have seen me, as my feet did not seem to touch the ground until I had caught up with the regiment and told Sergeant Carroll what I had seen. Then we both peered over the bank and saw any number of Johnnies among the trees and some up in them.

At this time we were getting near enough to the hill in front so that they had opened up on us with musketry, and our boys were beginning to fire back. Our skirmishers had fallen back in the rear of the line of battle. Just at this time I saw our Col. William G. Ely (and a better fighter never straddled a horse), in the rear of the center of the regiment. I made a rush for him and told him of the Rebs we had seen on our right.

The colonel was a very moderate talker, but a very decided one. He said, in his slow way, "Oh, no! Sergeant, there ain't any Rebs there!"

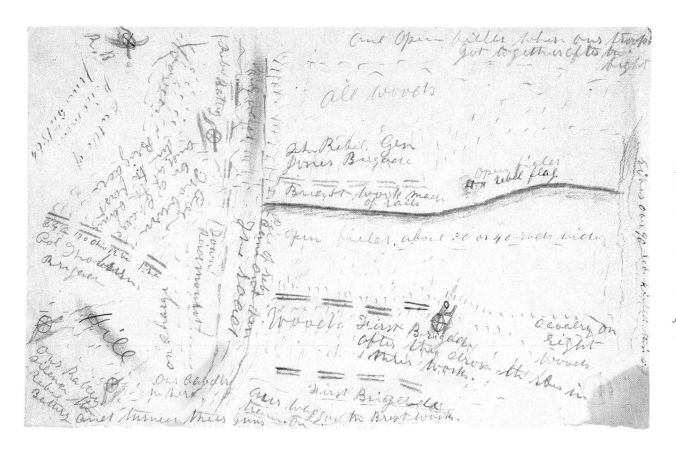

Musician J. Chapin Warner of the 34th Massachusetts, Thoburn's brigade, sketched this map of the Piedmont battlefield on the evening after the battle. Warner's unit played a large part in the victory, attacking on the extreme Federal left, repulsing a Confederate counterattack, and killing Rebel commander "Grumble" Jones. For most of the men, this was their first victory and prompted much celebration.

Sergeant August Goebe of the 28th Ohio Infantry was twice wounded at Piedmont. The 28th, a German-American unit, was raised in Cincinnati in 1861 by Colonel Augustus Moor and honed into a well-disciplined outfit under Moor's Prussian-style training. Although the regiment was due to be mustered out shortly after the Battle of Piedmont, it fought wholeheartedly there, losing 138 men killed and wounded. Goebe reenlisted as a veteran volunteer.

LIEUTENANT HENRY OCKER
28TH OHIO INFANTRY, MOOR'S BRIGADE

Ocker's unit had been supporting the artillery when the call came for it to rejoin the brigade, which had already launched one unsuccessful attack against the Rebels. Ocker and his comrades had fought at the Battles of Antietam and South Mountain in 1862, but he considered Piedmont "the hardest and bloodiest fight" the regiment had ever had. Ocker originally wrote his account in German and sent it back to his mother in the town of Diepholz, along with a full-length oil painting of himself.

Soon thereafter the first brigade, of which our regiment was a part, was ordered to advance by our colonel [Moor] and, reaching a bald hill, we stopped.—Here we were received by a murderous musket fire, and to obtain better cover, the regiment went down flat on their bellies and loaded the muskets lying on their backs. The other regiments of the brigade to our right and left could with this fire hardly hold their line and made off, leaving us behind alone, fighting

"After taking our place in line we were not allowed to fire, as we expected the enemy to assault us at any moment."

with 6 to 7 rebel regiments plus artillery.—Our artillery, by their excellent case shot fire, helped a great deal during the battle, but the horrible mass of fire-spitting cannon mouths which were aimed at the front of our regiment, brought us a great loss of men, dead and wounded, but no one gave ground, every one held his position, and so we fought for three quarters of an hour and were then ordered back, to be replaced by a line of skirmishers.—The regiment, crawling on their belly, continuing to fire, slowly retreated, until they had reached a covered position, then stood up, made a right turn-about and marched into the wooded area to the place where we were positioned and sat down.

PRIVATE J. L. HENRY
1st Tennessee (C.S.) Cavalry (Dismounted), Vaughn's Brigade

Henry's regiment served primarily in east Tennessee, its home area, under the highly regarded Colonel James Carter. In early June the 1st Tennessee, with most of Vaughn's brigade, was rushed by train from Bristol using a circuitous route that took them to Lynchburg, Charlottesville, and finally, Staunton, enabling "Grumble" Jones to concentrate troops rapidly in the face of the threat from Hunter.

Rebel brigadier general John C. Vaughn of Tennessee was no stranger to disaster. In 1863 most of his brigade was captured at the Battle of Big Black Bridge during Grant's campaign for Vicksburg. After being exchanged, Vaughn returned to east Tennessee and reorganized the brigade. At Piedmont, he lost almost 300 men killed, wounded, or captured. In spite of this high casualty rate, Imboden falsely asserted that Vaughn had refused to fight at Piedmont.

The 1st, 59th, and 31st Tennessee Regiments were ordered to reënforce the left wing, and the 43d Regiment and 12th Battalion were left on the right to support our artillery. On our way around to the left of our line the 1st Tennessee Cavalry, to which I belonged, was halted. While General Vaughn was making us a speech and we were cheering, the Yankees got our range with their batteries, and the limbs from the trees fell all around us, several of our regiment being killed and wounded.

We then had to face the enemy's fire, which was terrific, to get our place in the line of battle, and we lost many good men, killed and wounded. After taking our place in line we were not allowed to fire, as we expected the enemy to assault us at any moment, the fighting being at close range, and they had nothing to do but to deliberately shoot our frail defenses to pieces. Finally the expected assault came, and from the time they entered the field until they were repulsed in front of our lines their loss in killed and wounded was fearful. Soon they rallied, and after being heavily reënforced they made the second attempt to break our line, headed by the 1st New York Veteran Cavalry, and were again repulsed, that splendid cavalry regiment being almost annihilated.

In the third attempt to break through they massed almost their entire force and hurled it against our frail line, when our center, held by the 60th Virginia, gave way, and, pouring through the gap left in our line, we were almost surrounded and had to cut our way out and pass through a heavy crossfire.

PRIVATE THOMAS J. EVANS

54TH PENNSYLVANIA INFANTRY, THOBURN'S BRIGADE

Although at 40 years of age one of the oldest in his unit, Evans, a native of Wales, won the Medal of Honor for capturing the battle flag of the 45th Virginia Infantry at Piedmont. Charging directly into a gap in the Confederate line, his regiment encountered little direct resistance and swept along the length of the Confederate breastworks, rolling up the enemy line and taking hundreds of prisoners, including a brigade commander. Evans' medal was bestowed on December 4, 1864.

About noon the Captain ordered us to put bayonets on our rifles and then he moved the company up to the top of that ridge, where we lay down and fired a volley at the Confederates located in some woods on our front. We had surprised the Rebels on their flank and they were right mixed up. We had just loaded up when all of a sudden the Captain ordered us to charge them. We jumped up with a big yell and took out across an open field for all we were worth hoping those Rebels wouldn't start shooting before we could get in among them. When it came to shooting you couldn't beat those boys.

In front of me a Confederate officer in a gray uniform was waving his sword and shouting, "New Market! New Market! Remember New Market!"

"Boys, shoot that officer before he starts a rally!" shouted one of our officers.

Several of us cut loose at him and he spun around, dropped his sword, and fell to the ground. The Rebel soldiers that had been collecting around him disappeared. Suddenly the biggest Rebel I ever saw was right in front of me waving a flag.

"Rally, Boys, Rally!" he was shouting.

Well, I was glad my bayonet was on my rifle instead of at my side, but I had never used it before except as a candle holder or to roast a little meat. Now here I was with my rifle unloaded and about to attack this giant who was about the size of a full grown grizzly bear. I hauled off and hit that flag staff a right smart whack with the bayonet and it must have really stung that Johnny's hands. He sort of lowered the flag and I didn't know what else to do but grab the cloth with my left hand and pull.

"Let go Reb!" I shouted.

"Let go yourself!" says he.

We pulled back and forth and went around in a circle, him about to win since he was using two hands to my one. I finally managed to raise my rifle and says, "Drop that there flag or I will pin you to a tree!"

Well now, he saw it wasn't any use and gave up and I sent him to the rear because the minnie balls were flying around right thick yet and there wasn't any use of us both getting killed. I handed that flag to the Lieutenant and got off another shot or two before the Confederates started to retreat. We lit right in after them and drove them a piece, and that was all for that day.

SERGEANT FOUNTAIN G. SHACKLEFORD

36TH VIRGINIA INFANTRY, JONES' BRIGADE

Like most of the Virginia infantry at Piedmont, Shackleford's regiment had fought at Cloyd's Mountain on May 9, where it lost 111 men. Recruited in what became West Virginia, the 36th later battled the 1st West Virginia Infantry at Piedmont. The Yankee Mountaineers captured the 36th's battle flag and more than 100 officers and men. Shackleford avoided capture and fought throughout the Valley campaign, until he was wounded on September 19 at Winchester.

The fight continued until about the middle of the afternoon, when the right of the command gave way, and being hid from us by the woods, we knew nothing of it, when I looked to the right, the whole of our regiment had given away, and also on the left they were fleeing for safety. I called and said, Pat are you going to leave us here to be captured, while the rest of the command is seeking safety by retreating. After taking in the situation, "he told us to take care of ourselves." Not knowing what direction the enemy was, the most of our men made for the woods, with the expectation of receiving shelter; but instead of that they ran right into the arms of the enemy, and were all captured. A few others with myself, took straight across the cleared land to the bluff of the river. . . . I then let myself down a few feet, when I was out of sight of the enemy. The bluff being very steep, we had to be very cautious, and use saplings for hand hold to let us down; when down, we then had to cross the river, which we done by waiding. As we were in a hurry, we lost but little time. After crossing we had something like a half mile to go across an open field exposed to the fire of the enemy. I supposed they were engaged more in taking care of the prisoners than watching us, as but few balls whizzed passed, which warned us to seek a safer place than the one we had. We soon got to a place of safety, where we met up with three of our command. Among them F. S. Reynolds. Although just out of the fight, the boys had made up a joke on

The state colors of the 36th Virginia bears battle honors solely from actions in Tennessee and western Virginia. It was spared the fate of the unit's battle flag at Piedmont, only to be lost to Federal cavalry in September at Winchester.

Fred, and about the first thing spoken about was his crossing the river, which he did at two leaps, the first to the center and the next to the opposite bank, and that when he struck the center, the velocity being so great, he cleaned the water out to the ground which, of course splashed up into sprays above his head, and with the sun rays acting upon it formed a beautiful hallo, which they took to be a minature rainbow.

This Federal officer's belt was taken from the body of General "Grumble" Jones by Lieutenant James L. Dempsey of the 34th Massachusetts after the general's corpse fell into Union hands. It is probably the same belt Jones wore while serving in the prewar Regular Army on frontier duty in Texas and the Oregon Territory.

LIEUTENANT COLONEL CHARLES T. O'FERRALL

23D VIRGINIA CAVALRY, IMBODEN'S BRIGADE

O'Ferrall received his appointment to the newly formed 23d in late April 1864. He participated in most of the actions of the Valley campaign, but his regiment never performed as brilliantly as at New Market on May 15. On July 11 the 23d led Early's advance on Washington, D.C. Like many former Confederate officers, O'Ferrall was active in state politics after the war.

I was summoned to General Vaughan's headquarters. . . . He wanted me to take two ambulances and a small squad and go on down the road over which I had come the night before, until I met Hunter's advance, and then raising a flag of truce, present a communication addressed by him to General Hunter, asking for the delivery to me of the bodies of General Jones, Colonel Doyle, and Colonel Brown, who as I have said had been killed on the day before. . . .

With two ambulances and a squad of three men I started on my mission with my communication in my pocket. Six miles below Fisherville, if I remember the distance correctly, is Mowery's Hill. As I reached the top of it I saw the Federal cavalry advance a short distance beyond the Mowery homestead at the base of the hill. Instantly I ran up my white flag, and quickening my pace rode down the hill with my men. My approach was seen by the Federal officer, and with three or four men he advanced, and we met right at Mowery's house, under some trees by a stream of clear, cold water from his dairy, or springhouse, as it was called, that ran across the road. We saluted and introduced each other. He was Major Charles G. Otis, of the Twenty-first New York Cavalry. . . .

After the salutation and introduction I said: "Major, I am the bearer of a communication from General Vaughan, commanding the Confederate forces, to General Hunter, commanding the Federal forces. I desire to present it to General Hunter in person. Will you please com-

municate my desire to General Hunter?" He replied instantly, "Why certainly, Colonel."

So writing a note he called a courier and dispatched him with the note, with orders "to be quick." Very naturally the battle of the day before came up and we discussed it. Of course I admitted it was a Union victory, and explained how I thought it occurred. He was not disposed to exult at all. I discovered directly that he was a gentleman of the most refined feelings, and ever cautious not to wound unnecessarily the feelings of another, even though he might be an enemy—"a Johnnie Reb." He admitted to me that in all of Hunter's front attacks the Federals had been badly worsted, and that Hunter was preparing to withdraw and retire when he learned of the gap in our lines; that he then determined to try the movement which I have described, and fortunately for them it was successful, and won the fight for them; that its success was a matter of wonderment with him and the Federal officers generally, who knew of the position and proximity of our cavalry. We continued to chat; the day was very warm, and we were enjoying the shade from the sun, and the atmosphere cooled and freshened by the pearly brook that rippled by us. Suddenly an elderly gentleman, splendidly mounted, rode rapidly down the hill. Stopping where we were sitting he commenced to abuse in the most vigorous style "the d—— Yankees," and insisting that "the last one of these infernal rascals should be taken and strung up to that limb," pointing to a large limb that extended above us over the road.

As soon as I could I checked the old man by saying to him, "You must not talk that way; you should not abuse prisoners—men who are helpless. You evidently think these men are prisoners, but they are not—we are all here under a flag of truce." When he learned the men in blue were not prisoners I never saw such a change come over a man; his face grew ashy pale and he seemed to become limp and almost to reel in his saddle, but in a second he recovered, and wheeling his horse, and with "Good-day, gentlemen," he put spurs to his fine, fleet-footed animal and sailed away in the direction he had come, with his coat-tails standing straight out behind him. . . .

The man who was so abusive of the Yankees and wanted to hang those who were with me was George W. Mowery himself. He thought Otis and his men were prisoners, and when he learned his mistake he feared that his home was doomed, and fearing that he might be identified and his name disclosed, he determined to lose no time in getting away. He did not know me or any Confederate with me; I, however, knew him, but I had sufficient presence of mind not to call his name or to show in any way that I knew him.

As he was taking his rapid departure from us, and Otis and I were watching with interest the beautiful and graceful strides of his horse under the pressure of spur, Otis said with a jolly laugh: "That old fellow evidently has no use for us Yankees. There would not be many of us if he could have his way."

Later in the day the whole Federal army passed his house, and he suffered no material damage. If Hunter had known that its owner had expressed such sentiments as I have related, before the day closed lone chimneys would have stood as sentinels over the charred ruins of Mowery's house.

RICHARD MAUZY
Resident of Staunton

Mauzy owned and edited the Staunton Spectator, the town's newspaper. Like many Valley residents, he lost his property in Hunter's brief but ruthless occupation. Such depredations caused Union colonel Joseph Thoburn to write, "I deeply regret such a course; it can do us no good and is sure to bring us to disgrace and justly too. The innocent will be made to suffer and instead of favoring a return to Union sentiment, the inhabitants will become more incensed against us."

After a short while there came, tramp, tramp, about twenty rough-looking soldiers, who halted at the office and proceeded to enter, when I asked them what they wanted. They said they wanted to enter; when I told them I had the key, and at the same time showed the leader the protection given me. He glanced at it casually, and in a rough tone remarked:

"I have different orders from that, sir." and in they rushed on their mission of destruction.

I followed them in, and pointing to the old Alligator job-press in the front room, said—"that is a job press, I suppose you will not destroy that." They replied that they had printers with them who knew it to be a job-press. They passed that by, and entered the next room in which was the newspaper power press, on which my heart was set, and with bludgeons proceeded to utterly demolish it. I remained among them till I saw that press broken into fragments. I then left them to do their utmost, and went to Mr. Charley Cochran's tobacco store on West New street south of Main or Beverley. Whilst sitting with him, four or five federal soldiers rushed in and helped themselves, hurriedly, to pipes, tobacco, etc, and had not the politeness to thank him; and Charley, "like the boy the calf ran over, had nothing to say," his feelings being inexpressible.

After remaining there a while, I returned to the Spectator office, where I found that not only the newspaper press, but also the job-press, and everything in the office that could be, was destroyed. They even tore to pieces the blank newspaper, cases and type, etc., were thrown into the street to be run over by wagons, and you remember the bushels of printers pi lying on the floor. . . . In the office were the printing material of three different newspapers—Republican, True American, and Spectator—all of which were destroyed or converted into pi.

Colonel Edwin G. Lee, a former regimental commander, had been forced from active campaigning by poor health. He took charge of the military depot at Staunton on June 4, 1864. Learning of Jones' defeat at Piedmont, Lee evacuated as much of his supplies and equipment as possible in wagons and on trains to prevent its capture.

LIEUTENANT COLONEL CHARLES FITZ-SIMONS
21ST NEW YORK CAVALRY, McREYNOLDS' BRIGADE

Hunter expected his army to live off the land, and his cavalry—Fitz-Simons and the 21st New York included—combed the countryside taking food and horses from helpless Valley residents. Fitz-Simons was wounded on July 19 at Ashby's Gap when his regiment attempted to break through Early's rear guard.

After a toilsome night and a day, we gained the mountain source of Tye river. By following its bed, it led us on the morning of the 12th to a point overlooking the luxuriant valley of the James; from a height of two thousand feet we looked down upon the golden vale of Virginia. The rising sun, far eastward, like a chariot of fire, ascended the horizon, made more distant and magnificent by the disappearing mists of the morning. The Tye river, like a thread of silver, wound its way in graceful curves until it joined the James, far below us; broad acres of waving grain, gemmed with dew drops, gladdened our sight. Truly could we say with the poet: "The valley lay smiling before us."

We quickly descended to find that we were in a land of milk and honey. Here, indeed, was the Canaan we had sought for many weary days; here were the storehouses. . . . Paragraph three of Uncle David's general order, No. I, seemed like a prophecy of Jeremiah. Spring chickens, whose incubation had not been disturbed by the sound of cannon, were sacrificed in hecatombs; a whole regiment boasted a breakfast of ham and eggs at one small plantation. Honey, alas! here was the thorn among the roses. The average cavalryman is very careful in handling an apiary, but on this occasion some recruits brought down vengeance upon us, nearly causing a stampede of our whole force. It was indeed fortunate that none of the enemy were near while we were in disorder; not a man of the South, black or white, was to be seen; we had fallen upon an Adamless Eden! . . .

That morning, after first descending to the valley, I left my regiment at the foot of a slight rise of ground, which was crowned by a fine house. Myself and adjutant, having on rubber coats, called at the door and explained we were officers of the McCausland cavalry in search of Yankees. Asking the lady of the house for a drink of water, we soon found ourselves surrounded by a dozen or more females. This completed the only feature lacking in the landscape, to make it, indeed, a paradise on earth. One of the ladies, a saucy young girl, with bright eyes and yellow, curling hair, asked us what the Yankees were like, said she did not believe what we Southern soldiers told "about their being such horrid monsters," and with an inimitable air of coquetry vowed she was just dying to see a Yankee officer. . . .

. . . The adjutant, throwing back his coat said: "Have then thy wish!" At the same time a trooper who had stolen up by the back way was quietly leading off the old family horse, in the deft manner a cavalryman secures a fresh mount. The lieutenant's exclamation, illustrated by the capture of the horse, caused the truth to flash upon the group, and such a shriek went up as fairly rent the skies, followed by hysterical sobs on the part of our golden-haired friend. It took the combined eloquence of adjutant and colonel a long time to assure the ladies they needed to fear no harm; but by returning the horse and placing a guard over the house until the command had passed, we flattered ourselves we had left an improved impression of the Yankees.

COLONEL DAVID H. STROTHER
STAFF, MAJOR GENERAL DAVID HUNTER

Virginia native Strother's harsh indictment of VMI as a school for treason against the United States was instrumental in Hunter's decision to burn it down. The destruction wrought by Hunter in the Valley left deep physical and emotional wounds, creating bitterness that lasted well into the next century. But in the minds of Southern society, the burning of VMI far surpassed Hunter's other depredations.

We entered the town from the west. The cavalry of Averell were coming in from the south, and numerous stragglers of our infantry crossing from the burnt bridge were peeping about for plunder. We rode directly to the Institute and found the sack already far advanced, soldiers, Negroes, and riffraff disputing over the plunder. The private trunks of the cadets seemed to be quite fat and remunerative, and I heard that one soldier got one hundred dollars in gold from one of them. The plunderers came out loaded with beds, carpets, cut velvet chairs, mathematical glasses and instruments, stuffed birds, charts, books, papers, arms, cadet uniforms, and hats in most ridiculous confusion. The General stopped at the house of Major Gilham, a professor of the Institute, and told the lady to get out her furniture as he intended to burn the house in the morning. She was eminently ladylike and was troubled, but yet firm. The house was a state building and it was fair to destroy it, yet it was her only home and it was hard to lose it, but she was a soldier's wife and a soldier's daughter so she set us out some good applejack, apologizing that she had nothing better, and then went to move out her furniture to the lawn. . . .

. . . The General asked my opinion in regard to the destruction of the Institute. I told him I looked upon it as a most dangerous establishment where treason was systematically taught. That I believed the States Rights conspirators had with subtlety and forethought established and encouraged the school for the express purpose of educating the youth of the country into such opinions as would render them ready and efficient tools wherewith to overthrow the government of the country when the hour and opportunity arrived. Throughout the pamphlet literature of the school, addresses, speeches, and circulars, we saw one prominent and leading idea—that the Cadet in receiving this education from the sovereign state owed allegiance and military service to the state alone, and if he should be called to serve the Government of the United States he could only do so by the order and permission of the sovereign state of Virginia. The same infamous and treasonable doctrines were taught at the University of Virginia, and, while all the other educational institutions in the state had dwindled into insignificance, these two expressly used as schools of treason were fostered by the state authorities until they were prosperous and plethoric. To their joint influence might be traced the prevalence and fixedness of their monstrous doctrines among the educated men in the South. The catalogue of the Institute itself showed what a list of capable military officers had been there raised up against the government of the country. This was the great paramount reason for its destruction by fire.

There were military reasons besides. The professors and cadets had taken the field against government troops, as an organized corps. The buildings had been used as a Rebel arsenal and recently as a fortress. . . . The order was given to fire the building and all the houses and outbuildings.

As this order was executed, the plunderers came running out, their arms full of spoils. One fellow had a stuffed gannet from the museum of natural history; others had the high-topped hats of cadet officers, and most of them were loaded with the most useless and impracticable articles. Lieutenant Meigs came out with fine mathematical instruments, and Dr. Patton followed with a beautiful human skeleton. Some of the officers brought out some beautifully illustrated volumes of natural history which they presented to me. I, however, felt averse to taking anything and left them at Professor Smith's. My only spoil was a new gilt button marked "V.M.I." and a pair of gilt epaulettes which some of the clerks had picked up and handed to me. The burning of the Institute made a grand picture, a vast volume of black smoke rolled above the flames and covered half the horizon. . . .

. . . The Institute burnt out about two P.M. and the arsenal blew up with a smart explosion. The General seemed to enjoy this scene and turning to me expressed his great satisfaction at having me with him.

This picture depicts the VMI barracks after they were burned by Hunter's troops. Although the facility had been used for military purposes, its razing brought little gain to the Federal cause. On the contrary, the event served to heighten Southern resolve in the face of the Yankee military presence and provided an effective propaganda tool for Southern politicians and writers.

After the war this Model 1851 VMI Cadet rifle was found in the Maury River, where it had been thrown to keep it from Hunter's men. When Hunter occupied Lexington, his troops captured five cannons, numerous caissons, and a quantity of small arms and ammunition. The Federals also destroyed six barges laden with commissary stores and artillery ammunition.

"Your name will stand on history's page as the Hunter of weak women and innocent children."

Captain Henry A. DuPont of Delaware, an 1861 graduate of West Point, command-ed the Federal artillery brigade and, like a number of other officers, decried Hunter's destruction of VMI. DuPont's handling of the guns at Piedmont contributed greatly to that victory, and he later earned the Medal of Honor for bravery at Cedar Creek.

HENRIETTA LEE
RESIDENT OF SHEPHERDSTOWN

After Mrs. Lee's home in Shepherdstown was burned in July on Hunter's orders, she promptly penned this venomous letter to "Black Dave." Although the destruc-tion loosed upon the Valley by Major General Philip H. Sheridan several months later would be on a far greater scale, Hunter's penchant for burning revered insti-tutions and the homes of prominent families—including the Lexington residence of Governor John Letcher—earned him the everlasting ire of Virginians.

Jefferson County, July 20, 1864.
General Hunter:
Yesterday your underling, Captain [Franklin G.] Martindale, of the First New York cavalry, executed your infamous order and burned my house. You have had the satisfaction ere this of receiving from him the information that your orders were fulfilled to the letter; the dwelling and every outbuilding, seven in number, with their con-tents, being burned. I, therefore, a helpless woman whom you have cruelly wronged, address you, a Major General of the United States army, and demand why this was done? What was my offence? My hus-band was absent, an exile. He had never been a politician or in any way engaged in the struggle now going on, his age preventing. This fact your Chief-of-Staff, David Strother, could have told you.

The house was built by my father, a Revolutionary soldier, who served the whole seven years for your independence. There was I born; there the sacred dead repose. It was my house and my home, and there has your niece (Miss Griffith) who has tarried among us all this horrid war . . . to the present time, met with all kindness and hospitality at my hands. Was it for this that you turned me, my young daughter and little son out upon the world without a shelter? Or was it because my hus-band is the grandson of the Revolutionary patriot and "rebel," Richard Henry Lee, and the near kinsman of the noblest of Christian warriors, the greatest of Generals, Robert E. Lee? Heaven's blessing be upon his head forever. You and your Government have failed to conquer, subdue or match him; and disappointment, rage and malice find vent on the helpless and inoffensive.

Hyena like you have torn my heart to pieces! for all hallowed memo-ries clustered around that homestead, and demon like you have done it without even the pretext of revenge, for I never saw or harmed you. Your office is not to lead, like a brave man and soldier, your men to fight in the ranks of war, but your work has been to separate yourself from all danger, and with your incendiary band steal unawares upon helpless women and children, to insult and destroy. Two fair homes did you yesterday ruthlessly lay in ashes, giving not a moment's warning to the startled inmates of your wicked purpose; turning mothers and children out of doors, you are execrated by your own men for the cruel work you give them to do.

In the case of Colonel A. R. Boteler, both father and mother were far away. Any heart but that of Captain Martindale (and yours) would have been touched by that little circle, comprising a widowed daughter just risen from her bed of illness, her three fatherless babies—the oldest not five years old—and her heroic sister. I repeat, any man would have been touched at that sight but Captain Martindale. One might as well hope to find mercy and feeling in the heart of a wolf bent on his prey of young lambs, as to search for such qualities in his bosom. You have chosen well your agent for such deeds, and doubtless will promote him!

A colonel of the Federal army has stated that you deprived forty of your officers of their commands because they refused to carry on your malignant mischief. All honor to their names for this at least! They are men—they have human hearts and blush for such a commander!

I ask who that does not wish infamy and disgrace attached to him forever would serve under you? Your name will stand on history's page as the Hunter of weak women and innocent children; the Hunter to destroy defenceless villages and refined and beautiful homes—to torture afresh the agonized hearts of widows; the Hunter of Africa's poor sons and daughters to lure them on to ruin and death of soul and body; the Hunter with the relentless heart of a wild beast, the face of a fiend and the form of a man. Oh, Earth, behold the monster! Can I say, "God forgive you?" No prayer can be offered for you! Were it possible for human lips to raise your name heavenward, angels would thrust the foul thing back again, and demons claim their own. The curses of thousands, the scorn of the manly and upright and the hatred of the true and honorable, will follow you and yours through all time, and brand your name infamy! Infamy!

Again, I demand why you have burned my home? Answer as you must answer before the Searcher of all hearts, why have you added this cruel, wicked deed to your many crimes?

Henrietta E. Lee.

CORPORAL ADAM H. PLECKER
Botetourt (Virginia) Artillery, McCausland's Command

As Hunter closed in on Lynchburg, Confederate authorities gathered troops from throughout Virginia to confront the Federal army. Plecker had served in southwest Virginia since being exchanged following his capture at Vicksburg in 1863. In May 1864 his unit helped resist Brigadier General George Crook's raid. The following month the Botetourt Artillery once again hastened to the threatened area, riding the cars of the Virginia & Tennessee Railroad.

On arriving at Lynchburg, we were told to remain for further orders . . . we left next day. . . . On arriving at Amherst Station, fourteen miles out, we were informed that the enemy was in our front, destroying the road. Captain Douthat prevailed on the conductor to take his company on to the next station, or as far as he felt safe to go. Arriving at the next station, we could see the smoke from the burning depot at Arrington, six miles off. Midway between the two stations was a railroad bridge (a large wooden structure) over Tye River. Now, we knew if the enemy got to that bridge the loss would be great. "But what can we do here with guns on these cars and no horses?" said the

Brigadier General John C. McCausland (left), an infantry brigade commander, took over Brigadier General Albert G. Jenkins' mounted brigade after Jenkins was mortally wounded near Cloyd's Mountain. McCausland boldly delayed Hunter's advance on Lynchburg, buying time for the Confederacy to assemble a force large enough to hold that crucial supply and railroad center.

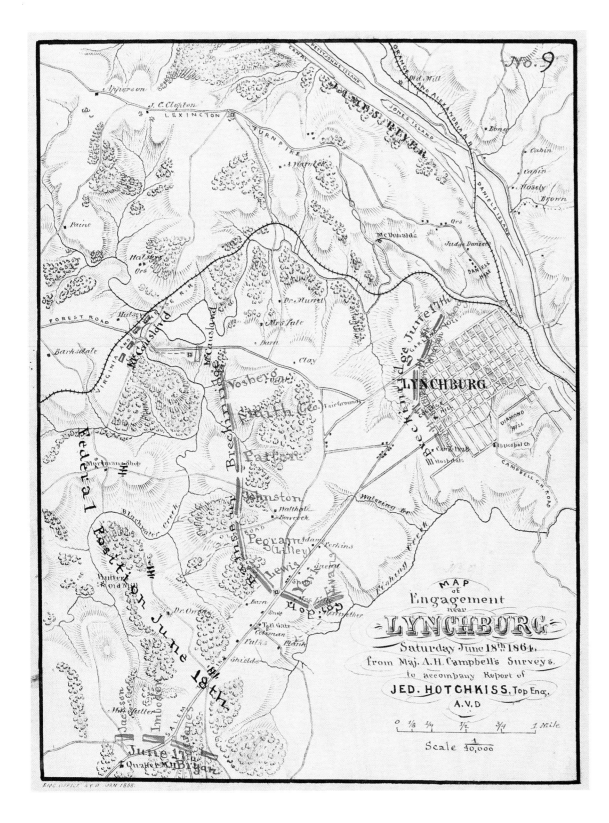

MAP
of
Engagement
near
LYNCHBURG
Saturday June 18th 1864,
from Maj. A.H. Campbell's Surveys.
to accompany Report of
JED. HOTCHKISS, Top Eng.
A.V.D.

Scale 1/40,000

Major Jedediah Hotchkiss, Stonewall Jackson's cartographer, now on the staff of Early's Second Corps, drew this map of the engagement at Lynchburg. On June 17 an advance by Hunter drove the weary Rebel cavalry behind the city's defenses. On the following day Hunter probed the enemy lines and confirmed that Jubal Early had arrived with reinforcements from the Army of Northern Virginia. Early then launched a sortie of his own, and although the action never became general, Hunter lost his nerve and retreated into the mountains of West Virginia.

captain. Some one said: "Let's rock them." Another spoke up and said: "There are small arms in one of the cars. I saw them put on in the city before we left." In a few minutes every man had a gun, with ammunition in his pockets, and started at a double-quick three miles to that bridge, got there at dark, and placed pickets. Captain Douthat asked me to take two good men and take position on a hill about five hundred yards beyond the bridge, in a road leading from the burned depot, and keep a good lookout should the enemy show up. "And when you are sure of your game, fire on them and fall back to the bridge," he said.

The night was very dark, and with woods in our front we could see nothing. About midnight we heard the tramp of horses on the hard road. We halted them when within proper distance, and asked who they were. They stopped, but made no reply. I asked again, "And if you don't tell me we will fire on you." At that they turned tail and went back at a rapid rate. We fired after them and still held our post. Now, I have every evidence to believe that it was the enemy coming to destroy that bridge. Shortly after daylight they came in contact with some of our cavalry, on the lookout for them, and were driven back across the mountain into Rockbridge County. After burying one of our men, who accidentally lost his life at the bridge, the company marched back to Lynchburg, twenty-three miles, as our train with guns had returned to the city soon after we left it. At Lynchburg we got horses and moved to a redoubt on Amherst Heights. On the morning of the 17th, the battery was ordered to the city, and lay all day on Church Street, every man at his post, awaiting orders to go on to the front, as the enemy was quite near the city at that time. At dark we moved to the inner lines on College Hill. Early the next morning we were ordered to move to the front lines, with four guns on the forest road, and two on the Salem Turnpike. Those on the forest road were just in time to drive the enemy back from the railroad and a railroad bridge over Ivy Creek they were trying to burn. They made several attempts to get to the road and bridge in the early part of the day.

During the early morning we met with an accident in the bursting of one of our guns, and Lieutenant Obenchain took the disabled gun and detachment back to the city to get a new one. On arriving at the depot, where a number of guns were parked, he was told by the officer in charge that he could not get one without the proper permit, and for him to go up into the city and see "Major So-and-So," who would give him an order on "Captain So-and-So," then to bring the order to him, and he would get the gun. Now, Lieutenant Obenchain was not a profane man, and it was hard to tell what was passing through his mind at that

time, but he told the officer that the case was very urgent; that the enemy was likely to enter the city any moment, and these guns would all go up with the city. A gun he had come for, and he was going to have it, regardless of the red tape, so he ordered his men to take charge of a gun and move rapidly to the front. With a smile he saluted the astonished officer, telling him to charge the gun up to the Botetourt Artillery. The gun arrived in good time to help drive the enemy back from the railroad and bridge. Finally they gave up it, placed a battery on the high grounds beyond the railroad, and spent the rest of the day shelling us. We replied in kind, and before daylight on the 19th, General Hunter was on the run for the mountains of West Virginia, with our battery in hot pursuit.

Jubal Anderson Early led Jackson's old Second Corps into Lynchburg. He ran a single train back and forth during the night of June 17 and ordered troops to cheer and bands to play, creating the impression that reinforcements were continually arriving. Hunter, already primed by wild rumors, fell for the ruse.

"The hurling and crashing of flying missles, the explosion of shells, and the yells of the victorious enemy, combined to make it one of the wildest battle scenes we ever witnessed."

LIEUTENANT COLONEL THOMAS F. WILDES
116TH OHIO INFANTRY, WELLS' BRIGADE

Wildes was born in Canada, the son of Irish immigrants. The family later settled in Ohio, where Wildes became a newspaper editor. He fought in the Valley throughout 1864, eventually commanding a brigade at Cedar Creek. Promoted to brigadier general, he served out the balance of the war in Tennessee.

The rebels were making a charge on our center, which they were driving back slowly. Two different regiments went forward in turn to check the rebel advance, but each was repulsed. By this time we had reached a position directly in the course of the regiment that had been last sent in, and was now falling back through us in disorder. Here we halted to stop the further advance of the enemy. We had hardly halted, before Colonel Washburn received an order to "charge with the 116th." We immediately formed for the charge, and went down upon the charging rebels, just as they were ascending a hill. We had the advantage in charging down, as they were charging up the hill, and we not only checked them, but they broke in wild confusion to their breastworks. Clambering over them, we pushed on to their second line, being now reinforced by the 5th West Virginia, under Colonel Enochs. Here we were met by a very heavy force well entrenched, and, lying down, we fought hard against desperate odds, waiting for help, which we felt would surely come, until we were assaulted on both

In 1862 Captain Edwin Keyes of the 116th Ohio Infantry raised his entire company in three days and commanded it until he was mortally wounded in the fighting at Lynchburg on June 18. Like many other wounded Federals, Keyes was left behind when Hunter retreated. The Confederates placed him in General Hospital No. 3 in Lynchburg, where he died from the effects of his wounds the next day.

flanks by infantry, and by grape and cannister from a battery, planted not five rods in our front. We then fell back to the first line of works we had taken, and on their face, fought again, until we were struck on our left by a large force which crossed over the works in the woods on that flank. We then fell back to a position in the woods, through which we had charged, where we remained for some time unmolested, and to which we carried most of our wounded. Among our badly wounded was Captain Edwin Keyes and Color Sergeant Fred E. Humphrey, both of whom we were obliged to leave behind us. . . .

. . . The Captain had a knee and an elbow shattered with musket balls, and he died at Lynchburg on the 19th of July, from the effects of these wounds. He led his company most heroically in the battle, and received his first wound in the knee, at the last moment, in holding his company against the charge made on our left, just before we fell back into the woods from the rebel works, and his second, in the elbow, just as we began to fall back. He was carried back by his men, and when he heard the command to halt given out along the line in the woods, he repeated it to his men and directed them to form in their places. As soon as it was learned that he was badly wounded, the officers and his men gathered about him to bid him farewell, for it was evident he could not be moved far. The rebels were now shelling the woods with great fury, and being still within range of their grape and cannister, also the rattle of small arms, the hurling and crashing of flying missles, the explosion of shells, and the yells of the victorious enemy, combined to make it one of the wildest battle scenes we ever witnessed.

COLONEL DAVID H. STROTHER
STAFF, MAJOR GENERAL DAVID HUNTER

Strother was uncomfortably familiar with the experience of fleeing from Rebels in the Valley. He had escaped Jackson with General Banks in 1862 and then again from Breckinridge with Sigel just a few weeks before Lynchburg. The retreat that began the evening of June 18 must have struck him as a particularly bitter reversal of fortune, coming as it did in the wake of the brief Federal mastery of the Valley.

The skirmishing fire was increasing and we heard the frequent report of telescopic rifles, an arm which had not before been brought to bear on us. The heavy balls came whistling back among the staff, one passing between the General and Stockton as they sat talking on horseback. The sound of these rifles suggested the presence of Richmond troops among the defenders.

Passing through the recumbent lines I perceived that everybody was dismounted and lying down. I therefore dismounted myself and tied my horse to a swinging limb. At some distance to the front I saw Colonel Wells and another person behind some large oaks reconnoitering. I could hear the balls whistling and clipping among the trees, made my observations but saw nothing additional except that the works had progressed and were very full of men. I also saw the spires of Lynchburg in the distance. While we stood there, several rifle balls struck the tree and scattered bark upon us. I called on Sullivan who was with Colonel Thoburn lying on the ground on some boards. Sullivan said he had heard the railroad trains coming and going all night, also cheering and military music which indicated the arrival of troops in the town. Since morning the lines were very much strengthened and were pressing him hard. He was sustaining himself with difficulty. He said he was ready to attack if ordered but he felt assured it would end in disaster. Thoburn spoke in the same strain and in somewhat more decided language. I said I had begun to suspect they were right and that I would represent their views to the General. . . .

Five prisoners brought in by Sullivan were questioned, which indicated beyond a doubt that Ewell's Corps commanded by General Early was in Lynchburg. These fellows were North Carolinians and said they had marched four days from Richmond to Charlottesville and had come thence by railroad last night. They represented the force in Lynchburg at thirty thousand men. The commanders acknowledged the position to be critical and all agreed that we must get out if possible. Crook was cool and matter of fact. Averell was excited and angry. He said to me, "I would give my head this night if we could have taken Lynchburg." I replied that the desire was past. We had but to make good our retreat. He said he was not afraid of them. I said neither was I and I be damned to them, nevertheless we should have to retreat. General Hunter immediately ordered the trains to move on the back track toward Buford's Gap. . . .

. . . The firing was lept up until dark and when it died, we started to Liberty. The troops were all withdrawn in silence and our picket line remained until midnight, when it also withdrew and overtook the main body in safety. We took off everything except about 150 wounded which Dr. Hayes had in a temporary hospital and left because he had no notice of the move. This withdrawal in the face of a superior force was well conducted and successful.

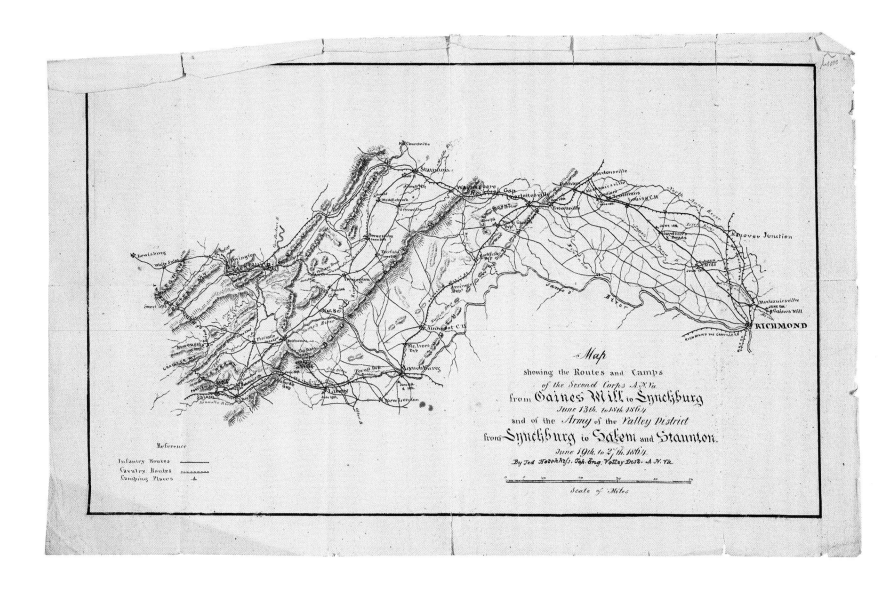

Map

showing the Routes and Camps
of the Second Corps A.N.Va
from *Gaines Mill* to *Lynchburg*
June 13th. to 18th. 1864
and of the *Army* of the *Valley District*
from *Lynchburg* to *Salem* and *Staunton*.
June 19th. to 27th. 1864.
By Jed Hotchkiss, Top. Eng. Valley Dist. A.N.Va

Scale of Miles

Reference

Infantry Routes
Cavalry Routes
Camping Places

BRIGADIER GENERAL WILLIAM G. LEWIS
Brigade Commander, Army of the Valley

Born in Rocky Mount, North Carolina, in 1835, Lewis was educated at Lovejoy's Military School in Raleigh and graduated from the University of North Carolina at the age of 19. He was placed in command of Hoke's brigade in the spring of 1864 and led it in the Valley until he was wounded at Stephenson's Depot on July 20. He was wounded again near Farmville two days before Lee's surrender at Appomattox. After the war, Lewis served for 13 years as the state engineer of North Carolina.

We are now far up in the Valley of Virginia, after a very tedious march from Lynchburg. If you will look on the map, you can easily see the route this corps has taken since it left the vicinity of Richmond. We passed along the Central R.R. through Louisa Court House, to Charlottsville. There we took the R.R. to Lynchburg. From that place we followed the Yankee army along the line of the Virginia & Tennessee R.R. by Liberty—through Bufords Gap, in the Blue Ridge & thence to Salem & Hanging Rock Gap—in some spurs of the Alleghany mountains. Failing to capture the Yankee force, who were

A New York native, Jedediah Hotchkiss moved to the Shenandoah Valley in 1846 at 17 and eventually settled in Churchville, Augusta County, where he ran a school with his brother. He studied topography and soon began drawing maps of Valley locales. This experience made him the ideal topographical engineer for the Confederacy's Valley District. Hotchkiss created the maps shown on the facing page and above, which depict Jubal Early's route of march from Richmond to Lynchburg and his progression down the Shenandoah Valley to Washington, D.C. Early's Second Corps left Richmond on June 13 and began arriving in Lynchburg four days later, just in time to confront Hunter. On July 5 Early crossed the Potomac and entered Maryland, arriving at the northern outskirts of Washington on July 11.

too swift for us, we turned towards Staunton, passing through Lexington, where the Virginia Military Institute was located, but now burned by the Yankees. At Lexington we were marched by Jacksons grave, which was covered with beautiful fresh flowers, as if some loving one remembered the dead hero every day by scattering sweet flowers over his last resting place. You have no idea what feelings passed over me as I went by his grave. There lay *the* great christian patriot & soldier, the unsurpassed warrior of his time, cold in death, & as harmless as the flowers that covered his grave. And the thought that Yankee Vandals had passed over his grave, who could never stand before him while alive, & passed in triumph as conquerors, stirred feelings within me, that I at least, would strike the hardest blows in my power to prevent such an occurrence again. I believe some of Jacksons spirit was instilled into the breasts of those hardy veterans who had followed him in so many hard marches, & fought with him on so many stubborn but victorious fields. This Valley of Virginia is one of the most beautiful countries in the world, & teeming with the prettiest ladies you ever saw. The roads were decked with them, who came from the surrounding country, to give a welcome & wave a nice white handerchieg, & smile sweetly at the "boys" who had rid them of the Yankee plunderers & thieves. Our march was almost an ovation. I paid considerable attention to some of the young ladies on the route. I believe I like ladies company now better than I did before I was married.

MAJOR JEWETT PALMER
36th Ohio Infantry, Hayes' Brigade

Palmer enlisted in August 1861 in the 36th Ohio, a regiment drawn from the Ohio River town of Marietta and originally commanded by George Crook. After seeing action at South Mountain and Antietam, the 36th went west with Crook and fought in the Battles of Chickamauga and Chattanooga, before returning first to West Virginia and then to service throughout the Shenandoah Valley campaign. During the retreat of Hunter's army, Palmer found his own unique form of misery.

The march that night toward Liberty from the city we had come so far to capture, and after lying in sight of its very spires for nearly thirty hours was solemn indeed. Nothing could be heard but the rumbling of the trains and the dull tramp of the column as it moved slowly along the rocky pike. Now and then, some fellow, faint and almost famished, would stumble over some cobbling stone and falling heavily to the ground his rifle could be heard to rattle upon the pike when it would again be recovered while a curse was uttered at the blundering which had caused such a failure and such suffering. The men were worn down and starved until they would go to sleep as they never had. About midnight as we were passing through a small village about ten miles from Lynchburg I went fast asleep in my saddle. The next thing I knew I received a tremendous lick across the lower part of the abdomen. Throwing up my arms I found upon awakening that I was embracing a huge apple tree limb while my horse not feeling like being left behind strove to go ahead, but the limb being so low almost grazed his back and having a saddle with rather a high [cantle], he could not succeed in passing on. As I was held in the saddle as firm as if a vise were acting on me, I was not long in recovering my senses, and, seizing the reins which I had dropped . . . I backed and relieved myself from a dilemma which, had not my horse been worn out and as willing to stop as to make a decided exertion to escape, might have proved a serious matter. I did not go to sleep again soon I assure you as I had enough to do to attend an overruling desire I had to vomit having completely upset my stomach in the battle of the apple tree limb.

Private James A. Bennett Sr. (left) served in Company G, "The Town Fork Invincibles," of the 21st North Carolina. Wounded first at Gettysburg, he fought with Early in the Valley until wounded in a skirmish with Sheridan's cavalry on August 29 near Smithfield. This wound cost him an arm and ended his military service.

LIEUTENANT COLONEL CHARLES HALPINE
Staff, Major General David Hunter

Seeking some consolation for the Yankees' arduous and humiliating retreat to the West Virginia mountains, Halpine later asserted that Hunter's raid to Lynchburg had been a success. He cited the damage inflicted on the Confederacy en route and the fact that Lee had been compelled to detach 10,000 men, 20 percent of his available infantry, to meet this threat to his rear at the same time that General Grant was maneuvering the Army of the Potomac toward Petersburg.

Beautiful, indeed, in its wild and forest-covered sublimity and ruggedness was the country through which we were now passing, had any of us been in the mood to enjoy such scenery. None of us were, however—at least not much; for some pounded corn, with a rasher of bacon or an onion, formed a feast only too rarely attainable even by the highest officers; while day by day the few cattle we had driven along ahead of each division began to fail, and there was literally no food—no cattle, sheep, hogs, or corn—in the ever-rising, ever-falling wilderness of mountains through which our diminishing column trailed its weary length like a wounded, all but dying, serpent. Each mountain-ridge that had risen before us seemed of interminable height. . . .

. . . We found one company, sharp-set by the pangs of hunger and half dead from fatigue, but carrying along with it a wooden-bedded billiard table which the boys thought would be "a nice thing to have in the house" if they ever got back to any Christian camp. "Hang me," said Captain Towne, our chief signal officer, "hang me, if I don't expect to see my rascals carrying a privy along with them, plank by plank, in hopes of setting it up for general delection when they reach Meadow Bluffs!" . . .

But mountain still towered above mountain, each apparently taller than the last; and from the top of each as we gained it, our saddened and sickening eyes dropped down into the deep gulfs of valleys, beyond which towered mountain-walls apparently blacker, steeper, loftier, more sterile and waterless than any we had yet traversed. The limited diet of mere fresh beef, too, without salt, corn, biscuit, or vegetables of any kind, began to revolt the stomachs of the weary men, and cases of aggravated diarrhœa soon became an epidemic. Still, as a whole, the men bore up wonderfully, such of the infantry as were not actually sickened growing more rugged, sinewy, bronzed, and soldierlike—confident that their sufferings were not in vain; that they had inflicted far greater loss on the enemy than paid for all they were enduring.

Major Jewett Palmer is seen above in a type of large, overpainted portrait photograph known as an imperial. Shown below it are his major's shoulder straps. Palmer was promoted to this rank on May 19, just as Crook's army went into bivouac following a grueling 50-mile withdrawal north after the Battle of Cloyd's Mountain.

LIEUTENANT JOHN H. WORSHAM

21ST VIRGINIA INFANTRY, TERRY'S BRIGADE

Worsham had fought in the Shenandoah Valley under Stonewall Jackson in 1862. After most of Jackson's old division was captured at Spotsylvania on May 12, 1864, the remnants of 14 regiments were consolidated into a single brigade that numbered fewer than a thousand men. Nevertheless, Worsham and his comrades would carry on Jackson's legacy of success in the Valley for three months in 1864, winning victories at Lynchburg, Monocacy, and Kernstown.

On the 28th we resumed our march down the valley and felt perfectly at home, since nearly all the valley from Staunton to the Potomac river was familiar to us, and many of its inhabitants old acquaintances. We stopped regularly at night and continued the march each day. On the afternoon of July 3d we reached Martinsburg, running in on the Yankees who were there, so suddenly, that they did not have time to move any of their stores. They were making big preparations to celebrate the Fourth, and many of the men had received boxes of good things from home and friends. The depot and express office were filled with articles of this kind. A guard was placed around these buildings and their storehouses. The express office was put in charge of a quartermaster who was an old friend of mine. At night I went there and inquired of the guard for him and he let me into the building. He was very glad to see me, as he had only one man to help him get these articles in shape, and asked me to help him; this I consented to do, if he would give me a barrel of cakes. He said "all right." I found one and carried it out and turned it over to my company . . . who were profuse in their thanks for the cakes, and soon fell asleep,—dreaming of little cakes, big cakes, and a mountain made of cakes.

The next morning was the Fourth of July, 1864! Gen. Early did not move us at the usual early hour, but issued to the men the good things captured the evening before. They were divided among the men as fairly as possible, F Company getting a few oranges, lemons, cakes and candy, and a keg of lager beer. We certainly enjoyed the treat, and celebrated the day as well as we could for our hosts, and regretted they did not stay to preside for us. We drank their health with the wish that they would do the like again. This was the biggest Fourth of July picnic celebration we enjoyed during the war. We took up our march and crossed the Potomac river at Shepherdstown.

KENNEDY PALMER. Co. H. 13TH VA. INFT. Vols
1861 To 1865 *Aged 17.* RICHMOND, VA.

Kennedy Palmer enlisted in the "Winchester Boomerangs," a company of the 13th Virginia Infantry, in 1861. He was captured in May 1862 near Shepherdstown during Jackson's 1862 Valley campaign. Exchanged and returned to service, he was severely wounded on July 4, 1864, in skirmishing with Federal troops at Bolivar Heights, near Harpers Ferry, as Early's army prepared to cross the Potomac River.

PRIVATE BRISCOE GOODHART
Loudoun Virginia (U.S.) Rangers,
Clendenin's Cavalry Detachment

Goodhart's unit was raised in and around the Unionist town of Waterford in Loudoun County, the heart of the territory dubbed "Mosby's Confederacy." The Loudoun Rangers squared off against Mosby's partisan rangers several times but generally got the worst of it. Goodhart was captured at Charles Town in 1863 and exchanged in March 1864. When Hunter retreated into West Virginia, small units like Goodhart's were left to confront Early's advance into Maryland.

It was learned last night that the enemy was concentrating at Monocacy Junction. Gen. Tyler ordered the entire garrison to put themselves in marching condition. The streets of Frederick presented a scene of great activity and some confusion. It was known to both soldiers and citizens that a large Confederate army was camped within 10 miles of the city, and that a battle was inevitable in probably less than 24 hours, and possibly in their own beautiful city. Gen. Tyler's troops moved out on the Baltimore pike, about 9 o'clock p.m., crossing the stone bridge over the Monocacy River and turning sharply to the right, continued down the stream to the Junction. The movement was made as quietly as possible, and, of necessity, was tedious. Several stops were made during the night, so the infantry and trains would be well up. We arrived about 1 o'clock a.m., and lay down on the ground, holding our horses by their bridles. We had been under fire for six days and nights, and as soon as we struck the ground were sound asleep. The sun rose clear and beautiful on the morning of the 9th. Looking west across Monocacy River, about one mile distant, lay Early's army, having arrived during the night. It was now settled beyond a doubt—both armies were encamped on ground where was to be fought a battle.

Federal soldier Charles W. Reed made this pen-and-ink drawing of Jubal Early demanding $200,000 from the elders of Frederick, Maryland, on July 9. Reed depicted the event as occurring in the rain, but one Virginian later wrote that it was "a beautiful day in this beautiful country." After Early made his demands, he left the details in the hands of staff officers and turned his attention to the enemy forces gathering on the far bank of the Monocacy River.

Monocacy

With Jubal Early's Confederate invasion force in a position to threaten either Washington or Baltimore, Lew Wallace began shifting Federal troops from the Baltimore defenses to Monocacy Junction, just south of Frederick, Maryland. The Monocacy River provided a natural barrier to Early's advance and enabled Wallace to guard the principal highways leading east to Baltimore and south to the capital.

On July 7 and 8, as Wallace skirmished with the vanguard of Early's column west of Frederick, Union reinforcements were arriving at the junction by train. Two veteran brigades from the VI Corps of Grant's army under the command of Brigadier General James B. Ricketts were particularly welcome, as most of Wallace's men were either inexperienced garrison troops or hastily organized militia.

By the morning of July 9 Wallace had pulled back to the heights east of the Monocacy where, with fewer than 7,000 troops, he prepared to give battle to a Rebel force that numbered between 12,000 and 14,000. Guessing that Washington was the enemy's intended goal, Wallace placed his least experienced troops—Brigadier General Erastus B. Tyler's brigade—on the National road, guarding the stone bridge that carried the highway east to Baltimore.

The bulk of his force he positioned two miles farther south, astride the B&O Railroad and the Washington-Georgetown pike. He fronted it with a strong skirmish line on the west bank of the Monocacy, screening the approaches to the bridges carrying the railroad and the pike, and he placed a battery of artillery on the heights overlooking the spans. But Wallace could not guard the entire stretch of the Monocacy to its confluence with the Potomac, and he knew that his left flank would be vulnerable should the Rebels find a fording place.

On July 9 Early's three divisions marched out of Frederick and soon ran into the forward Yankee positions. Heading east on the National road, Major General Robert E. Rodes' division encountered Tyler's Federals on a ridge just west of the highway bridge, while Major General Stephen D. Ramseur's division tangled with the Yankee skirmish line near Monocacy Junction. Unwilling to risk a costly assault on the Federal bridgeheads, Early pondered his options.

At about 10:30 a.m. McCausland's Virginia cavalry brigade located a farm ford a mile south of the Union left flank. Brushing aside a small Union cavalry detail, McCausland's horsemen crossed the river and came into line. Confident that the enemy facing him were nothing but nervous militiamen, McCausland dismounted his troopers and sent them forward in a charge. But the deadly volleys of Ricketts' VI Corps soldiers brought the Rebels to a standstill. A second foray was also thrown back.

When Early learned of the cavalry's crossing and repulse, he directed Gordon's division to follow up McCausland and assault the Federal left. Gordon's battle-hardened brigades forded the Monocacy and deployed in lines of battle behind the cover of a hill. Then they swept over the crest and stormed the Yankee position.

Holding the high ground, Ricketts' troops savaged the Rebel ranks with a deadly fire that stymied Gordon's two leading brigades—led by Brigadier Generals Clement A. Evans and Zebulon York. With casualties mounting, Gordon took direction of Brigadier General William

R. Terry's Virginians and led a charge that smashed through the Yankee brigade nearest the river. With Ricketts' line unhinged, Wallace had no option but to order a retreat northward, yielding the Washington pike to the enemy.

In the meantime Ramseur, having skirmished all day long against the Federal troops west of the Monocacy, finally managed in the late afternoon to cross the river on the iron railroad bridge, linking up with Gordon's troops and snagging several hundred prisoners. But the majority of Wallace's defenders made good their escape, gaining the road to Baltimore, where Tyler still held Rodes' division at bay. Early settled for having rooted the Federals out of their blocking position and prepared to resume his march on Washington.

While the precise number of Confederate casualties at Monocacy is uncertain, it seems likely that Early lost somewhere between 900 and 1,000 men, 700 of them from Gordon's division, which bore the brunt of the fighting. The Federal loss totaled some 1,300, more than 500 of whom were captured or missing.

Lew Wallace had been unable to halt Early's offensive, but by delaying the Rebels for a full day, he had bought precious time for reinforcements from Grant's army to bolster the defenses of the nation's capital.

The climactic phase of the Battle of Monocacy on July 9 began at 4:00 p.m., when Gordon's Confederate division managed to dislodge Ricketts' brigades from their position on the Thomas farm, and Ramseur's division finally drove stubborn Federal skirmishers back across the railroad bridge.

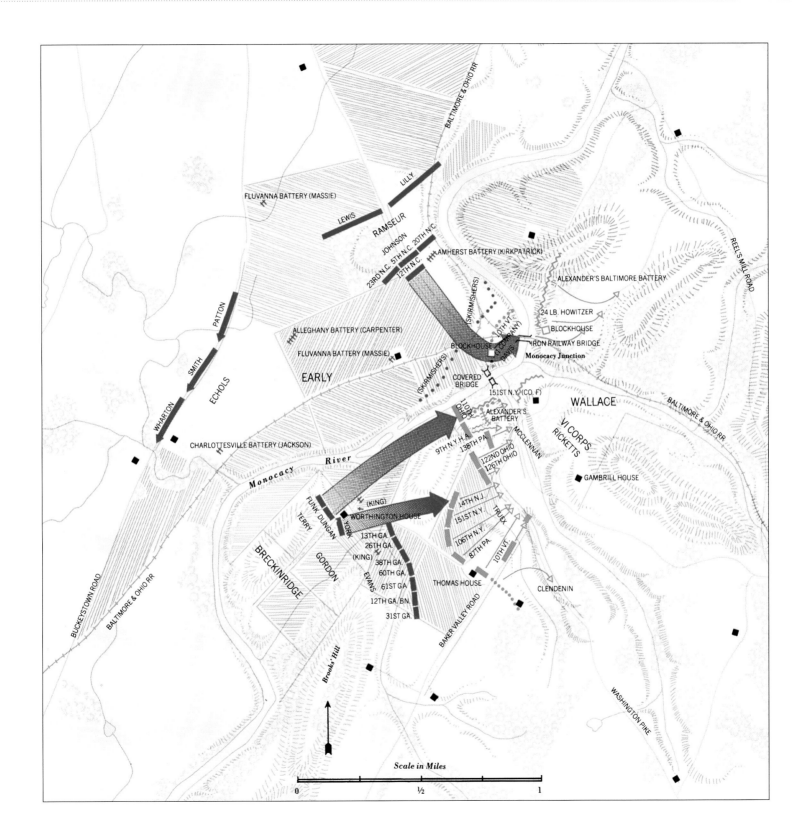

FLUVANNA BATTERY (MASSIE)

LILLY

LEWIS

RAMSEUR

BALTIMORE & OHIO RR

JOHNSON

23RD N.C. 5TH N.C. 20TH N.C.

12TH N.C.

AMHERST BATTERY (KIRKPATRICK)

REEL'S MILL ROAD

ALEXANDER'S BALTIMORE BATTERY

(SKIRMISHERS)

24 LB. HOWITZER

10TH VT. (1 COMPANY)

BLOCKHOUSE

PATTON

SMITH

WHARTON

ECHOLS

ALLEGHANY BATTERY (CARPENTER)

FLUVANNA BATTERY (MASSIE)

EARLY

BLOCKHOUSE

DAVIS

IRON RAILWAY BRIDGE

Monocacy Junction

(SKIRMISHERS)

COVERED BRIDGE

151ST N.Y. (CO. F)

WALLACE

BALTIMORE & OHIO RR

CHARLOTTESVILLE BATTERY (JACKSON)

10TH OHIO

ALEXANDER'S BATTERY

VI CORPS
RICKETTS

Monocacy   *River*

9TH N.Y. H.A.

138TH PA.

McCLENNAN

122ND OHIO

126TH OHIO

GAMBRILL HOUSE

BUCKEYSTOWN ROAD

BALTIMORE & OHIO RR

FUNK DUNGAN

(KING)

WORTHINGTON HOUSE

14TH N.J.

151ST N.Y.

TRUEX

BRECKINRIDGE

TERRY

GORDON

EVANS

YORK

13TH GA.

26TH GA.

(KING)

38TH GA.

60TH GA.

61ST GA.

12TH GA. BN.

31ST GA.

106TH N.Y.

87TH PA.

10TH VT.

THOMAS HOUSE

CLENDENIN

BAKER VALLEY ROAD

Brooks' Hill

WASHINGTON PIKE

Scale in Miles

0   ½   1

MAJOR GENERAL LEW WALLACE

COMMANDER, FEDERAL
MIDDLE DEPARTMENT

The son of an Indiana governor, Wallace was a Mexican War veteran and lawyer who began his Civil War service as commander of the 11th Indiana Zouaves. But his promising military career foundered when Grant accused him of over-caution and incompetence at the Battle of Shiloh. By effectively confronting Early at Monocacy, Wallace hoped to redeem his reputation.

The men of my staff had nothing to say to me, and but little to one another. Like myself, they were impressed with the situation, and waiting. They knew as well as I that in all probability the preparation going on behind the screen of woods in the south would be decisive; and with them, as with me, the deliberation with which it was being conducted was ominous enough to edge their expectation with anxiety. Occasionally they remitted their watchfulness to follow the sound of a shell flying invisibly over the fields. . . .

The woods across the fields showed signs of renewed life. In the fringing of scattered trees, by looking closely, I could see what I thought moving figures. Now and then these appeared in patches of sunlight of greater transparency than the general mass of late afternoon shadows, helping my glass bring them distinctly to view—men with slouched hats, and in dust-colored clothes—very reliable telltales, all of them, but not to be compared in that respect to the flashes electrically emitted by gun-barrels suddenly sunstruck. I passed the glass to the officer nearest me, and said, simply:

"They are coming."

And then to an orderly, the horses having been again taken down the hill: "Bring up the horses. We may have to ride."

"Yes," said Colonel Catlin, after a long look, "they come, and no mistake."

"Only see how long the line is!" said another of my officers.

And sure enough, out of the ragged fringe of trees there came a thin line of skirmishers—I say *line* out of grace, for there was no "dressing on guides"—that extended from the river up to the Thomas mansion, and beyond it, though how far I could form no idea on account of obstructions to the view; far enough, however, to overlap the extreme left of Ricketts' left regiment. And then, was the extension of the skirmishers a proper measure of the front of the main line advancing behind it? My hope, already faint, began shrivelling up like a child's rubber balloon while the air goes whistling out through an unlucky rent.

I turned the glass to where Ricketts was in holding, his brigades lying down, and looking for the most part like a far-stretched blue thread. The regiments on his left—two it seemed—were on the run, taking intervals in the direction of the Thomas house, a desperate expedient, but the only one left the good soldier, conscious of the necessity of saving his flank by equalizing fronts as best he could. But how thin the formation looked! I shivered, thinking of what would happen to it in the face of the rush of a solid line of battle.

And presently the slouch-hatted skirmishers began firing. Then, as at a signal, the battle broke from its leash. All the guns on the thither side of the river awoke, reminding me of sleeping dogs responding to a kennel-cry. And again, drowning the crackle of the more distant skirmishers, and the yelping, they searched the low places and the high everywhere behind, over, and in front of Ricketts. In the common crash above the block-house we were not considered unworthy special attention. With a mighty *swishing*, comparable to nothing else I know of, though nearest the ragged tear of rushing locomotives, the missiles rent the air over our heads seemingly not more than an arm's-length too high. The tempest spent, we counted one another, thankful for another escape; and when I got a breathing time to give attention to the situation in the field proper, the skirmishers were giving place to a line of battle emerged from the woods, and reaching from near the river's bluff out of sight almost solidly. I saw the flags in furious waving, and the mounted officers galloping to and fro in the rear. Then I became interested in the number of regiments moving into action, and while trying to count the flags in sight, the whole long array under them began firing. This brought them to a slower movement; whereupon a misty, pale-blue envelopment which I knew to be musketry smoke dimmed them to the eye; while out of it arose the inevitable "*Yelp, yelp, yelp,*" a vent to battle passion strangely unlike that of any other of the great fighting Anglo-Saxon families.

Major Benjamin Franklin Eakle of the 14th Virginia Cavalry was among 150 casualties sustained by General McCausland's brigade in the initial assault on Wallace's defenses at Monocacy. Shot through the torso while leading his dismounted troopers against the veteran Yankee infantry of James Ricketts' division, Eakle was taken to a hospital in nearby Frederick, Maryland. He recovered from his wound but was captured at Nineveh, Virginia, in November.

CORPORAL RODERICK A. CLARK
14TH NEW JERSEY INFANTRY, TRUEX'S BRIGADE

After repulsing McCausland's cavalry, the 14th and the four other regiments of Colonel William Truex's brigade helped slow the onslaught of Gordon's division but were eventually flanked and driven from the field. Wounded, Clark was left behind when his comrades retreated. A sailor and boatbuilder from New Jersey, Clark lost his left leg and later married the Maryland girl who nursed him.

It was certainly a grand sight as they advanced, in good order, with their numerous battle-flags waving in the breeze. We began firing at once, but it made no difference. On they came with quick step until they got within 300 yards of us. . . . I was hit in the left ankle by a minie-ball, completely crushing the joint. I started to retreat, but found I could not walk; so I stood there until two of my comrades placed me on their gun, and, with my arms around their necks, started to the rear with me. But ere they got 20 steps I was struck with another minie-ball under the shoulder-blade just to the right of the back-bone, penetrating the right lung, stopping just under the skin in my breast. It felt about the size of a cannon-ball. I don't know how long I lay uncon-

scious, but when I came to the rebels were all around me. Our men had retreated to the Washington pike, and were making it hot for me as well as the rebels. Although very weak I managed to crawl about 20 feet to the fence. . . . I never heard minies fly so fast or sound so spiteful as they did there, cutting the weeds and throwing the dirt all over me. Behind the rail fence were a good many rebels firing at our men. Two of them were right behind me, and as they fired the muzzles of their guns were within a few inches of me, and to prevent burning my face I put my hat over my eyes. I had just taken my hand away when a ball from our men struck the hat, and came so close that it burned my forehead, passed on, and killed a rebel stone dead. I thought at the time that the ball had struck the rail, but after the fighting was over I

Captain James W. Conover, Captain Henry I. Covine, and First Lieutenant William H. Craig (left to right, above) were among 140 casualties the 14th New Jersey sustained at Monocacy—40 percent of those present for duty. Covine was killed outright, Conover mortally wounded, and Craig permanently disabled by a leg wound.

saw that it had hit one of the rebs just over the eye. Now my worst trouble began. I was dying with thirst, and to make matters still worse, a big rebel came along and pulled off my shoes; the pain caused was almost unbearable. When he discovered the bullet-hole through the one, he threw it down in disgust and said it was a d——n shame to spoil so good a shoe.

"It was one of those fights where success depends largely upon the prowess of the individual soldier."

MAJOR GENERAL JOHN B. GORDON
DIVISION COMMANDER, ARMY OF THE VALLEY

After fording the Monocacy near the Worthington farm, Gordon's men advanced to support the wavering Rebel cavalry. Deploying behind Brooks' Hill, his three brigades dressed their lines, then attacked. Gordon was a charismatic leader whose face bore the scar of a Yankee bullet—one of five wounds he had received at Antietam.

*E*n échelon by brigades from the right the movement began. As we reached the first line of strong and high fencing, and my men began to climb over it, they were met by a tempest of bullets, and many of the brave fellows fell at the first volley. But over they climbed or tumbled, and rushed forward, some of them halting to break down gaps in the fence, so that the mounted officers might ride through. Then came the grain-stacks. Around them and between them they pressed on, with no possibility of maintaining orderly alignment or of returning effective fire. Deadly missiles from Wallace's ranks were cutting down the line and company officers with their words of cheer to the men but half spoken. It was one of those fights where success depends largely upon the prowess of the individual soldier. The men were deprived of that support and strength imparted by a compact line, where the elbow touch of comrade with comrade gives confidence to each and sends the electric thrill of enthusiasm through all. But nothing could deter them. Neither the obstructions nor the leaden blast in their front could check them. The supreme test of their marvellous nerve and self-control now came. They had passed the forest of malign wheatstacks; they had climbed the second fence and were in close proximity to Wallace's first line of battle, which stood firmly and was little hurt. The remaining officers, on horseback and on foot, rapidly adjusted their commands, and I ordered "Forward!" and forward they went. . . . the swell of the Southern yell rose high above the din of battle as they rushed upon the resolute Federals and hurled them back upon the second line.

The Union lines stood firmly in this second position, bravely defending the railroad and the highway to Washington. Between the two hostile lines there was a narrow ravine down which ran a small stream of limpid water. In this ravine the fighting was desperate and at close quarters. To and fro the battle swayed across the little stream, the dead and wounded of both sides mingling their blood in its waters; and when the struggle was ended a crimsoned current ran toward the river.

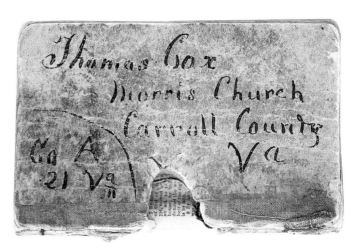

This Bible, carried in the pocket of Private William A. Cox of the 21st Virginia Infantry, was pierced by a Minié ball that mortally wounded Cox as he advanced with General William Terry's brigade in the third wave of Gordon's assault.

PRIVATE DANIEL B. FREEMAN
10TH VERMONT INFANTRY, TRUEX'S BRIGADE

The Battle of Monocacy provided a memorable 22d birthday for Freeman, a farmer from Brookfield, Vermont. One of 75 men under Lieutenant George Davis, Freeman took position on the left flank of a skirmish line guarding Monocacy Junction and the western approaches to the highway and railroad bridges. Despite the odds against them, the skirmishers managed to fend off Ramseur's division for seven hours. They yielded only when Wallace ordered a retreat. Two months later, at the Battle of Winchester, Freeman suffered a crippling wound in his left ankle.

Towards 11 o'clock another effort was made to dislodge us, and Gen. Lew Wallace, in command, ordered the Pike Bridge, over the river, burned, which left the skirmishers under Capt. Davis cut off from the rest of our troops, with no way of retreat except to swim the river or cross the railroad bridge 40 feet in the air, stepping from tie to tie.

The enemy shortly moved a large part off by the Buckeystown road, a mile east of us, to a ford below, crossed, formed line-of-battle, and charged our men on the other side of the river.

Again and again, with two and three lines-of-battle did they charge, to be each time hurled back defeated. . . .

I was now left alone, my comrade having been carried off, wounded, and every time I raised my head above a certain rail a bullet would hit the rail, embankment of dirt, or go whistling past.

. . . Corp'l Wright sent to post me as a videt outpost and relieve the comrade on duty there,

some 200 yards to our left, in the cornfield.

As we came to this comrade, Wright stretched up to take observations, and was shot through the head. We carried him back to the reserve, and I returned to the outpost alone just in time to see in the distance across the river the enemy on their fourth charge, with as many lines-of-battle.

On and on I saw them come, and our troops were being withdrawn. I heard Lieut. Wilkie calling to me to come in quickly. As I crossed the pike I saw our reserve on the railroad bridge, and a little to the rear was Lieut. Wilkie urging me on.

As I neared the depot and looked back along the railroad I saw one of my comrades under the Pike Bridge fighting a dozen Johnnies charging down the railroad toward him. He was riddled with lead.

I sped on, paying no heed to the orders to halt. I reached the bridge and, stepping from tie to tie, crossed over in safety under a crossfire from others of the enemy at the bend in the river a few rods below.

Capt. Davis ordered us to fall in behind the railroad, after getting across, and I fired one or two shots more, and heard the order: "Every man for himself!"

Commander of the Federal skirmishers defending the Monocacy bridges, Lieutenant George E. Davis— seated second from right with fellow soldiers of the 10th Vermont—later received the Medal of Honor in recognition of his valiant stand. "I have not words to express my admiration," General Wallace wrote. "From every point of view it was heroism."

PRIVATE ALFRED S. ROE
9TH NEW YORK HEAVY ARTILLERY, McCLENNAN'S BRIGADE

Fighting as infantry, Roe's unit sustained 200 casualties at Monocacy—the heaviest loss of any regiment in the battle. The 9th's commander, Colonel William H. Seward Jr., was among the wounded. Son and namesake of Lincoln's secretary of state, he narrowly escaped capture when Terry's Virginia brigade drove the New Yorkers from a ridge overlooking the Washington pike. Roe, a 19-year-old schoolteacher, was less fortunate; he spent the next seven months in a Rebel prison.

To tell the truth, I didn't realize that we were whipped effectually. I knew that things were mixed, but I confidently expected to find an orderly line somewhere which would stem the tide of retreat. Had I known then, as I afterward learned, that our general officers had for some time been making their way towards Baltimore, using for their trip the train standing on the track, I think I should have taken much longer steps. Wheeler and myself kept together till we reached a little branch of the Monocacy, through which he went regardless of depth, but I, not thinking the exigency sufficient for such carelessness, endeavored to encounter as little moisture as possible. Once across, I shouted my comrade's name, and even ran up and down the stream for a little way, hoping to see him, but without avail. Lee had surrendered before I saw him again. On I went over the railroad, following the greater number; but where it was to end, I hadn't the remotest notion. All this time, shot of assorted sizes was falling about us. The rebel artillery was giving us canister as fast as possible, and every few seconds some poor fellow would throw up his hands and go down, but the puffs of dust all about me, indicating the fall of a shot, told me that only one missile in many score hurt any one. As I struck a wooded road, I saw before me a poor fellow staggering like a drunken man. His path could be traced by the blood streaming from his wound. Coming up with him, I found that one side of his face had been shot away, giving me a clear insight into his mouth. He appeared to be dazed or bewildered, and well he might be; but he still clung to all his equipments. "Why don't you throw away some of your things?" I at once asked. Apparently the idea had not occurred to him before, for he speedily dropped his gun, and, with my aid, was soon free from all his impedimenta. Straightening up, he shot ahead at a wonderful rate, completely distancing me. There were so many men all about me that the idea of running had not once entered my head. In fact, running from a field of battle did not comport with the dignified manner with which I thought troops ought to withdraw from a situation where they had been whipped. Another time I should have known better; but one must have experience in war as well as in anything else. By the roadside I passed my friends Foster and Searls; the latter badly wounded, and Foster trying to help him. I never expected to see Searls again in this world, and so bade him "good-by." . . .

My bump of curiosity, coupled with an acquisitive faculty, was the cause of my ruin or capture; it's all the same thing. Anything lying around loose was, in those days, accounted legitimate plunder. An exceedingly plethoric knapsack lying by the roadside tempted me beyond resistance. Had I realized the nearness of the foe, I would have thrown away my own burdens and have made haste from that locality. But all this is hindsight; what I lacked then was foresight.

The knapsack was a rich one. It must have been the property of one of the hundred day men who made up a part of the defending force, for no man who had had any experience in marching would have tolerated for an hour such a load. The owner, too, was a Dutchman. This I knew from the German Bible and other literature in it. He also chewed tobacco, as I inferred from the large plug of "Navy" which it contained. I helped myself to an excellent pair of stockings and to the tobacco, already wondering with what one of the boys I would trade that, and for what, when my investigations and meditations were rudely interrupted with, "Look here, Yank!" Looking upward, I found myself gazing into the mouth of a six-shooter, held in the hand of a stalwart cavalryman. Resistance was out of the question, at least so it seemed to me. In fact, I was too much surprised for anything else than unconditional surrender.

A prisoner! One-half the meaning of that word I had never imagined, much less realized. "Let's have your money; damned quick, too," were the greeting words of my captor. At this I produced an old weather-beaten purse that a man belonging to an Ohio regiment had thrown away some weeks before. Its contents were just thirty-five cents in scrip. The disgust depicted on the cavalryman's face at this exposition was most intense.

"Is that all you've got?"

"Every cent," was my reply.

"Well, keep it then. It isn't worth taking."

Small though the amount was, I was nothing loath to do this; for with us, at the front, considering the infrequency of pay-day, money was money. This small remnant was some remaining from enlistment; for no paymaster had ventured near us. . . . However, I had no watch, nor other valuables, so I did not net my captor very much.

PRIVATE GEORGE W. NICHOLS

61ST GEORGIA INFANTRY, EVANS' BRIGADE

*The first of Gordon's brigades to become engaged, General Clement Evans' Geor-
gians were savaged by Yankee volleys as they advanced through a wheat field on the
Thomas farm. With many of their officers killed or wounded, Evans' regiments
halted and returned fire against Ricketts' Federals, who used the banks of the
sunken Washington pike as an improvised breastwork. Only after Zebulon York's
and William Terry's brigades joined the attack was Gordon able to break the stubborn Yankee defense. Nichols recalled the carnage in his 1898 regimental history.*

It made our hearts ache to look over the battle-field and see so
many of our dear friends, comrades and beloved officers, killed
and wounded. Our loss was terrible, while the Yankees lost but few.
I only saw three dead Union soldiers and I did not see one that was
wounded, though I did not go over the field. We could not see a Yankee on our part of the line during the whole advance. All that we could
shoot at was the smoke of their guns, they were so well posted. It was
called our victory, but it was a costly one, for it cost Evans' Brigade over
five hundred men, in wounded and killed. It was said that it was raw
troops that we were fighting, but I never saw old soldiers shoot better.
The Sixty-first Georgia Regiment went into the battle with nearly one
hundred and fifty men, and after the battle was over we could not stack
but fifty-two guns by actual count.

Our beloved Colonel J. H. Lamar and Lieutenant Colonel J. D. Van
Valkinburg . . . were both killed on the field. We truly mourned the loss
of these good men and noble Christian commanders.

Colonel Lamar was quite a young man and a military graduate, and
was very profane when the war begun, but thank *God!* I hope and
believe that he died a Christian. He had joined the church and often
led in the prayer service at divine worship. His life seemed to be the
life of the humble followers of Christ.

It looked like half of the Twelfth Georgia Battalion were killed or
wounded. Company D had the sad misfortune of getting Lieutenant
James Mincy severely wounded. He was carrying our battle flag. He
had picked it up after the fifth man had been shot down while carrying
it in this battle and he was likewise shot down at once. He had already
been wounded at Manassas and *severely* wounded at Gettysburg. Here
he was shot through the left lung, the ball just missing his back bone.
Bloody froth from his lungs would come out of his mouth and nose, and
in the front and back where the ball passed through. He has since told

me that the Yankee doctors drew a silk handkerchief through him and
treated him *very* kindly. . . .

Here I saw one of Company A of our regiment, Thomas Nichols,
(though no relative of mine) with his brains shot out. When I saw him
he was sitting up and wiping his brains from his temple with his hand.
I went to try to render him some assistance and did so by giving him
some water. He seemed to have some mind, for he said he wanted
to go back to Virginia and get a horse and try to get home and never
to cross the Potomac again. He lived twelve hours before death came
to his relief.

*Brigadier General Clement A. Evans was wounded through the left arm and
side as he spurred his horse along the line of his brigade. The shot drove a sew-
ing kit in Evans' pocket deep into his body; although a surgeon was able to cut
out the bullet, bits of pins and needles were still being extracted a decade later.*

In the wake of Early's foray against Washington, Leslie's Illustrated gave front-page coverage by their "special artist" to the Confederates' destruction of U.S. Postmaster General Montgomery Blair's estate near Silver Spring, Maryland. Blair's home was gutted by fire—whether accidentally or in retaliation for Yankee depredations in the Valley remains unclear. The artist depicted a group of Rebel soldiers carousing on the grounds with liquor and cigars looted from the mansion, while an officer scrawls a parting message. One such note, written on the flyleaf of one of Blair's books, read, "Now Uncle Abe, you had better be quiet the balance of your Administration, as we came near your town this time to show you what we could do. But if you go on in your mad career, we will come again soon, and then you had better stand from under."

CAPTAIN SEATON GALES
STAFF, BRIGADIER GENERAL WILLIAM R. COX

Through the day on July 10 Early's army pushed toward Washington, D.C., covering more than 30 miles. Torrid weather and choking dust took their toll on the men. Hundreds fell by the wayside, lagged behind, or wandered off to forage in the lush Maryland countryside. Soon after passing the Blair family estate at Silver Spring, the vanguard of Early's force—including Cox's North Carolinians—crossed the District of Columbia line and engaged outlying Union skirmishers.

July 10.—Through the pretty village of Rockville and on into the District of Columbia, realizing the strange and anomalous fact, that the nearer we approached the Federal seat of Government, the more emphatic were the indications of sympathy which we encountered. Arriving at "Silver Spring," the famous and magnificent suburban villa of the Blairs, between three or four miles from Washington, we at once deployed into line of battle and moved forward, when lo! before us were the tremendous and almost impregnable fortifications of the city, while the minarets of the metropolis gleamed in the distance, the massive dome of the capitol, capped with the colossal statue of Liberty, towering eminently among them. A shout of exultation rang along the lines, which was responded to by a storm of monster shells from the Titanic siege guns in the forts, which was kept up at intervals throughout the day. Our skirmishers advanced and met those of the enemy and an animated engagement prevailed between them until night. At times our lines approached within 300 or 400 yards of the works. The casualties on either side were not heavy.

I took occasion to visit the splendid residences of the Blairs and to explore the elegantly ornamented grounds. The espacious Spring House contained hundred of crocks of the finest milk which quenched the thirst of many a weary "rebel" that day, while the statuettes, paintings, books and furniture feasted many an eye. All the dwellings in the vicinity had been precipitately abandoned by the inmates, who, it would appear, hardly knew of our coming before we were upon them. To have required that our boys should not, now and then, appropriate an occasional trophy of their visit, would have been demanding too much. I remember listening for hours to the swelling strains of our national airs, as some of the men gifted with a talent for music, drew them forth from grand octavo pianos, which the fair Union damsels would doubtless have thought desecrated by the touch, had they known it.

Lieutenant Colonel Samuel McD. Tate commanded the 6th North Carolina Infantry—part of Ramseur's division—in the fighting at Fort Stevens. Wounded three times during the war, he survived to become a successful railroad executive.

PRIVATE DAVID T. BULL
147TH OHIO NATIONAL GUARD INFANTRY,
FORT STEVENS GARRISON

A farmer, Bull was among nearly 84,000 guardsmen who volunteered for a 100-day tour of duty in the summer of 1864. Though often derided by the battle-hardened veterans of the Army of the Potomac, the "Hundred Days Men" helped hold the defenses of Washington until reinforcements from Grant's army arrived. Bull served at Forts Reno and Stevens, and on July 12 he saw President Lincoln come under fire.

I did not think that I would be called out so soon to go and see Rebs, the Johneys we call them, but last Sunday night at half-past twelve o'clock, we was called out and left for Fort Reno and there was put in Fort and we could see the Rebs fall on all sides. We had the Sixth Army Corps in the front a skirmishing and they soon drove them back and when they drove them back far enough our cannon opened out on them and you can bet that they run like sheep. . . . After we had routed them there they went down to Fort Stevens about four miles from Fort Reno and we was ordered down there the same day and when we got there we found them hard at work. They had drove our men in 300 yards of the Fort and we laid in the rifle pits all night awaiting for the Johneys to come up and try to take the Fort but they stayed back and I tell you if they had come up we could have whipped fifty thousand and I don't think that our force was more than fifteen thousand. But a Tuesday morning, we sent out a new line of skirmishers and we stood in our rifle pits and seen some warm work about four o'clock in the evening the Johneys massed a heavy force in front of the Fort, thinking that our force would not shell them thru fear of killing our own men. There was a large force of them gathered around a house in front of the Fort and there was a sharp shooter got up in the top of the house and thought he would kill some of our men that was on the parapets. Old Abe and his wife was in the Fort at the time and Old Abe and his doctor was standing up on the parapets and the sharp shooter that I speak of shot the doctor through the left thigh, and Old Abe ordered our men to fall back. When our men fell back far enough, the cannon in the Fort opened on them and fired the house, shelled them till they was in full retreat and then the Sixth Army Corps went after them and run them clean out of hearing. A Wednesday morning we got up and there was not a Johney to be seen. We heard only of them that was left on the field dead or wounded and we have not seen a Johney since and I don't think they will try any of this fort again.

Fort Stevens (left), the northernmost of some 70 earthen fortifications guarding the Federal capital, had a perimeter of 375 yards and mounted 17 cannons and mortars. The salvos of Fort Stevens' artillery, heard at the White House just five miles south, drew President Lincoln to the scene. On July 12 the president attracted Rebel fire when he climbed atop the parapet for a better view of the action. Surgeon C. C. V. Crawford of the 102d Pennsylvania was wounded at the president's side (above).

CAPTAIN GEORGE W. BOOTH

STAFF, BRIGADIER GENERAL BRADLEY T. JOHNSON

As Early and Wallace battled at Monocacy, Johnson led 1,500 Confederate cavalry on a raid toward Baltimore. After disrupting enemy communications, Johnson hoped to travel on to Point Lookout, the Federal prison camp at the mouth of the Potomac River, and free the 10,000 Rebels held there. The daring plan proved impossible, and the raiders rejoined Early in front of Washington, as Booth recalled.

We approached through the Green Spring Valley to within a few miles of Baltimore, which was in a state of great excitement, apprehending capture. A small party under Lieutenant Blackistone, of the 1st Maryland, was sent to the country place of Governor Bradford, near Charles street avenue, with orders to burn the house in retaliation for the destruction by Hunter of Governor Letcher's house at Lexington, in the Valley, a few weeks previous. While waiting for this detachment to return we struck the establishment of Painter, the then well-known ice-cream man, about daybreak, and found his wagons loaded with this product, just about starting for the Baltimore market. It was a most ludicrous sight to see the ice cream dished out into all conceivable receptacles, and the whole brigade engaged in feasting on this, to many, a novel luxury as the column moved along. The men carried it in hats, in rubber blankets, in buckets and old tin cans—in fact, anything that would hold the cream was utilized. No spoons were at hand, but as fingers and hands were made before spoons, the natural and primary organs were brought into play. A number of the men from southwest Virginia were not familiar with this delicious food, but were not slow in becoming acquainted with its enticing properties and expressing themselves as being very much satisfied with the "frozen vittles," as they termed it. It was not the intention to do more than to threaten Baltimore, our objective point being Point Lookout. We, therefore, passed around the city, crossing the Baltimore & Ohio Railroad about Woodstock and from thence headed toward the Washington Branch at Laurel. On learning that a considerable body of infantry was at this point we passed farther on and crossed the railroad at Beltsville, six miles nearer to Washington. Near Beltsville we found a large number of government mules, some several hundred; these would serve admirably to mount some of the prisoners, and they were at once driven up and secured. We had stopped at this point to feed, and had just mounted and reformed the column and started to march on the Marlboro road, when Johnson received a mes-

sage from General Early directing him to abandon the enterprise and rejoin him at once at Silver Springs, the Blair place, on the Rockville road out of Washington, and stating he would hold on for us until 9 o'clock that night. . . . By dark we were skirting the outer lines of earthworks around Washington, but the night concealed our movements and we were not molested. . . . It was with no little relief, therefore, when, shortly after 9 o'clock on the night of July 12th, I struck the Rockville road and reported our arrival to General Early, who was mounted and observing his infantry as they marched along the road in the retirement from the position they had occupied for the past two days in front of the Capital.

A cousin of Confederate partisan leader Harry Gilmor, Hoffman Gilmor (seated) and his friend Joshua F. C. Talbot fell in with Major Gilmor's 2d Maryland Cavalry during the raid on Baltimore. Along the way they had their photograph taken, clad in the brigandish attire affected by many of Harry Gilmor's band.

mishers, who were under cover of bushes skirting the west bank of the river. On crossing we captured a rebel captain and fifteen men. We learned from these prisoners that Early's whole force was close by. The other two brigades soon crossed, and Thoburn forming with the 1st, our brigade, on the left; the 3d in the centre, and the 2d, with about 1,000 cavalry, on the right, moved forward to a position a short distance from the river. Companies B, C, D and K of our regiment were put out as skirmishers, and advanced under Lieutenant Colonel Wildes in search of the enemy. We did not have to search very long. Breckenridge, with two divisions, advanced against Thoburn's left and centre, and Rhodes against his right, pushing the whole line back to the cover of a stone wall along the bank of the river. The 1,000 dismounted cavalry on our right broke in confusion and retreated across the river, when our regiment, on the extreme left, was hurried to the extreme right. We found on our arrival a large body of rebels between the stone wall and the river, bearing down heavily on the right of our position, and the gallant 4th West Virginia fighting to maintain its position against desperate odds. Colonel Washburn fell desperately wounded at the head of the

Captain James B. Root of the 21st New York Cavalry was wearing this shirt when, on July 16, he was wounded through the arm and chest near Purcellville, Virginia, during a charge on one of Early's wagon trains that was retreating back to the Valley.

LIEUTENANT COLONEL THOMAS F. WILDES
116TH OHIO INFANTRY, WELLS' BRIGADE

Believing Early's army to be in full retreat, on July 18 General George Crook ordered Thoburn's division to ford the Shenandoah near Snicker's Ferry and harass the Rebel rear guard. When Early turned on his attacker, Thoburn was compelled to wage a desperate stand lest his force be driven into the river. The Federals managed to fend off repeated Confederate assaults, but at a cost of 422 casualties, many of them from Wildes' regiment.

On the morning of the 18th, we advanced through Snicker's Gap to the Ferry. About 2 o'clock, General Crook directed Colonel Thoburn to cross the Shenandoah river at Island Ford with his two brigades and the third brigade of the second division. Our brigade was the first to cross, which we did under a severe fire from some rebel skir-

At Snicker's Ferry Colonel James Washburn of the 116th Ohio was shot through the head by a bullet that entered his left eye and exited behind his right ear. Despite the loss of his eye and partial paralysis of the left side of his body, Washburn was able to return to duty and finished his wartime service as military commander of Wheeling, West Virginia.

regiment just as he reached the right. Hurrying forward and assuming command of the regiment, Lieutenant Colonel Wildes stationed two companies under Captain Mallory between the wall and the river. They charged and drove back the rebels, who had been so closely pressing Colonel Vance. Now hastily throwing up a breastwork of stones and logs across this space, the Captain opened a deadly fire upon the rebels in his front, and drove them out. The rest of the regiment as effectually opened on those in front of the stone wall. . . . Soon the rebels returned again to the charge, but we were prepared for them. Every man in the two regiments felt that in driving that column of rebels back depended his life. The river at our back was too deep to more than walk slowly through, and so escape that way was out of the question. Run we could not, if we would. Nothing was left to do but to fight.

MAJOR GENERAL STEPHEN D. RAMSEUR
DIVISION COMMANDER, ARMY OF THE VALLEY

On July 20 some 2,500 Union infantry and cavalry struck Ramseur's division a stunning blow at Stephenson's Depot. When Averell's cavalry flanked the Confederates, their line broke. Ramseur was excoriated by the Southern press, but in this letter to his wife he blamed his troops for the rout.

ear Strasburg Va
July 23rd 1864
Our trip into M'd. was a success. I see the Richmond papers are "pitching into" Gen'l. Early for not taking Washington—If he had attempted it he would have been repulsed with great loss, and then these same wiseacres would have condemned him for recklessness. The fight of the 20th at Winchester where Divn. was engaged ought to have been a *victory*. Our men for some unaccountable reason became panic stricken & after a fight of five minutes ran off of the field in wild

disorder. I did all in my power to stop them—but 'twas impossible. Officers who are acquainted with all the facts not only do acquit me of all blame but unhesitatingly declare that had the troops behaved with their usual steadiness we would have gained a glorious victory. I am sure I did all that mortal man could do—Yet—newspaper editors & stay at home croakers will sit back in safe places and condemn me. I do hope my Darling Wife that you will be as little affected by these things as I am. I must request that you will endeavor to pass all such things by without notice. I am sorry I was unable to procure you any goods in M'd. A pair of kid gloves with the compliments of Col Pendleton Genl Early's Ad't Genl is about all I have to send you. We are now preparing for another advance—hope we may be as successful in our military movements and even more so in procuring stores. . . . The papers mention a rumour to the effect that Grant has been killed by a shell—If so, I think we have cause for rejoicing! The news from Northern Ga. looks bad. I hope however that Gen'l Hood will be able to drive them back. From the TransMississippi we have glorious news. All of La. except New Orleans, all of Arkansas & Texas in our possession. Price at the head of a large & growing Army, moving into Missouri—Oh! If we can be successful at Richmond & in Ga, I believe we can see the beginning of the end of this horrible war.

The daughter of a North Carolina planter, Ellen Richmond married her cousin Stephen Ramseur in October 1863. The West Point–educated general described his bride as his "long cherished ideal of womanly perfection." In the summer of 1864 the two were expecting their first child, and Ramseur hoped that a decisive Confederate victory in the Shenandoah would permit him to return home on a leave of absence.

CAPTAIN GEORGE P. RING
6TH LOUISIANA INFANTRY, YORK'S BRIGADE

Marching south from Winchester with two Federal divisions, General George Crook was dealt a staggering blow on July 24 when Early struck both of his flanks near the village of Kernstown. After a brief stand the poorly positioned Union line gave way in confusion, losing 600 killed or wounded and another 500 taken prisoner. Advancing with a skirmish line in front of Gordon's division, Ring was astonished and thrilled by the Yankees' collapse. He described the pursuit of Crook's demoralized command in a letter to his wife in New Orleans.

When we had arrived within five miles of Winchester, to our surprise, (as we had been told that the enemy had left) we saw the troops being placed into position and soon after the sharp quick sound of the minie was heard, affording palpable evidence that there was work ahead for us. Our Division filed off at exactly the same point as last year and the thought struck me rather forcibly, I wonder if we will continue the coincidence and I be fortunate enough to get another nice eight month furlough wound. About twelve oclock all our troops having reached their positions we heard a rapid fire on the right, where Gen Breckinridge's Division was posted followed soon after by the well known yell of the Confederates that spoke as plainly as the "handwriting on the wall" that we were driving them before us. Soon the wished-for order reached our Division which was next to Breckinridge's to advance and our Gallant Gordon . . . led us at a quick step towards the foe who could be plainly seen flying through the stubble field, about a mile in our front. Passing under a heavy fire of artillery from a high hill (the same on which I was wounded) we came up with our double quicking friends and our sharpshooters gave them a fire that covered the ground with killed and wounded. Securing a number of prisoners we pressed on as fast as the nature of the ground would admit and the fires from their artillery would allow. . . . We finally arrived at the suburbs of Winchester about 4 oclock P.M. . . . Halting just at the edge of the city, our Sharpshooters were sent on through the city and on emerging from the town we found the enemy drawn up in line of battle, with cavalry Artillery & Infantry in position. . . . I thought that at last we will have some hard work to do and I awaited the advance of our Infantry with some anxiety—while sitting on my horse behind the line of sharpshooters, I saw for the first time since I have been in service a charge of cavalry and I could hardly contain myself and resist the strong impulse, that I, under the exciting scene had to gallop over and take part in the affair. It was thrilling while it lasted which was only a few minutes as the enemy broke and changed their base after McClelland's style in 62. Soon I saw the head of our division and giving the sharpshooters orders to advance to my utter astonishment the moment our men emerged from the rock walls behind which they had been sheltered, than away started our Yankee friends and I can assure you darling that of all the tall travelling I have ever seen, they did some of the tallest from that time until night. Our men, when they saw the enemy so quietly slipping away from a position that would have cost us a great loss of life, breathed a sigh of relief and with many humorous remarks about the race we were running again took up the pursuit which until darkness came upon us and gave us the welcome privilege of throwing our wearied frames upon our Mother Earth, and forget in sleep all about wars and battles and recall in our dreams thoughts of home and our dear ones left behind.

This flag of the 14th West Virginia Infantry bears the coat of arms of that state, established in 1863 by Virginians loyal to the Union. The unit lost 59 men while covering the retreat of Crook's army from Winchester to Martinsburg.

MAJOR JEWETT PALMER

36th Ohio Infantry, Hayes' Brigade

Under Crook's battle plan at Kernstown Colonel Rutherford B. Hayes was to wheel his brigade from the Federal left toward the center, rolling up the Rebel right. But Hayes' own left and rear were quickly enveloped by Gabriel Wharton's Rebel brigade, and the Yankees put to rout. Palmer described the debacle.

At 3 P.M. our line of battle, owing to the negligence of the cavalry, was flanked by the enemy—he having sufficient force to lap both our flanks and still maintain a line of battle in our front equal to our own—and the 36th being on the extreme left of the army, was the first to receive the withering fire of the whole rebel line! We were cut down by the score, Capt. Ford fell almost upon the first fire shot through the heart and Lt. Putnam went down shot through both legs. Besides these enlisted men went down as I never before saw them from our regt. I was shot through the left thigh before I had been in five minutes and seeing the line in the act of giving way, began hobbling to the rear. Luckily I got sight of the orderly with whom I had intrusted my horse and by a sign attracted his attention. I succeeded in getting onto my horse and soon after reached an ambulance into which I crawled being by this time (I had traveled two miles) very sick, so sick that I could have remained on horseback but little longer. The trains immediately began moving to the rear of Winchester and continued to move back until 11 oclock at night.

Captain William R. Ford (above, right) and Lieutenant George W. Putnam (right) were among the 136 casualties suffered by the 36th Ohio at Kernstown—the heaviest loss among Federal regiments. Major Palmer erroneously reported Ford killed; badly wounded and captured, the captain was discharged after his release.

SURGEON ABNER E. MCGARITY
61ST ALABAMA INFANTRY, BATTLE'S BRIGADE

Lacking effective cavalry and with his infantry in disarray, Crook retreated from the battlefield at Kernstown, abandoning Winchester and Martinsburg to the enemy, and crossed the Potomac River at Williamsport. On July 27, as Crook licked his wounds at Harpers Ferry, McGarity wrote his wife a glowing account of the recent Confederate victories. The doctor was taken prisoner at Cedar Creek in October and confined at Point Lookout prison.

Martinsburg, W. Va., July 27th, 1864.

Well, My Love we are still wandering about up here, catching and frightening Yankees, gathering up wheat etc. We went back as far as Strasburg (forty four miles from this place), and lay there two days. We went from Snickersville, where we fought on the 18th to Strasburg, sending Gen. Ramseur around by Winchester, where he was surprised and sustained a right sharp little loss. . . . That and the loss of the wagons when on our way from Leesburg . . . is all the ill luck we have had since we left Richmond. Since Ramseur's misfortune everything has gone well. We left Strasburg on the morning of the 24th (Sunday) and marched rapidly to within four miles of Winchester, where we deployed and engaged the enemy. He was quite easily dislodged, when he quit the use of powder and tryed the virtue of flight. The race was very interesting indeed. We pushed him thro W[inchester] and *on, on* till darkness overtook us, when we had to halt. We drove him ten miles, considerably faster, no doubt, than he ever travelled before, causing him to burn a great many wagons and a good deal of Artillery. He was so much crowded that he had to leave a great deal without touching the torch to it, which fell in our hands. I have not heard the number of killed, wounded, and captured, but suppose it would amount to some eight hundred or a thousand. We got quite a number of wagons, some artillery and horses and other property. Our loss I do not suppose was over one hundred. It was quite a pretty affair. I rode right along with the line of battle all the way, and by so doing, I captured a splendid saddle. So much for my gallantry. It was, however, not much dangerous to keep with the line as the enemy ran too fast to fight much. The only danger was shells, and they didn't have time to throw many of them. When we halted the men were completely exhausted. They had travelled twenty seven miles, ten of which they were running thro fields, over fences, ditches, etc. and fighting.

John Chapman Goodgame began his wartime service as a sergeant in the 12th Alabama Infantry and by the summer of 1864 had been promoted to lieutenant colonel in command of the regiment, which served in Battle's brigade. "His name is an exceedingly appropriate one," a subordinate wrote, "as he is a gallant, unflinching officer and soldier."

CAPTAIN GEORGE W. BOOTH
STAFF, BRIGADIER GENERAL BRADLEY T. JOHNSON

On July 30 at dawn, 24 hours after crossing the Potomac, McCausland and 2,800 Rebel cavalry—including Johnson's and Gilmor's Maryland troopers—arrived at Chambersburg, Pennsylvania. McCausland told the citizens that unless his force was given $100,000 in gold or $500,000 in currency the town would be burned. The money was not forthcoming, and Chambersburg was put to the torch.

At about 11 o'clock, the specified hour, McCausland gave the order to fire the town. The troops in the town at this time were a portion of our brigade, the 21st Virginia, under Col. W. E. Peters, a high-minded gentleman of culture and attainments and who for years has been occupying a chair in the faculty at the University of Virginia. General Johnson and myself had talked over the order, which was very repugnant in character to both, and had been hopeful the dire alternative would not be forced upon us. It was impossible, however, to arouse the citizens to a realization of what was coming. . . . On my delivering the order to Colonel Peters he hesitated for a moment, and then said: "I would be glad if you will give my compliments to General Johnson and ask him to relieve me of this duty; it is something so hurtful to my conscience and so utterly opposed to my ideas of a soldier's duty that I cannot bring myself to its execution without violence to my convictions." I felt for this honorable man and knew General Johnson himself would appreciate the protest, and, therefore, readily consented to bear the message. On making report to General Johnson, he directed me to order Colonel Peters, with his regiment, out of town and to send for Gilmor. In a short while Harry came dashing in with his command, and the order was given him, coupled with the injunction that no plundering would be permitted, but that the burning must stand as a stern act of retributive justice, and no property was to be molested except boots

or shoes and clothing for the troops as found in the several stores. Whether this restriction was properly carried out I cannot say; a fearful example to the contrary was exhibited by General McCausland himself, whom I saw coming out of a store with an armful of books, and I remember the disgust with which General Johnson and myself remarked so grave and flagrant an impropriety. It is not in derogation to the memory of Gilmor that I chronicle he entered upon his sad and disagreeable function with promptness and with zeal. He was not troubled with compunctions which afflicted Colonel Peters; in fact, he was a different type of mental and moral manhood. No more gallant and brave a trooper was there in the confederate service than Harry Gilmor, but he

Chambersburg's South Main Street stands in charred ruins in the aftermath of McCausland's raid. The town's business district was gutted, with nearly 600 buildings destroyed and 2,000 people left homeless. C. A. Newcomer, one of the Federal soldiers pursuing McCausland's retreating column, later wrote of observing "desolation on all sides. . . . strong men with bowed heads, women wringing their hands and the little children clinging to their mothers' dresses and crying."

was a rugged character, and it required the taking off of a very considerable of the rough exterior before the brightness of the hidden diamond became apparent. . . .

The burning was systematically done; door after door was opened and fires kindled, and in a little while the heart of this thriving town was in flames. The distress of the citizens, especially of the women and children, was heartrending and exemplified the hellish nature of war. It was a sight never to be forgotten and I pray God may never be witnessed again in this fair land of ours. After a while these distresses and sorrows so appealed to the men that a number of them ceased their work of destruction and engaged with the stricken citizens in efforts to subdue the flames and to rescue property, and when in the course of the afternoon the troops were withdrawn and moved out of the town, I remained among the very last in the effort to clear the town of those who were under the influence of liquor. Some several, however, remained and fell victims to the enraged populace when our troops had retired. The horrible story of the punishment inflicted upon these unfortunate wretches who, through their own vices, became a prey to the revengeful passions of the people I will not recall. It is enough to say the whole episode is one of regretful experience and unutterable sadness.

Renowned among Confederates as a dashing partisan leader, Major Harry Gilmor commanded a battalion of Maryland cavalry in McCausland's Chambersburg raid. The general ordered Gilmor to round up 50 of the town's leading men and present them with his ransom demand. "The citizens," Gilmor said, "positively refused to raise the money, laughing at us when we threatened to burn the town."

PRIVATE WILLIAM H. BEACH
1ST NEW YORK CAVALRY, TIBBITS' BRIGADE

On August 4 General Averell's 1,800 Federal cavalry crossed the Potomac in pursuit of McCausland's raiders, who had left a trail of destruction and chaos across western Maryland before withdrawing into West Virginia. Moving under cover of thick fog, at dawn on August 7 Averell led his troopers toward the sleeping encampment of Bradley Johnson's brigade. A company blacksmith with one of Averell's units, Private Beach recalled the stealthy and daring advance.

Calling his leading officers together, [Averell] informed them about where the two brigades of Confederates were encamped, and gave minute instructions. The column moved forward several miles and halted. The General himself, taking Capt. T. R. Kerr of the 14th Pa. Cavalry and a few picked men, went forward stealthily on foot and captured the two mounted videttes. From these they learned where the reserve picket was, and that it was commanded by a Lieutenant Carter. Captain Kerr, taking fifteen mounted men, made a wide detour, striking the road beyond the picket and approaching it from the direction of Moorefield. When near the picket he was challenged and answered, "Relief." Then, dismounting his men, Kerr asked, "Where is your picket, Mr. Carter?" "Under a tree here in the field," was the reply. "Any straw?" "Plenty." Keeping up a conversation, Kerr and his men surrounded the tree under which the men were sleeping, and taking their arms which were leaning against the tree, passed them out of the way. "Any news, Mr. Carter?" "No; none of our scouts have come in lately. The last we heard of Averell he was coming on this side of Romney." Noticing Kerr's movements, he asked, "What's your hurry? What do you want? Who are you?" Kerr replied, "We're Yanks, and want you." Carter exclaimed, "My God! Averell's here!" After a little demonstration he surrendered. Averell himself stepping forward said, "Mr. Carter, I am Gen. Averell, and I think you are not to blame for this. Gen. McCausland ought not to have placed you five or six miles out here when he knew I was coming near at hand." Carter, blaming himself instead of McCausland, said, "Oh, it is not so far as that, not more than two or three miles." "Well," said Averell, "then he ought to have sent out patrols once in a while to see whether you were all right." "He has done that, and I thought this was a patrol when I heard it coming." Leaving the prisoners under guard and moving in toward the camp, they met the unsuspecting patrol coming out, and captured it entire. The road was now clear, and the entire command moved rapidly forward. It was now near daylight. A heavy fog had befriended Averell, interfering with the enemy's hearing as well as seeing. The command in three columns, one in the road and one on each side, was riding over the camp before the Confederates, who were just bestirring themselves, could know what was being done. Capt. Rumsey, riding at the head of one of the columns, came upon a vidette, one of a line of videttes posted some distance in front of the camp. The vidette was sitting on his horse, holding the reins in his left hand, his cocked revolver in his right, a blanket pinned with a thorn over his shoulders, with his mouth wide open and his eyes open wider still. He sat there without moving a muscle until our men were right upon him. Even then he didn't stir, but looked at the men and said "Good mawnin'." The captain did not have time to stop and talk with him. He was a very civil enemy, and did not in the least try to hinder the column, which got into the camp before he did.

BRIGADIER GENERAL BRADLEY T. JOHNSON

BRIGADE COMMANDER,
ARMY OF THE VALLEY

On August 5 Johnson's brigade made camp north of Moorefield on the McNeill estate "Willow Wall." The unsuspecting troopers were caught completely off guard by Averell's onslaught. Asleep in an upstairs bedroom of the home, Johnson narrowly avoided capture by the charging Federal cavalry.

A graduate of the West Point Class of 1855, William W. Averell had battled Indians on the Southwest frontier and seen extensive wartime action as a regimental and brigade commander of cavalry. His victory at Moorefield netted 400 prisoners, an equal number of horses, three flags, and several cannon.

We went to Moorefield, where we camped the evening of the 6th of August. . . . I was sound asleep at daylight, August 7th, when my adjutant jumped into my room. I was on the second floor of the McNeil House with my jacket and boots off, lying on the floor. . . . "General, the Yankees are in the camp!!" In one twist I was in boots, jacket and hat. . . . I reached the ground floor in two jumps, and was out of the front door. But along the road, ten steps off, was a column of horsemen in blue, at carry sabre, moving at a trot. I turned for the back entrance. Five or six gentlemen in blue came bouncing up the steps and into the hall, pumping their Spencer carbines at every jump.

Well, there are many gymnastic exercises and many plans of getting men into condition for speed, but my observation then was that five Spencer carbines ten yards behind a man, pouring five continual streams of bullets around and over him, are the most exhilarating tonic that was ever invented. I went down the steps in one jump, over a four and a half foot fence in another. As I got into the open, a man fell from his horse. I was on the horse in a breath, galloping to get ahead of the Yankee column to my command, yet untouched. I reached the 8th and the 21st Virginia, crossing the South Branch of the Potomac. I formed the 8th and held it for, say fifteen minutes, while the 21st was forming in the rear. The momentum of the blue horsemen was irresistible, though. They rode over everything; they rode over me with the 8th; they rode over Peters with the 21st, wounded and captured him . . . and nearly routed McCausland and me off the face of the earth.

"I Want Sheridan"

On July 31, 1864, President Lincoln and General Grant held a private conference at Fort Monroe, Virginia. The business of their meeting was Rebel commander Jubal Early, who had sown panic in his advance to the doorstep of Washington and who still roamed free in the Valley, making a mockery of Federal efforts to corral him. What Union general, Lincoln wanted to know, could stop "Old Jube"?

The next day, Grant announced his choice —Major General Philip H. Sheridan, the 33-year-old commander of the Army of the Potomac's Cavalry Corps. "I want Sheridan put in command of all the troops in the field," Grant informed chief of staff Henry W. Halleck, "with instructions to put himself south of the enemy and follow him to the death."

On August 6 Sheridan arrived at Monocacy Junction to take command of a newly created Army of the Shenandoah, a consolidation of the

forces of four different commands. He received an army that would be unprecedented in size for the Valley—35,000 infantry soldiers when fully assembled, supplemented with 8,000 cavalrymen in three divisions. Clearly, Grant had confidence in his appointee and was giving him ample manpower to carry out his mission.

A West Pointer, Sheridan had distinguished himself as an infantry division commander during the bloody battles of Perryville and Stones River in late 1862. In the fall of 1863 he fought at Chickamauga and, later, at Chattanooga, where he led his division up Missionary Ridge under heavy fire, breaking the enemy's line— and greatly impressing his superior, Grant.

When Grant went east in 1864 to take over as general in chief, he brought Sheridan with him to command the cavalry of the Army of the Potomac. In May, Sheridan sealed his reputation by leading his Cavalry Corps on a ride around Lee's entire army—during which his men killed the great Rebel cavalry leader Jeb Stuart.

Sheridan scarcely looked the part of a dashing horseman. He was short, compact, and oddly proportioned. James E. Taylor, a special artist for *Frank Leslie's Illustrated Newspaper*, recorded that Sheridan's "body and arms were long while his pedals were disproportionately short—'duck

Men of the 2d West Virginia Cavalry ride up to their camp at the Hackwood farm, about two miles from Winchester. A few months earlier, on September 19, the farm had been the setting for some of the hardest fighting of the Valley campaign.

legs,' in fact." President Lincoln, whose own appearance was frequently caricatured, described Sheridan as "a brown, chunky little chap, not enough neck to hang him, and such long arms that if his ankles itch he can scratch them without stooping." Furthermore, Sheridan's head seemed abnormally large and misshapen. And his voice rasped when he got excited.

But he radiated energy, and he inspired in his men an absolute devotion. Captain George B. Sanford, a Federal cavalryman, likened Sheridan's influence on the battlefield to "an electric shock. He was the only commander I ever met whose personal appearance in the field was an immediate and positive stimulus to battle."

On August 10 Sheridan marched his new army south. The Yankees reached Berryville that evening, forcing Early to fall back on Winchester. When Sheridan resumed his advance next day, the Rebels evacuated the town while fending off Federal cavalry probes. By nightfall on August 12, Early had taken up position at Fisher's Hill, and Sheridan's men were bivouacked four miles to the north, along Cedar Creek.

Both commanders then paused to await reinforcements. Two divisions—one of cavalry and one of infantry—had yet to join the Yankee army. Early was expecting a combined force under the command of Lieutenant General Richard H. Anderson consisting of an infantry division led by Major General Joseph B. Kershaw from the Army of Northern Virginia's First Corps, a division of cavalry under Major General Fitzhugh Lee and an artillery battalion. With their arrival, Early's army, which already consisted of a Second Corps of three divisions as well as a division from previous Valley forces, would grow to nearly 20,000 men.

Grant, concerned that the entire Rebel First Corps was moving to reinforce Early, instructed Sheridan not to attack until he had accurate in-

formation about the enemy's strength. When on August 14 a courier from Grant arrived confirming that large Rebel forces were on their way to join Early, probably by way of Front Royal, Sheridan decided he had no choice but to fall back north of Winchester. He was also increasingly concerned about his supply line, which had already come under attack by Colonel John S. Mosby's partisan rangers. The first Federal troops began pulling back on the evening of August 15.

Burning all the hay, wheat, and provisions found on his route, Sheridan moved to the east side of the Valley and established a line from near Charles Town to Berryville. His retrograde movement seemed to follow the familiar pattern of previous retreats by timid Union generals, and it drew a torrent of criticism. Suddenly the North was gripped by fresh fears that Early was about to resume marauding in Maryland.

But Sheridan, aware of public dismay over the recent lack of major Federal victories, was unwilling to jeopardize support for the war by risking battle without a clear superiority in numbers. Amid cries for his removal, Sheridan explained to Grant that the withdrawal, in addition to its cautionary element, was meant to entice the Confederates northward again so that he could maneuver around them and get in position to spring a giant trap. "There is no occasion for alarm," he assured Grant.

Early refused to take the bait. Instead of heading for the Potomac River fords, he lashed out against Sheridan's rear guard on August 21, and the next day he followed the Yankees retreating through Charles Town.

Here Early's pursuit ended, however, for Sheridan's men were now well emplaced back in the fortified positions they had marched forth from two weeks earlier. Instead, the Rebel commander fell back on a familiar strategem.

He assumed that Sheridan, when threatened with a flanking movement, would pull back as his predecessors had done. So, on August 25 he headed north to cross the Potomac once again.

Ordering Kershaw's infantry and McCausland's cavalry to engage the Federal line and hold it in place, he sent Fitzhugh Lee's cavalry toward Williamsport and the rest of his infantry, under Breckinridge, north to Shepherdstown. Sheridan, however, suspected that the fighting on his front was a diversion. He dispatched his cavalry chief, Brigadier General Alfred T. A. Torbert, with two divisions to reconnoiter.

About eight miles south of Shepherdstown, Torbert's troopers ran into Breckinridge's infantrymen. Both sides were startled by the encounter, but soon the Federal horsemen, outgunned and outnumbered, were fleeing toward the Potomac.

Early once again had an open route into Maryland, but this time he dared not take it. He knew that Sheridan would have learned from the cavalry the exact location of the Confederate army and was in a position to trap it. Early gave up his invasion plans—for the moment—and returned to his base at Bunker Hill.

On August 26 Grant sent Sheridan some encouraging news. Assaults by the Army of the Potomac near Petersburg had inflicted 10,000 casualties on Lee's army in the past two weeks. Lee, Grant predicted, would have to recall the reinforcements that he had sent Early. "Watch closely," Grant wrote, "and if you find this thing correct, push with all vigor."

Just as Grant had foreseen, Lee sent for Anderson's command, except for Fitz Lee's cavalry, which he allowed to stay with Early. Accordingly, on September 3 Kershaw's infantry marched toward Berryville, headed for the Blue Ridge passes. But on the way the Confederates collided with Crook's VIII Corps, and after a sharp clash, Kershaw and his men withdrew back toward Winchester.

At dawn the next morning, Early arrived on the scene with three divisions, intending to attack what he thought was only a detached force. But when he realized it was actually the left wing of Sheridan's well-prepared army, he pulled his entire force back to Winchester and formed a line east of the Valley Turnpike facing the Federals. There he decided to sit tight for a while and see what developed.

Sheridan was also waiting—for Kershaw to leave the Valley. But as days turned into weeks and nothing happened, Grant grew exasperated with the delay, and on September 14 he set out for Charles Town to meet with Sheridan personally, a plan of attack in his pocket. By the time he arrived two days later, however, the situation had changed.

Sheridan had learned from a spy that Kershaw had indeed finally left the Valley, and he had a battle plan of his own. He intended to strike toward Newtown, south of Winchester, and cut Early off from the upper Valley. Grant listened to his enthusiastic junior's scheme and, impressed with what he heard, uttered a two-word directive: "Go in."

Early, in the meantime, had revived his invasion plan. Despite the removal of Kershaw's division and the presence of a superior Federal force just six miles away, Early remained confident. Again he boldly divided his army, preparatory to once more striking the B&O Railroad and entering Maryland. Leaving Ramseur's division in front of Winchester and Brigadier General Gabriel C. Wharton's division at Stephenson's Depot four miles north, Early started toward Martinsburg on September 17 with the divisions of Rodes and Gordon.

Sheridan, informed by his cavalry of these surprising developments, determined now to strike the two divisions Early had left behind around Winchester. While Major General Horatio G. Wright's VI Corps and Brevet Major General William H. Emory's XIX Corps attacked Ramseur head-on from the east, two cavalry divisions under Brigadier Generals William W. Averell and Wesley Merritt would swing far north, keep Wharton occupied, and await the opportunity to hit Early's left and rear. Crook's VIII Corps would stand in reserve. If the plan succeeded, half of Early's force would be destroyed and the other half trapped in the lower Valley.

On September 18, the day before Sheridan was to attack, Early was in Martinsburg, 20 miles to the north. There he had a stroke of luck: He happened upon a copy of a Federal message that referred to Grant's recent visit to Sheridan's headquarters. Early realized that Grant's presence could mean only one thing: imminent action. Shaken, he immediately ordered the two divisions with him to make a forced march back to Winchester.

They had not yet arrived when Sheridan launched his attack against Ramseur the next morning. But fortunately for the Rebels, the Federal advance became snarled when men and wagons choked the approach to the battlefield, a narrow defile called Berryville Canyon. It was noon before Sheridan got his troops deployed in a battle line. By then the divisions of Rodes and Gordon had joined Ramseur's men in the Rebel line.

At a signal from Sheridan his divisions surged forward under heavy Confederate artillery fire. When the XIX Corps on the right made more progress than the VI Corps, which was also veering left to follow the Berryville Pike, a gap appeared in the center of the Federal line. Gordon and Rodes, seizing the chance thus offered, counterattacked through the opening and began driving the Federal troops back.

For a moment, the Rebels threatened to break through. But Sheridan's numerical advantage enabled him to rush reinforcements forward. The Rebel advance was soon pinched off, and the Federal lines restored. Hundreds of Rebel troops were taken prisoner, and General Rodes was mortally wounded.

The battle began to turn in Sheridan's favor in the early afternoon. The two divisions of the VIII Corps, under Colonel Joseph Thoburn and Colonel Isaac H. Duval, arrived on the field and came into line to the right of the embattled XIX Corps. Meanwhile, Merritt's and Averell's cavalry divisions had advanced on Winchester from the north, pushing back the Rebel horsemen posted on the Confederate left flank and dogging the heels of Wharton's division, which Early had recalled to the battlefield.

At 4:30 p.m. the Federals drove forward all along the front. The VIII Corps divisions struck at the Confederate line where it angled back into an L shape, while the Union cavalry descended on Early's left flank and rear. The Rebel line broke, and by nighttime the battered remnants of Early's army were in full retreat southward along the Valley pike.

As night fell, the town of Winchester changed hands for the final time of the war. In what came to be known as the Third Battle of Winchester, Early lost more than one quarter of his army, about 4,000 men, half of them taken prisoner. Sheridan's losses, about 5,000 men, were proportionately smaller and more easily made good.

Nevertheless, Early was still full of fight. He made a stand at Fisher's Hill but was put to flight again by a Federal flanking move. The Confederates then withdrew well south to Port Republic and sought refuge in the shadow of the Blue Ridge Mountains.

Gratified by this great victory, Grant and

Sheridan concluded that the war in the Valley was over and turned their minds to a plan for a grim sequel. Grant had earlier proposed total destruction of the Valley's productive capacity, and Sheridan now told his chief, "I think the best policy will be to let the burning of the crops in the Valley be the end of this campaign, and let some of this army go elsewhere." Grant agreed, and Sheridan thus opened a new and bitter phase of the campaign that would create a legacy of hate among the Valley people.

On September 29 Sheridan ordered his cavalry to put the torch to all the "forage, mills, and such other property as might be serviceable to the Rebel army" between Staunton and Harrisonburg. Soon after that wave of destruction was carried out, an incident occurred that would provoke more burning. On October 3 Sheridan's topographical engineer, 22-year-old Lieutenant John R. Meigs, was riding with two orderlies near the town of Dayton when they were ambushed by Rebel horsemen. Meigs and one orderly were killed.

General Early later claimed it was a fair fight by Confederate cavalry scouts in uniform, but the Federals called it murder. In a fury, Sheridan ordered every house within five miles of Dayton burned to the ground.

Then, on October 5, near Harrisonburg, a line of blue-clad riders stretching for 20 miles across the Valley began moving northward, toward Strasburg, burning as they went. They torched every source of food—barns, granaries, haystacks, and mills. Sheridan later reported the destruction of 2,000 barns, 120 mills, and a half-million bushels of grain and the confiscation of 50,000 head of livestock.

The destruction enraged Early, whose army had lately been reinforced by the return of Kershaw's division, though the combined force still numbered fewer than 20,000 men. On October

I he led his men back into the Valley, spoiling for a fight. For the next three weeks, he dogged the Federal army down the Valley, probing and skirmishing, although his forces were further bloodied in the process.

By October 17 Sheridan's troops had settled into camp on the banks of Cedar Creek, north of Strasburg near the village of Middletown. That afternoon General Gordon, along with two other officers, left the Rebel camp around Fisher's Hill and climbed a nearby mountain to take a look at the Federal encampment.

From his lofty vantage point, Gordon perceived an enormous opportunity. If the three divisions of his Second Corps could negotiate the steep, thickly wooded terrain and cross the North Fork of the Shenandoah River undetected, they could surprise and roll up the Federal army. Early concurred and also ordered Kershaw's and Wharton's divisions to move up on Gordon's left and be ready to cross Cedar Creek. At nightfall on October 18, Gordon's men began their flanking movement, advancing silently in single file along a path through the woods.

At first light Kershaw's Rebels forded the creek, formed a line of battle, and charged. A few minutes later Gordon's command, already across the North Fork, surged forward. The surprise was complete. As the yelling Rebels swept through the camps of the nearest Federal force, the VIII Corps, the Yankees fled in a panic, leaving clothes, guns, and everything else behind. Then Gordon's victorious troops, joined by those of Kershaw, converged on the XIX Corps camp, flanking the earthworks and capturing hundreds of prisoners.

By this time the men of the Federal VI Corps, farthest to the rear, were fully alert to the peril and had readied themselves to meet the onrushing enemy. They doggedly held their line against repeated Rebel charges. As

the sun rose, the Confederate juggernaut lost momentum. Many of the Rebel soldiers left the ranks to plunder food and clothing from the overrun Federal camps.

General Sheridan had not been present. He was returning from a Washington conference and had spent the previous night in Winchester. In the morning, alarmed at reports that the sound of cannon fire could be heard farther south, he mounted his horse and galloped up the Valley pike on a ride that would enter legend. As Sheridan rode past fleeing Yankee soldiers, the men saw him, stopped and cheered, and turned around to follow him back to the front. "Come on back, boys!" The general called out. "Give 'em hell, goddamn 'em. We'll make coffee out of Cedar Creek tonight!" He reached the fighting at about 10:30 a.m. and immediately began to re-form his army.

Within two hours Sheridan had a solid line facing the slowing Rebel drive. Riding along his front he yelled to his men, "We'll raise them out of their boots before the day is over!"

At 4:00 p.m. Sheridan signaled a counterattack, and his line moved foward. At first the Confederates blocked the advance, but then they began to give way, stubbornly contesting every foot of ground. But when Brigadier General George A. Custer's cavalry thundered around the Rebel left, the Confederate front began to crumble. Panic set in, and it spread along the Rebel line. Soon the rout was on. Only Ramseur's division in the center held its position. Then, as the Federals pressed in from three sides, Ramseur was mortally wounded and his line disintegrated.

Hounded by Federal cavalry, Early's troops fled. By nightfall his shattered units had fallen back to Fisher's Hill and would soon retreat farther up the Valley—never to recover from the counterblow struck by Sheridan at Cedar Creek.

ORDER OF BATTLE

CONFEDERATE

Army of the Valley Early

Second Corps

Gordon's/Evans' Division
Atkinson's/Lowe's/Evans' Brigade
Terry's Brigade
York's/Peck's Brigade

Ramseur's/Pegram's Division
Pegram's/Hoffman's Brigade
Godwin's/Davis' Brigade
Johnston's Brigade

Rodes'/Ramseur's Division
Battle's Brigade
Cook's Brigade
Cox's Brigade
Grimes' Brigade

Wharton's Division
Forsberg's/Otey's Brigade
Patton's/McDonald's Brigade
T. Smith's Brigade

Kershaw's Division
Conner's/Goggin's Brigade
Humphreys'/Moody's Brigade
Wofford's/Sanders' Brigade
Bryan's/Simms' Brigade

Cavalry F. Lee/Rosser

Lomax's Division
G. Smith's Brigade
Ferguson's/McCausland's Brigade
Johnson's Brigade
Jackson's/Davidson's Brigade

F. Lee's/Rosser's Division
Wickham's/Munford's/Owen's Brigade
Rosser's/Dulany's/Funsten's Brigade
Payne's Brigade

FEDERAL

Army of the Shenandoah Sheridan

VI Corps Wright

1st Division Russell/Wheaton
Campbell's Brigade
Upton's/Hamblin's Brigade
Edwards' Brigade

2d Division Getty
Wheaton's/Warner's Brigade
Warner's/Grant's Brigade
Bidwell's/French's Brigade

3d Division Ricketts/Keifer
Emerson's Brigade
Keifer's/Ball's Brigade

Army of West Virginia (VIII Corps) Crook

1st Division Thoburn
Wells'/Wildes' Brigade
Curtis' Brigade
Harris' Brigade

2d Division Duval/Hayes
Hayes/Devol's Brigade
Johnson's/Coates' Brigade

XIX Corps Emory

1st Division Dwight/McMillan
Beal's/Davis' Brigade
McMillan's/Thomas' Brigade

2d Division Grover/Birge
Birge's Brigade
Molineux's Brigade
Sharpe's/Macauley's Brigade
Shunk's Brigade

Cavalry Corps Torbert

1st Division Merritt
Custer's/Kidd's Brigade
Devin's Brigade
Lowell's Brigade

2d Division Averell/Powell
Schoonmaker's/Moore's Brigade
Powell's/Capehart's Brigade

3d Division Wilson/Custer
McIntosh's/Pennington's Brigade
Chapman's/Wells' Brigade

"It has now arrived at that point when officers must expose themselves freely if they would have their commands do their whole duty."

BRIGADIER GENERAL EMORY UPTON
BRIGADE COMMANDER, VI CORPS

Upton earned his star by launching a brilliantly conceived attack at Spotsylvania in May 1864. He led his brigade in a timely counter-attack on September 19 at Winchester, sealing a breach in Sheridan's line. Later that day, after he had taken over as division commander, he was knocked out of the Valley campaign by a serious leg wound.

Headquarters Second Brigade, Harper's Ferry, August 9, 1864. My Dear Sister: A new campaign will be inaugurated to-morrow under the command of General Sheridan. How soon it may develop the enemy, and what may be its consequences no one knows, but I trust it will be successful. General Sheridan has the appearance of great nerve, and hitherto has been quite successful. For one, I am better pleased with his appearance than that of any other commander under whom I have served. How humiliating was the reverse at Petersburg, and how disgraceful on the part of division commanders to abandon their troops! I have never been reckless, but I am sure it is a praiseworthy quality when so few of our higher commanders expose themselves as much as duty requires. It has now arrived at that point when officers must expose themselves freely if they would have their commands do their whole duty; so, whatever I may do, you must not attribute it to rashness, but to a soldier's sense of duty.

Major General Philip H. "Little Phil" Sheridan had his own way of inspiring his men in battle. At Winchester he exhorted the 49th Pennsylvania to "kill every son of a bitch" as the regiment prepared to charge the enemy. Then, wrote one of his men, "he went off like a streak of lightning and seemed to be smiling all the time."

In this sketch by Illustrated London News artist Frank Vizetelly, Lieutenant General Richard Anderson's reinforcements for Early's army ford the South Fork of the Shenandoah at Front Royal on August 16. Once across the river they ran into Wesley Merritt's cavalry division, which had been shadowing the Confederate movements. Near Cedarville the Yankee cavalry drove back William T. Wofford's Georgia Brigade with heavy losses before Merritt ordered his command to break off the fight to rejoin Sheridan.

PRIVATE JAMES J. WILLIAMSON

43D BATTALION, VIRGINIA CAVALRY

Williamson eloquently describes a typical action by his unit, which was better known as Mosby's Rangers. Mosby's command harried Federal armies throughout the latter part of the war, but its activities, although a deadly threat to isolated Federal detachments, failed to alter the overall course of events in the Valley.

On the morning of the 13th we moved out in the direction of Berryville, and nearing the pike discovered the long line of wagons moving towards Berryville. A portion of the train had just hauled out of park near a stream, where it had been halted to water the animals. A fog, which the morning sun had not yet dispelled, partially concealed us from the enemy and gave time to bring up our little force. . . .

. . . The Federals did not at first seem to realize their situation and made no preparations to repel an assault. As the curtain of fog lifted they could plainly see us, being only a little over 200 yards distant, but evidently mistook us for their own men. A shell from our gun struck a forge in the road, and bursting, aroused them and scattered the guard. A second exploded in the midst of their wagons and caused a stampede among the drivers. The third shot was followed by a charge. The cavalry had fled at the first fire, and the infantry now retreated, some taking refuge in the woods, and behind stone fences, from which they kept up an incessant fire until dislodged by a charge or a shell. . . .

The head of the train was at Berryville and extended for a long distance along the pike. Mules were taken from the wagons and the wagons then set on fire. The whole line presented a scene of the wildest confusion. The booming of cannon, the bursting shell, the rattling of musketry and the sharp crack of the pistols mingled with the yells and curses of the contending forces; the braying of mules and the lowing of cattle were heard together with the cries and groans of the wounded. In the road, horses and mules were dashing wildly about like mad; wagons upset—some blazing or smoking. Teams running off at a furious pace, which it was impossible to check, would attract the notice of some of our men, who, riding alongside, would set fire to the wagon, and as the smoke curled up, the frightened mules rushed frantically along until they fell exhausted or were released by dashing the wagon against a tree or some obstacle in the road.

. . . The long line of prisoners, mules, horses and cattle stretched out along the road. Our men, wild with excitement and elated with their success, gave vent to their feelings with shouts and yells and merry songs, the braying mules and lowing cattle joining in the chorus. The bright new captured uniforms of the Federal officers transformed our dusty rebel boys for the time into the holiday soldiers of peaceful days; and the citizens along our route, though well used to raids and the passing of armies through the country, gazed on the scene in mute astonishment, seemingly at a loss whether to stand or run on the approach of the cavalcade. . . .

In retaliation for our attacks, the Federal soldiers, acting under orders from their superiors, proceeded to wreak their vengeance on the defenseless citizens, and the burning and destruction, commenced by Hunter, was resumed.

On August 19 Mosby's men killed or mortally wounded 15 men from a detachment of the 5th Michigan Cavalry who had been burning civilian property in retaliation for Rebel raids. Some 200 of the partisans surprised the Yankees in the act and were so enraged that several of the Federals were shot after they had thrown down their arms.

Captain William H. Chapman (left) commanded the detachment of Mosby's Rangers that descended on the Yankee "house burners." Chapman had killed a Federal cavalry picket on the night of August 18, which had in turn goaded Custer into ordering the burnings. Praised by Mosby for his role in the Berryville raid and other actions, Chapman was promoted to lieutenant colonel in December.

MARY GREENHOW LEE

Resident of Winchester

The sister of Confederate spy Rose Greenhow and a vehement secessionist, Lee was well known to the men of Jubal Early's army and hosted Early, Gordon, and other prominent officers at her home throughout the summer campaign of 1864. She also spent uncountable hours taking care of sick and wounded Confederate soldiers in the hospitals of Winchester.

Our scouts, in their search for information last night, captured a picket-post of the Fifth Michigan Cavalry, near Castleman's Ferry. There were but 4 men on post: 1 was killed, 1 wounded and the remaining two captured.

As Captain Chapman moved on with his command, he saw the house of Mr. McCormick in flames, and learned that it had been set on fire in retaliation for the killing of the picket.

A little further on, the Rangers came upon another, the residence of Mr. Sowers. Here the women and poor little children were gathered in a forlorn and weeping group in a corner of the yard, gazing on the blazing pile of what was once their happy home. As our men rode up and looked upon the pale, upturned, pleading faces and met the looks of utter despair there pictured, they felt that it would be mockery to offer sympathy or express regret, and driving their spurs into their horses, they dashed on in pursuit of the destroyers. On they went, like bloodhounds on the trail. Soon they came in sight of the houseburners, who were then in the act of destroying the residence of Colonel Morgan. They had already burned the hay, wheat, barn, etc., and had set fire to the house. Worked up to madness by this scene, as well as what they had just witnessed, the Rangers closed in on the enemy and neither asked nor gave quarter.

August 17, 1864

Wednesday 2 o'clock—Before day break I was roused by the rapid passing of ambulances and troops and went down to the parlor windows entirely in dishabille to enjoy my favorite sight—the retreat of the enemy. The street and pavement were filled with a disorderly rabble as in the Bank's rout, it became so jammed with men and wagons that they halted before our door and filled the porches. Some got into the yard and were robbing the peach trees; one of the girls called in an officer and I flew upstairs for my dressing gown and went out and told them they ought to be ashamed to steal when they were running so fast. This was the 19th Corps which passed before breakfast; knowing I could not go to sleep, I took time to unpack one of the trunks I had packed when our army left us. After breakfast I made all my arrangements to be ready for our men and then went on the front porch and from that time till half past one o'clock there was a continuous stream of troops; first came Hunter's Corps commanded by Crook. I went out on the parapet which projects into the pavement and scanned the faces of the men as they passed close to me and I was surprised at their good behavior. Could scarcely imagine they were the same men who had ravaged so large a portion of our country; except to ask for bread, which I did not give them, they did not speak to me. Then came the 6th—Sedgwick's old Corps—the brag Corps of the Army of the Potomac; they made a much better show than the 8th— The music was exquisite and there were so many bands. General

Sheridan, who commands the whole expedition and Wright of the 6th Corps passed our door. All have gone now except the Cavalry, the main body of which is I suppose in the rear; the stragglers who are going along now say three companies of Chambersburgh men are coming and that they will burn the town; a few hours will decide whether it is a mere idle threat; one house has been fired, but it was put out. One of the soldiers came up to me this morning and asked if I remembered the 110th Ohio and on my expressing my forgetfulness, he said he was one of Milroy's men; I asked him what he had come back here for; he replied, "To burn the town." Some others tried to get into conversation, but I never allow a Yankee to speak an unnecessary word to me. Some of them again tried to rob the peach trees before my eyes and

This sketch by Vizetelly depicts Anderson's force pursuing Sheridan after the Federals fell back north in mid-August. Visible in the distance are columns of smoke rising from buildings put to the torch by Sheridan's retreating army. Anderson, who served only briefly in the Valley, loathed his fellow general, Early.

when I said I would call an officer, they ran off through the garden, breaking down a portion of the fence in their exit. The movements of today are inexplicable and until our army comes the mystery will remain unsolved. Why the largest army that has ever been here (50,000 as a rough guess) should retreat in a panic before Early's handful, with scarcely a skirmish I cannot understand.

PRIVATE THOMAS J. WATKINS

14TH NORTH CAROLINA INFANTRY, COX'S BRIGADE

Watkins and his comrades were involved in heavy skirmishing around Charles Town on August 21. The Rebels drove in Sheridan's skirmish line, but the Yankees counterattacked and retook the line. For a while it looked as if a general engagement might boil up, but Early declined to assault the strong Federal position, and Sheridan abandoned Charles Town that night, falling back to Halltown. Even so, almost 500 men were killed or wounded in the fighting.

At midnight, we sent out scouts to determine the enemys position. We found their pickets on the hill in our front, on an old country road, the old rail fence, on both side of the road, but that the army was retreating in the direction of Charlestown our Regiment was ordered to go forward and throw down the fences, so as our line of battle could more readily pop over.

The ridge was covered with loose stones, when we began tearing away the fences, the Yankees began rocking us, we retaliated, it was drizzling rain, and as dark as Egypt, neither side could see the other.

We being the most numerous at this point, we soon convinced them that we were as good throwers of rocks as they were, during the throwing, some one struck a fat Dutchman in his bread basket, he cried out, "Oh, I am kilt, mein Got, I am kilt." It would have made a preacher laugh to have heard the old fellow; seeing we could beat them with rocks they began firing on us, we took our guns and gave them a reception they were not looking for, nor prepared to receive. The main line on our side hearing the firing advanced, but the enemy had already retreated; we killed several of their pickets when we fired on them; we advanced and struck the road leading into Charlestown and run into their cavalry camp. They not expected us, was run out of their tents in their night clothes, we captured several prisoners and their camp. They charged us but seeing we were infantry they retreated in their night apparrell, leaving the outer garments in our hands, with camp and supplies of two Divisions of Cavelry.

James Taylor, pictured here early in the war (inset) wearing the uniform of his regiment, the 10th New York Infantry, or National Zouaves, later accompanied Sheridan's army throughout the Valley campaign in the late summer and fall of 1864 as a special artist for Leslie's. This Taylor sketch depicts the retreat of the Federal cavalry through the streets of Charles Town on the morning of August 22 under heavy fire from Early's artillery. Taylor traveled with the division of Brigadier General James Wilson during this part of the campaign.

Winchester Augt 21st 1864.

My Dearest wife —

I have been full of anxiety about you all, since the occupation of Clarke by the miserable demons who I hope have now left there — have heard nothing definite from there. Our army is in motion this morning, and again advancing. I hope to see you soon. Have not time to write more. Good bye.

Your fondly

Saml J. C. Moore

Captain Samuel J. C. Moore, whose family resided in Berryville, wrote this note to his wife as Early's army was advancing past the town on August 21. Moore had fought in the 2d Virginia Infantry of the Stonewall Brigade and had been wounded at Second Manassas. In 1864 he was serving as an inspector general on Early's staff when, upon the death of Colonel Alexander "Sandie" Pendleton on September 22, he was appointed Early's adjutant general.

ANONYMOUS

5TH WEST VIRGINIA INFANTRY, HAYES' BRIGADE

On September 3 Sheridan began shifting his army south out of its entrenchments at Halltown at the same time as Anderson's command, summoned by Lee, was marching east to leave the Valley via Ashby's Gap. Around sunset the Rebels collided with Crook's two Federal divisions near Berryville. Kershaw reacted quickly and launched an attack that, as this unknown chaplain describes, drove Colonel Joseph Thoburn's division back in confusion toward Berryville.

The fight began in the most innocent way in the world. The boys had no idea of it.—Their only thoughts were of rails and roasting ears. They had just "confiscated" a modest little quantity from a friendly cornfield, for supper. We were out about 18 miles from Harper's Ferry, and just at the edge of Berryville—a pretty, little, deserted, tumble-down, torn-down, secesh town. We had been marching since 4 o'clock in the morning, with an hour for dinner, then a short march and a long halt, and we were told to go into camp for the night, about 4 o'clock. At the last part of getting the corn picket firing began to get interesting, and plainer and plainer; but we thought nothing of it, for we didn't believe any considerable portion of the enemy were

about. Pretty soon, just as the water began to be hot enough to put the coffee in, the General's bugle began to blow, "pick up and get out here," for that is the translation the boys give to the trumpet-call of the "assembly"; and in a minute the aid on the white horse came and spoke something low to Enochs, Lieutenant Colonel in command, which made him say, "fall in," at the same time that the General's horn blew it. We were all astonishment, and the boys looked ruefully at the nice green corn they had to leave; for we didn't believe there would be any fight. If there was, we thought that the line of skirmishers ought to hold the rebs in check until we got our suppers, even if they didn't want to stop for any supper. But the bugle blew, "fall in," "fall in," and the firing was evidently coming nearer and faster; and I observed that I thought Crook's aid was more anxious to get the boys out of that little valley and up towards that stone-wall plateau, than I saw cause for. Enochs told me he guessed there would be no fight; we would probably be ordered out to support skirmishers, and lay in line of battle, and have plenty of time to feed the horses, and roast corn then; and for me to see that none of the officers or men were left behind here, to make it all "close up."

The attack was so sudden and vigorous, and the two regiments of skirmishers driven in so quick, that the regiment and in fact the whole brigade was moved up the slope towards the firing, while I was putting a bridle on my horse. . . .

The rebels had come down the road from Winchester. Our boys were hurried out to meet them, all unconscious of what was coming. . . . Our regiment formed under a heavy cross-fire, by a stone wall, the door-yard of which was upon a level with the top of the wall. Our skirmishers ran through this yard, and jumped right down from this wall, over the ends of the boy's guns—their skirmishers and line following them, firing and yelling. They first found out there was "something besides a regiment of cavalry," by hearing our boys snapping caps as they were stooped down under the wall, to dry out their guns for the big shooting they were about to have to do in a few minutes. . . . The rebels . . . had a lot of cannon behind them which threw shells so savage at Thobern's regiments . . . that they pretty much all scattered and came running back like a flock of chickens, at which some cruel old woman shakes an apron. At least that's the way it seemed to me. Like the chickens in another thing, a good many hadn't any guns.

I arrived on the field just in time to see this part of the show which I watched with philosophic interest, for it was my first sight of a "grand skedaddle" and being a preacher it didn't occur to me that our dear Confederate Brethren (for I want to compose history that will be readable to our Copperheadish Fellow Citizens) would of course rush up there and occupy the stone ridge, which these men had just left, and thus get a near sideways-fire at where I sat so safely.

It didn't occur to me till this afternoon where the bullets came from that made it so unhealthy for me. But soon they came whizzing one by one, like drops before a big shower, back where I was.

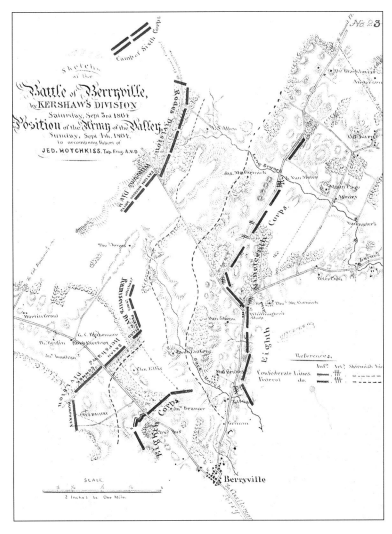

This map by Jedediah Hotchkiss depicts the positions of the two armies just after the fight at Berryville. Following Kershaw's initial success, Crook's reserves counter-attacked and drove the Rebels back. Then a brisk, inconclusive firefight illuminated the evening darkness. Colonel Rutherford B. Hayes wrote, "I suppose I was never in so much danger before, but I enjoyed the excitement more than ever before."

This field desk belonged to Captain James C. Selby of the 36th Ohio Infantry, of Hayes' brigade. Despite the loss of an arm in the brutal fighting at Chickamauga, Selby returned to duty only to be mortally wounded at Berryville.

BRIGADIER GENERAL BRYAN GRIMES
BRIGADE COMMANDER, ARMY OF THE VALLEY

Grimes unconsciously tempts fate in this letter to his wife when he suggests that she is tired of hearing that he is well and might wish for different news. Grimes began the war as a major in the 4th North Carolina and was elevated to brigade command upon the deathbed request of General Junius Daniel, mortally wounded at Spotsylvania.

Stevensons Depot
Sept 10th 64

Another day of comparative quiet has passed and I have seated myself to write you the same routine letter that I am well—you are doubtless tired of that song and wish that I would change it to another but unless I were to give you a sort of diary of everything that is said and done around me have nothing that will either interest or amuse you—We have had a spell of very rainy weather and fortunately have been encamped so near a house as to take advantage of its comforts and have slept in this house and on a bed for the past three nights and found it very luxurious with the exception of numberless little vermin crawling and biting but War service accustoms us to all little discomforts but the supply of Coffee Milk and butter which we have had supplied us by these people has been delicious and I could even stand their crying babies and the ugly women for their sakes—We are now becoming very much in need of clothing and shoes there being at least two hundred barefooted men in my Command and I am using every effort to get them shod and the poor fellows are in rags and tatters, but few having suits . . . and most cut a most ludicrous and ridiculous figure in the eyes of these Union people who are used to seeing the yankee soldiers equipped in apple-pie order or "cap a pie" order but with all our nakedness we have put up a most beautiful fight and the men go into it with spirit and I myself feel twenty years younger after being in

a fight for a few minutes and for the time being forget even my darling wife and think only of killing the detested hated yankees and driving them off our soil—Tomorrow we will break up our encampment and again go in the direction of Bunker Hill, when we move up the enemy fall back, and when they come in force we edge off to toll them up the Valley where we expect to reap the fruits of a Victory if they come on us and if we were to fight them here they would fall back into their holes too securely and have no long road to travel—So far Gen'l Early has been very Successful indeed in all his Manoeuvres.

REBECCA M. WRIGHT
RESIDENT OF WINCHESTER

Wright belonged to one of the few Unionist families in Winchester, and her sympathies were known to Sheridan by way of General Crook. In need of information on Early's strength, Sheridan sent Tom Laws, a freed black man who regularly passed through the Confederate lines to go to the markets in Winchester, with a message requesting Wright's assistance. Sheridan later rewarded Wright for her help by securing her a government job in Washington, D.C.

Just at noon on the 16th of Sept. 64, while occupied with duties in my schoolroom, in our home in Winchester Va. I was aroused by a knock on my door, which I answered at once and found an intelligent looking colored man, about 30 years of age who asked for Miss Wright and said "you are Miss Rebecca the one I want to see, your sister is in sympathy with the rebels"—I then asked what he wanted, he did not reply at once but in the most careful manner observed the surroundings, when he said he wished to see me privately. Impressed by his earnest manner I took him into another room where we were alone, when he looked carefully around and closed all the doors. I was some what alarmed as he was a stranger and there were only my mother and myself in the house, and in a very positive manner demanded his errand. He immediately told me he had a note for me from General Sheridan who wanted me to give him all the news I could of the rebel force and handed me a little package rolled in tin foil which he had carried in his mouth with instructions to swallow it if he was molested in the way through enemy picket lines. I told him I did not know anything about the rebels, but he talked on so intelligently and with so much confidence in the ultimate success of the Union cause, giving such good reasons for thinking and talking as he did, that I concluded he must be sincere and not trying to entrap me into any trouble. While he was talking I was tearing open the foil, when he said, "O don't tear the foil you will want it to wrap your answer in"—evidently noting the change in my thoughts, for he said, "I will go now Miss Rebecca, and come again at 3 o'clock and I *know* you will have a line to send the General. You must know something, living right in the lines." Then I went at once to my mother. We were almost overwhelmed at the thought of the great risk, we were running if betrayed or on the other hand if action should be taken on the information I would give, but we loved the old flag and concluded to imperil even life if need be in complying with his request. All I knew had been obtained as follows. Two evenings before a rebel officer, a convalescent who boarded with one of our neighbors, had asked the privilege of spending the evening with us. he had often noticed us from his windows which overlooked our garden gathering flowers, was lonely and desired a little variety. but a sorry call it proved for his cause, for after the usual remarks between entire strangers the only subject I knew to talk of was the war, so we talked of it. I asked questions (never thinking of using the information he gave me) and he answered, then when Gen Sheridan asked me I knew what to tell him. When the colored man returned and I handed him my reply rolled up in the foil he looked so pleased, but did not say one word, leaving quickly and quietly. Meantimes on the following day and the quiet sabbath the 18th I wondered what became of the man and my note and when I was wakened on Monday morning by the booming of cannon almost my first thought was whether my note had anything to do with the fighting and in the afternoon when the streets were filled with troops, cannon, wagons and ambulances filled with the poor suffering wounded and buildings were on fire all around us (the fire, kindling our own fence several times) my mother asked me with tears in her eyes, if I thought what I had written had anything to do with this battle. I was overwhelmed having thought of it all day long and hiding my face in my hands shuddering I replied "O no no!" I don't suppose he ever received it, but I wondered still and the shells fell so near we went down cellar for safety, for it was most terrible day of all our experience in old Winchester.

This Taylor sketch depicts the meeting between Tom Laws and Rebecca Wright in her Winchester home on September 16. A Quaker, Wright taught school in the room shown. She provided Sheridan with the information that Kershaw's infantry division and Cutshaw's artillery battalion had left Winchester to return to Lee at Petersburg. Sheridan had been waiting for just such a reduction in Early's strength, and when he received this intelligence he decided that the time was right to attack, leading to the Federal victory at Winchester.

Winchester

Jubal Early was in Martinsburg with Gordon's division on a foray to wreck Union railroads—having posted Rodes' division 10 miles south at Bunker Hill—when he realized that his remaining force back in Winchester was in imminent danger of attack from Sheridan's Yankees. He turned his troops around and began a forced march south. They arrived on the field in time to confront Sheridan, but the Federals—some 35,000 strong—retained a numerical advantage of 2 1/2 to 1.

The vanguard of Sheridan's force—Brigadier General James Wilson's cavalry division—led off the Federal attack by riding west toward Winchester in the predawn darkness of September 19. Shortly before sunrise, the troopers forded Opequon Creek and moved up a narrow gorge that later came to be known as Berryville Canyon. As Wilson's horsemen engaged the outlying units of Ramseur's division, which Early had left behind to cover the eastern approaches to Winchester, Sheridan's infantry followed. Soon, however, Berryville Canyon was congested by a jumble of marching men, artillery caissons, supply wagons, and ambulances. The resulting delay gave Early time to brace for the onslaught.

While Sheridan's infantry slowly deployed on the plateau east of Winchester, Early hastened Gordon's and Rodes' divisions into line with that of Ramseur. Meanwhile Breckinridge, with Wharton's division and McCausland's cavalry, remained north of the town around Stephenson's Depot to protect the far left flank of the Rebel line.

By 10:30 a.m., as heavy skirmishing flared up all along the front, Sheridan's force had taken position on a line stretching from Redbud Run on the north to Abraham's Creek on the south. At 11:40 a signal gun boomed, and the Yankee lines stepped off in a synchronized attack.

Pushing forward on the Federal right, Brigadier General Cuvier Grover's 8,000-man division of the XIX Corps made some headway, but it was thrown back when Gordon's division counterattacked. The commander of the XIX Corps, William Emory, brought Brigadier General William Dwight's division forward to shore up the line, but the Federals were unable to gain a decisive advantage, as the battle seesawed across an open field between two patches of woods.

Meanwhile Horatio Wright's VI Corps had advanced on the Union left and center. The VI Corps divisions of Brigadier Generals James B. Ricketts and George Washington Getty angled toward the left as they moved forward, and a gap opened between them and the XIX Corps to their right, into which Gordon and Rodes hurled their Rebel divisions. Brigadier General David Russell's division charged forward from the Union second line and plugged the hole; both Rodes and Russell were killed in the bloody clash. But Russell's successor, Brigadier General Emory Upton, managed to flank the Rebel attackers, and the VI Corps line stabilized.

Finally, around midafternoon, both armies ground to a halt and the fighting diminished mostly to artillery exchanges. Early was led to believe that the battle was just about over. Sheridan, however, was not finished. He instructed Crook to take his infantry divisions on a swing to the north and probe for the Confederate left flank. There, Breckinridge, having been driven back from Stephenson's Depot by heavy pressure from the Federal cavalry, was now linked up at right angles with Gordon to form an L-shaped Confederate line. When Crook realized that he was beyond the Rebel left, he ordered an attack. At the same time, Sheridan issued orders for a renewed frontal assault all along the line. Galloping before his troops, Sheridan cried out, "Crook and Averell are on their left and rear—we've got 'em bagged, by God!"

The sheer weight of the Federal numbers gradually wore down the defenders. Ramseur's and Rodes' divisions, hearing the roar of Breckinridge's battle with Crook in their rear, began falling back toward Winchester. Then Merritt and Averell launched a massive cavalry charge that slammed into Breckinridge and around his line to lance into the Confederate rear. The Rebel line disintegrated, and Early's soldiers fled through the streets of Winchester, pursued by saber-wielding horsemen.

This third and bloodiest battle that Winchester witnessed during the war cost Sheridan's force 5,000 men. Early's loss was most likely comparable, if not higher, but it included a large proportion of prisoners and stragglers. The Federals had won a handsome victory—and, they believed, a decisive one. But although his army was badly battered, Jubal Early was in fact far from finished with his fight to hold the Valley.

At Winchester on September 19, Sheridan sent massed infantry to push back Early's line east of the town. Simultaneously, Yankee cavalry drove Breckinridge back from Stephenson's Depot and, with the VIII Corps, enveloped the Rebel left. Sheridan then unleashed a general assault that routed the Rebels.

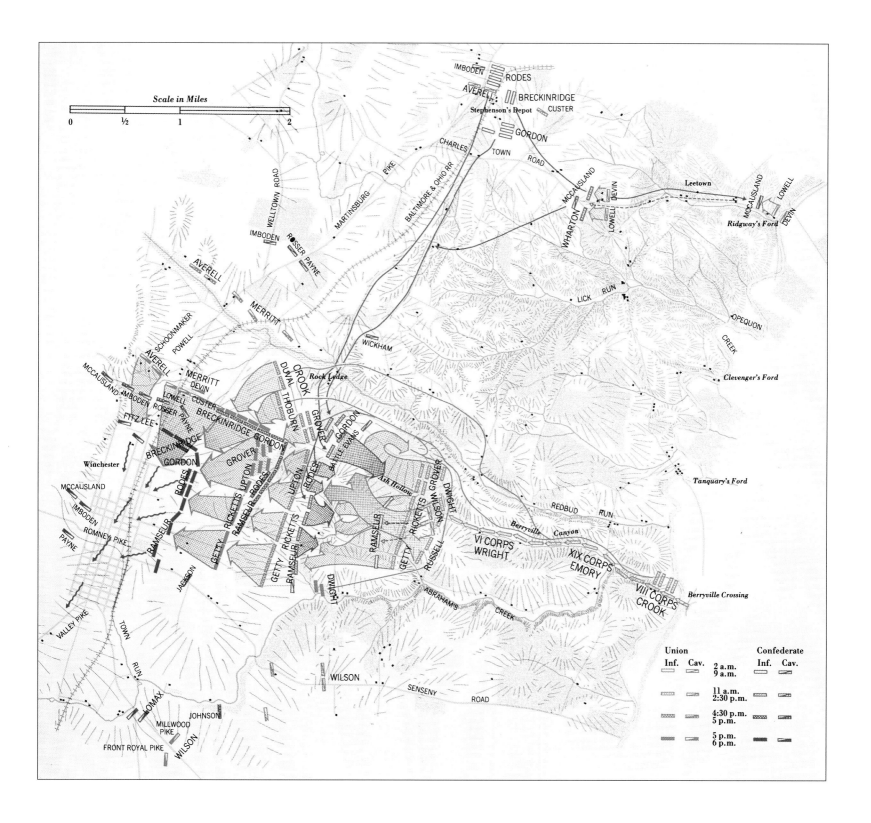

Scale in Miles

0   ½   1   2

Union
Inf.   Cav.

Confederate
Inf.   Cav.

2 a.m.
9 a.m.

11 a.m.
2:30 p.m.

4:30 p.m.
5 p.m.

5 p.m.
6 p.m.

BRIGADIER GENERAL JAMES H. WILSON

Division Commander, Army of the Shenandoah

An 1860 West Point graduate, Wilson served as an engineer officer on Grant's staff at Vicksburg. At Grant's request Wilson was placed in charge of the Federal army's cavalry bureau and later given command of the corps' 3d Cavalry Division. His troops spearheaded Sheridan's attack at Winchester.

*I*t started at two o'clock and [Mcintosh's brigade] was soon in contact with Ramseur's division, occupying the same position it held when our first advance was made. Without waiting for daylight, I put Pierce's battery of horse artillery, supported by Chapman's brigade, in a position to the right and then ordered McIntosh with his entire force, mounted and dismounted, to rush the enemy's works, which he did in the finest possible manner, breaking through and driving back the enemy all along the line. But Ramseur, a classmate of mine, and an accomplished soldier, quickly recovered from his surprise and in turn led his men against us with firm determination to regain his lost ground and entrenchments. A fierce mêlée of charge and countercharge ensued, in which both sides put forth their best efforts. Every man of the division became sharply engaged and, as every man seemed to know the importance of success, but few orders were necessary. Both brigade commanders fully understood that we had to hold the captured entrenchments, and must continue to hold them till our infantry arrived, and hold them we did. With my staff and escort of Indiana troopers we were in the midst of it, firing and slashing right and left wherever we could see a rebel soldier. I discharged twelve shots from my revolvers at close range and then, with bugles blowing, drew my saber and charged with the men as best I could.

In the midst of the excitement, before we knew what would be the result, a little waif of a boy, not yet in his teens, and known only as Jimmie, rode up to me, crying as though his heart was broken: "General,

give me a squadron. The rebels have captured Billy Brinton [lieutenant colonel commanding the 18th Pennsylvania Cavalry] and I want to charge and bring him out." But everybody was engaged and there was no squadron, even for this little paladin to lead. Brinton really was a prisoner, but that night he rolled under a hedge and escaped, rejoining us well up the valley the next day. . . .

In the midst of the fighting Colonel Sandy Forsyth of Sheridan's staff rushed upon the field, exclaiming: "This is splendid; you have got a bully fight on hand!" Then, waving his hat, he dashed into the thick of it, but, being an experienced soldier, his enthusiasm soon cooled down, and, recognizing the importance of making good our position, he swung about and, galloping to the rear, called out as he passed me: "What you need here is infantry and I am going to hurry it forward as rapidly as possible." With this he disappeared, but, withal, it was eight o'clock before the Sixth Corps arrived on the position we had captured.

Lieutenant Colonel William Brinton (above), a prewar member of the elite City Troop of Philadelphia, fell into Rebel hands for a brief period while leading the 18th Pennsylvania Cavalry in a charge on Ramseur's division. In 1881 Brinton disappeared without a trace during a failed business venture in Argentina.

Colonel Charles C. Blacknall (left) of the 23d North Carolina had been captured at the Battle of Gettysburg. Exchanged in March 1864, he rejoined his regiment, which was posted as Ramseur's picket line, on September 19. The line was driven back by Wilson's cavalry, and Blacknall, trying to rally his troops, was wounded and taken prisoner. Refusing amputation, he succumbed to infection on November 6.

a small piece of woods on the Berryville road. By this time, our sharpshooters and the Yankees were hotly engaged. The Yankees were in strong force about 200 yards from our front. Our artillery now came up and were heavily engaged. . . . We had to send three companys to help the sharpshooters and about this time Gen. Fitz Lee and Gen. Ramseur rode up behind our line. Gen. Lee was riding a white horse. Gen. Ramseur said that he thought that there were only cavalry in our front and told Gen. Lee that if he wanted to advance his line that he would take Pegram's brigade and drive them off. Gen. Lee told him

PRIVATE GEORGE Q. PEYTON
13TH VIRGINIA INFANTRY, PEGRAM'S BRIGADE

Rushed forward to bolster Brigadier General Robert D. Johnston's North Carolinians, the five Virginia regiments of Brigadier General John Pegram's brigade were still deploying when Wilson's cavalry charged their line. The Yankee troopers, fighting on foot and using their rapid-firing Spencer carbines to deadly effect, drove both Confederate brigades from their isolated position. Peyton was captured later in the day. He survived the war, became a successful builder, and died in 1932.

I laid down and went to sleep, but before day I heard all sorts of curious sounds. There were loud explosions followed by shrieks and yells and all kinds of noises. When I became fully awake, I found that the explosions were Sheridan's cannon firing on our camp and the explosions and sounds were the shells bursting over the camp. We hustled out, rolled up our fly tents, grabbed our guns and formed a line of battle and waited for orders. We did not wait long, but moved to

Captain Henry W. Wingfield (above) of the 58th Virginia Infantry was captured when Pegram's brigade temporarily collapsed before the assault of Wilson's dismounted cavalry. Wingfield was confined at Fort Delaware prison until June 1865. A former schoolteacher, he later became a professor at Randolph-Macon College.

"We saw surgeons taking out and examining the bright, keen knives; laid on a table was a victim undergoing amputation of the leg, which with other mangled men, and pools of blood, showed too plainly what was going on at the front."

he thought that there were more than cavalry in our front and we had best wait a while before we charged them. "Let us wait a while" said he "and see what's what." Old Gus said "I like what Gen. Lee said 'Let's see what's what.' Let us take that as our motto." In a little while our sharpshooters had to fall back again to the fence. It was curious to see the occupations of the men while lying on this hill side waiting for the Yankees to charge us. Some talking, some were reading, Lieut. Newman read aloud from an old magazine. . . . A terrible commotion started on our front. We were to move by the right flank and get behind some piles of rails on the left of the Berryville road. We went at [it] quite quick. When we reached the piles of rails we saw a long line of Yankees advancing. The men ran behind the rails and some low bushes. Trainham, the color bearer, had gotten back from home where he had been since 12th May and he rushed out with the flag crying "Let's charge them" but the officers ordered [him] back in the line. We had fired only a few rounds from the rail piles when the Tarheels on our right commenced running and nothing the officers could do would stop them. They cried, they cursed, and used their swords, but all to no purpose. The whole line gave away and left both our flanks exposed. Soon we saw three lines of battle coming around our left flank and had gotten in our rear before we saw them. We commenced falling back right off. . . . I looked back at the way that I come and here I saw a magnificant sight. Coming down the hill on the other side of the branch were three solid blue lines of Yankees extending as far as I could see and all firing as fast as they could pull their triggers. They were dismounted cavalry. As imposing as this sight was, I did not view it many seconds as I was anxious to get beyond the top of that hill as soon as I possibly could and so I hurried on.

CAPTAIN GEORGE CARPENTER
8TH VERMONT INFANTRY, McMILLAN'S BRIGADE

While the Union cavalry battled the outlying Rebel skirmish lines, Carpenter's regiment and the bulk of Sheridan's infantry struggled through the narrow pass later dubbed Berryville Canyon. The Vermonters had joined Sheridan's army at the outset of the Valley campaign after two years' service with the XIX Corps in Louisiana. A resident of Northfield, Vermont, Carpenter was the 8th Vermont's sergeant major until commissioned captain of Company C in August 1863.

At the appointed time the march was begun under cover of the darkness, and as we filed out of camp the column turned toward Winchester. While halting for a little rest just after daybreak, we heard that sound which I believe strikes a chill through the bravest man that lives, and causes him to feel that his heart is sinking down, down, till it seems to drop into his boots. I mean the dull rustling of air which is hardly more than a vibration, but which to the experienced listener betokens artillery firing at a distance.

Pressing forward at a rapid march we entered a deep, wooded gorge, and while there got the order to quick-step and then double-quick, while the noise of fierce strife beyond and out of the woods gave a fearful meaning to the haste with which we were urged forward. In this defile was established a hospital; and as the regiment passed, we saw surgeons taking out and examining the bright, keen knives; laid on a table was a victim undergoing amputation of the leg, which with other mangled men, and pools of blood, showed too plainly what was going on at the front.

In a sketch by Alfred Waud, mounted orderlies bearing the headquarters guidons of the VI Corps splash across Opequon Creek with corps commander Major General Horatio G. Wright and his staff. By 7:00 a.m. the lead brigade of Wright's column had crossed the stream and was making its way up Berryville Canyon to support Wilson's cavalry. But it took two more hours to get the rest of Wright's men across the Opequon and up the canyon, a delay that gave General Early time to prepare his defense.

PRIVATE ISAAC G. BRADWELL
31st Georgia Infantry, Atkinson's Brigade

Returning from Martinsburg, Early arrived at Winchester with Major General Robert Rodes' and John Gordon's divisions in time to support Ramseur's line. Rodes engaged the VI Corps in the center of the field and Gordon slammed into the flank of the XIX Corps on the Federal right, driving back two brigades of General Cuvier Grover's division. Bradwell described the fighting and the repulse of the Yankees.

Early marched his weary soldiers back halfway that night, and at two o'clock in the morning we were again on the pike. By eight o'clock we could see to the south the white puffs of smoke in the sky made by the exploding shells, indicating that Rodes was engaged with the enemy. The pike was given up to our wagon trains, and the infantry marched alongside in fields and woods, with a line of skirmishers to the left to protect us from a sudden attack from that direction. Veering to the left from the pike, we came to a body of woodland. The brigade was formed for battle in a deep ravine in the edge of this, with high ground in front of us that obstructed the view more than thirty feet away, and our old reliable sharpshooters were thrown out to develop the enemy's position. Almost immediately Sheridan's whole line, extending far to the right and left, was upon them, and these brave fellows came running back to us in a panic, causing our men to laugh at their disorder. Some said: "What's up?" To this they replied: "You'll soon see."

Colonel Lowe, of our regiment, in command of the brigade, sitting on his horse, could see the long blue lines of the enemy advancing and ordered the brigade to move forward. This we did, and to our surprise we met face to face long lines of splendid infantry advancing, apparently unaware of our presence. The entire brigade brought down their guns, and a flame of fire flashed along its entire length; at the same time a dreadful yell arose that stampeded the enemy the length of our line. We rushed at them and took advantage of their fright and were driving them in fine style through the woods as we did at the Wilderness when, glancing to the extreme right, to my horror I saw the regiment on that part of the line in great confusion giving ground, and then the next. The center and left were still driving the enemy; but the left, seeing themselves outflanked, gave way also, and there was nothing now for all to do but fall back or be surrounded and cut to pieces.

When our regiments reached the ravine in great disorder, General Rodes's Alabamians (Rodes had just been killed) were forming there,

and General Gordon, who had the greatest confidence in his old brigade, seeing our disorder and not knowing the cause, galloped to and fro among them crying: "What in the world, men, is the matter? Fall in here with General Rodes's men and fight." . . . They did so as the word was given to advance, and when we reached the top of the high ground we were face to face again with our enemy. These brave Alabamians rushed at the enemy like tigers, and for a time the two lines were so near each other that the paper of their cartridges flew into our faces. At one point to my left the lines came together, and I saw the ensign of one regiment snatch the colors out of the hands of a Federal soldier and drag them along on the ground, while he held his own standard aloft. They pressed them back through the woods to the open field, and there the majority of them stopped, for they were now without the splendid leadership of General Rodes. But the rest continued to press the fleeing enemy across the open field until they reached the protection of the forest beyond.

Zebulon York (above) was born in Maine but moved to Louisiana and became one of that state's wealthiest planters. York was promoted to brigadier general in June 1864 and led the hard-fighting Louisiana Brigade at Monocacy and Kernstown, and at Winchester, where his third wound of the war cost him his left arm.

LIEUTENANT WILLIAM H. ROOT
75TH NEW YORK INFANTRY, BIRGE'S BRIGADE

Advancing with only light opposition, the six regiments under Brigadier General Henry W. Birge were suddenly flanked by Gordon's division. Another brigade from Grover's division came to Birge's aid, but both were soon sent reeling back to their starting point with the Rebels in hot pursuit. Root, a 21-year-old farmer, must have been especially glad to avoid capture during the rout, having only recently returned from 10 months in a Confederate prison camp.

"I never felt so bad in my life–
I felt as though we were disgraced
and had probably lost the day
and I cared little whether I was
shot or not."

We forded the Opequon creek and formed line of battle at about 10 A.M. The troops were formed in three lines and the 75th were in the first line, and in about an hour the order was given to advance. The ground was rolling and we had to advance first through a piece of woods, then across an open field to another piece of woods in the edge of which we found the enemy. They commenced firing [on] us when we first came into the open lot, but we steadily advanced in good order without wavering or returning the fire until within about two hundred yards from them when the whole line started on a double quick, and the rebs left on a run. Before this our men were falling very fast, but this move relieved us somewhat.

The line advanced in splendid style until we reached the other edge of the woods—when they opened a withering fire of grape and canister from a masked battery in our front that staggered us somewhat. The left of our brigade which was our regiment did not connect with the brigade on our left and the rebels were advancing in splendid style in front of the gap this formed, and they were already on our flank when the line on our right broke and ran in the greatest confusion followed by the whole line, and in spite of the effort by the officers it could not be rallied till it had recrossed the woods and open field, and then only partially. I never felt so bad in my life—I felt as though we were disgraced and had probably lost the day and I cared little whether I was shot or not—only when I was going back I thought about being shot in the back and turned and walked backwards. This was the first time the 75th had ever run and I felt the disgrace. It was a real panic and nothing else, but I guess it was a good thing for us—for though I did not know it at the time, we were flanked on the right as well as the left and would probably have been taken prisoners.

Lieutenant Joseph G. Strong (above) of the 28th Iowa Infantry had been shot in the shoulder while serving with the XIX Corps in Louisiana and was wounded again at Winchester five months later. His unit, one of four midwestern regiments in Colonel David Shunk's brigade, was swept away by Gordon's onslaught.

As field officers ride along their embattled line in this sketch by Alfred Waud, troops of Grover's division attempt to stem the counterattack of York's Louisiana Brigade, who fire from the so-called Second Woods (background). On the back of the sketch Waud noted that Grover's men "had to fall back in a hurry, losing severely." Brigadier General William Dwight's division came to Grover's support and shored up the line, as the XIX Corps struggled to hold its ground.

SURGEON HARRIS H. BEECHER

114TH NEW YORK INFANTRY, BEAL'S BRIGADE

The first of Dwight's regiments to emerge from the eastern belt of timber and into the open field beyond, Beecher's unit pushed through the demoralized survivors of Grover's division and squared off against the oncoming Rebels. In a matter of minutes 188 of the 350 New Yorkers fell—the heaviest loss of any Federal regiment in the battle. Beecher recounted the carnage in his 1866 regimental history.

Finally, away across the fields came the faint notes of a distant bugle. The strains were warbled forth from hundreds of brazen throats, and instantly the immense army silently and majestically commenced to move slowly forward. In front of the Regiment, the Second Division was seen to disappear in the forest. Soon our men began to tramp in the shade of huge trees, where nothing was heard save the rustling of multitudinous feet, and the crackling of little twigs upon the dry leaves. It seemed as though every one was holding his breath, in the dread stillness that preceded the impending crash.

Now a few shots were heard a short distance ahead, and immediately the solemn woods roared and echoed with the crash of thousands of muskets. Then yells and shrieks, the hissing noise of missiles, the heavy, deep base of artillery, the humming of fragments of shells, joined in the confusion of unearthly sounds. So suddenly did the battle of the Opequan open, that many were struck down before they had time to realize their danger. The line kept moving forward during these exciting moments, struggling through a deep thicket. A light gleamed through the trees in front, and quickly the men came out into the sunshine. Before them was a broad, undulating field, and there, upon the opposite edge, along the border of a forest, was a long line of rebels in full view, save when the smoke of their volleys partly obscured them.

Our men took but one quick, nervous glance, and perceived the terrible situation. The Second Division was routed, and was pouring back across the field upon our lines. As soon as the steady and well-formed column of the One Hundred and Fourteenth was exhibited to the rebels, they desisted from shooting upon the fugitives, and concentrated their whole fire upon this single unprotected Regiment. The result was perfectly horrible, revolting, heart-rending. It seemed but an instant of time before scores of our noble men were lying bleeding upon the ground. Still the heroic Regiment kept moving forward in the open field, leaving its tract distinctly marked with the prostrate bodies of brave comrades. The men were restrained from firing, because the Second Division had not all retired from in front of them.

With inflexible determination, the rapidly thinning ranks struggled forward, breasting not only a deluge of lead and iron, but a torrent of frantic fugitives and wounded men. It was a moment of such delirious excitement and terror, that men before accustomed to the sights and sounds of battle, quivered and paled at the prospect before them. Once a visible shudder passed through the line of the Regiment, and it appeared to be wavering, but Colonel Per Lee rode up and down before the men, and making himself heard above the din of conflict, encouraged and strengthened them with cheering words, as well as by his gallant example. But in a moment he, too, was struck down, and Major Curtis assumed command. The Major's horse had been killed, and on foot he was compelled to direct movements.

The doomed Regiment had not proceeded in this stubborn manner more than five hundred feet from the forest, before it was discovered that it was all alone in the unequal contest. Immediately the remnant of the command was halted, and down the men laid flat on the grass. . . .

. . . Our Regiment presenting the only exposed line, received the converging fire of an entire Brigade of rebels. Not only in its front but upon either flank the enemy's balls were pouring, while over the heads of the men was a perpetual halo of fire and smoke from bursting shells.

As they were reclining on the ground, they began slowly and deliberately to deliver their fire upon the enemy. Loading their pieces upon their backs, they rolled over and took careful aim upon the distinct forms of the rebels across the field. The effects of their firing must have been terribly galling upon the enemy; still he held his line in plain sight, waving his blood-red battle-flags in token of defiance. On the other hand, our boys seemed to have enjoyed no exemption from his atten-

While leading the advance of the 114th New York, Colonel Samuel R. Per Lee (above) was shot through the neck by a Minié ball and severely bruised by a shell fragment that slammed into his chest. The 45-year-old merchant from Norwich, New York, recovered from his injuries and three months later resumed command of the regiment. Per Lee's gallantry earned him the brevet rank of brigadier general.

tions by lying upon the ground. The veterans of Stonewall Jackson fired amazingly low, so that the grass and earth in front of the Regiment was cut and torn up by a perfect sheet of lead. Their bullets sought the hiding places of the men with fatal accuracy, and by ones and twos and threes, they went crawling to the rear, with their blue clothes defaced with streaks and clots of crimson gore. Blood was on everything—was everywhere. Blood was bedraggled upon the pure grass—was spattered upon bushes—was gathered in ghastly puddles upon the ground. Upon one side was a sigh and a groan; on the other followed a shriek. Here was heard a few parting words of endearment; there a dull heavy *thud*, as a ball entered the vitals of some fated comrade.

CAPTAIN JOHN W. DE FOREST
12TH CONNECTICUT INFANTRY, McMILLAN'S BRIGADE

The 8th Vermont and De Forest's 12th Connecticut, double-quicking from the First Woods, came into line alongside the 114th New York but were quickly pinned down by a deadly fusillade. A wealthy New Englander who had spent six years abroad and written several books recounting his travels, De Forest kept a richly detailed journal of his wartime experiences. In later years he achieved a degree of fame as a novelist and playwright.

It presently appeared that our little column was needed in various places at once. Contradictory orders repeatedly changed our direction and position. We were countermarched, filed to the right, filed to the left, double-quicked and halted till we thought that the generals had lost their wits. At last we fronted upon an open knoll at the western edge of the wood and looked out anew upon Grover's field of battle.

An obstinate and bloody struggle was still going on there; but as a spectacle the scene would have disappointed a civilian. No long lines or massive columns trampled those undulating fields; the combatants on both sides were lying low in the herbage, or behind fences and thickets. The only signs of battle were long stretches of smoke from musketry, and graceful, rolling masses of smoke from the batteries.

The commanding officer of the 12th Connecticut, Lieutenant Colonel Frank H. Peck (right), was a Yale-educated lawyer whose bravery and skill had endeared him to his soldiers. Wounded at Winchester a week before his 28th birthday, Peck succumbed the following day to shock and loss of blood after sending a last message to his family: "I die cheerfully in the performance of my duty and at the front."

Meanwhile the unseen Rebel guns on our right still enfiladed us, sending most of their shells screaming through the branches above our heads, but occasionally aiming low enough to do mischief.

Here we sat down for some minutes and awaited orders. Bradbury had got up two more of his brass howitzers and was putting them in position to repulse infantry. Generals Emory, Grover and Dwight, surrounded by staff officers, lounged on their horses nearby, and watched the deadlock of the battle.

Erelong the Twelfth lost its only field officer present, Lieutenant Colonel Frank Peck, a brave and able commander. He had just received instructions to charge and had called out, "Officers, rectify the alignment." I was leaning against a sapling hardly thicker than my wrist, and felt it shaken a yard or two above my head by a shell which screeched over me and instantly burst. The crash nearly deafened me for a moment, but the splinters whizzed forward without hitting me. In the next instant Peck dropped slowly from his plunging horse, while two of Bradbury's horses reared and fell dying, and an artilleryman staggered to one side with a ghastly face. The missile had done its ferocious work with frightful swiftness and clamor.

"This is a slaughterhouse," I heard General Emory say. "But it must be held; it is the key to the whole position."

A moment later, under command of our senior captain, Clark, afterwards major, we made our advance in company with the Eighth Vermont. . . .

Trotting into the open, we wheeled slightly to the right and double-quicked for nearly a quarter of a mile across the meadows, pulling up occasionally for breath like Caesar's veterans at Pharsala, and then hurrying on again at the best speed possible. Of course there was soon no such thing as a battalion line; we were a loose swarm, the strongest in front and the feeble in rear. One veteran skulker, who had cunningly dodged fate in various battles and skirmishes, met his deserts in this advance. He slyly plunged for shelter into a hollow made by the uprooting of a tree; but his lieutenant, Mullen, promptly spanked him out of this ambush with the flat of a sabre. Right unwillingly the skulker straightened up and trotted onward to meet the bullet which was hastening to grant him a soldier's death. Not many others fell in this hasty and shapeless scramble; indeed, it seemed to me that the enemy fired at us very little. Probably they expected us to charge home, and therefore reserved their ammunition for close quarters.

Presently we reached the line indicated for us and dropped panting among the men who held it. . . . They constituted a slender line, needing re-enforcement as well as ammunition, and by no means a match for the force which confronted them. We were scarcely among them when they began to leave us, running in a stooping posture for the nearest cover visible and generally making for the forest where Grover was reforming his division. . . .

. . . It was a hot job where the Eighth Vermont and Twelfth Connecticut lay. The musketry commenced with violence shortly after the two regiments reached their line. Every few seconds a groan, a sharp cry, a plunge of some bleeding wretch rearward showed how rapidly our men were being disabled. Once, by Clark's order and with the usual instructions of "Steady, men, aim low," we sprang up and delivered a crashing volley.

For a short while our antagonists were silenced; perhaps they expected to see us come on with the bayonet. Then, little by little, on our side first, the fire-at-will recommenced. The men in both lines were nearly all cool, old soldiers who knew their deadly business. They loaded on their backs, leveled through the grass *à fleur de terre,* and fired with deliberation, usually aiming at a puff of hostile smoke.

After serving several months as inspector general of Ricketts' division, Major Peter Vredenburgh (left) requested transfer back to the 14th New Jersey and rejoined the unit just before Winchester. Vredenburgh was a bright, congenial, and popular officer whose death in that battle "was deeply felt by the men," one soldier recalled.

LIEUTENANT ENOCH COWART

14TH NEW JERSEY INFANTRY, EMERSON'S BRIGADE

The 14th New Jersey, its ranks thinned by the fight at Monocacy, was nearly annihilated when Ricketts' division began to lose touch with the XIX Corps to its right and had to rectify its alignment under heavy artillery fire. Cowart was one of two officers in the regiment who survived unscathed.

About 12 oclock the fight opened with brisk musketry and severe cannonading. I rode up where the signal station was placed on a high bluff commanding a fine view of the valley, and the scene of Battle, and with the aid of two good glasses we could see distinctly the movements of the two armies engaged. We watched the Union Banners & Colors as they waved to and fro and the day being cool and fine & clear the prospect was truly grand and imposing. . . . During the hardest struggle the 19th [corps] wavered and were in part flanked by the enemy and compelled our whole line to fall back a short distance. This struck a thrill of doubt in our mind but our forces soon rallied and drove back the Rebel forces. The Rebel Batteries worked finely and made sad havoc in our ranks being on open range. Gen Sheridan then resolved to charge them and the order was made. Major Vredenburgh was at the head of the 14th on horseback. His remark last to them was, "Boys we are the guide on the left of the line in this charge, advance on double quick, keep your ears open to the orders, and I will do the best I can for you." The words were just uttered when a shell or some say a solid shot struck him, tearing away the left side of his neck and passing out through his shoulder, the ball glazed the left ear of his horse. He threw up both arms and fell back, his head striking first on the hard ground of the turnpike road. Lt B. Ross was near him and fell back to the rear with two other men to render him assistance, he, the major, covered his face after he fell with both hands and with a little heaving of the breast expired.

In this Waud sketch, troops of Colonel J. Warren Keifer's brigade, preceded by a line of skirmishers, advance through the underbrush of Ash Hollow, a ravine opposite the center of the Confederate line at Winchester. Deploying on the right of Ricketts' division, Keifer initially gained ground but was stalemated by Rodes' counterattack.

CAPTAIN ROBERT E. PARK

12TH ALABAMA INFANTRY, BATTLE'S BRIGADE

Ordered into the fray by Rodes, Brigadier General Cullen A. Battle led his five Alabama regiments through the gap between Ricketts' division and William Emory's XIX Corps, rolling up the right flank of Keifer's brigade and throwing the Federal advance into disarray. Many of Rodes' men were unaware that their leader had been killed at the outset of the attack. Park was also a casualty; a bullet broke his left leg, and he spent the rest of the war in Northern hospitals and prison camps.

The enemy soon ran precipitately before us, and officers and men were in the utmost confusion. We raised our well known "Rebel yell," and continued our onward run, for we actually *ran*, at our greatest speed, after the disordered host in our front. We could see they had a much larger force than ours, but we cared not for numbers. We had never regarded superior numbers since we entered service; in fact, rather enjoyed it. . . . As we moved forward we passed scores, yes, hundreds, of dead and wounded Yankees, and a large number of prisoners were captured. We passed entirely through the woods, and into the open space beyond, when we halted for a moment, and then formed our line in the edge of the woods. While the lines were being established, Major Peyton, A.A.G. to General Rodes, rode up, and an indescribable, unexplainable something, I know not what, carried me to his side as he sat upon his horse. I had heard nothing, not even a rumor nor whispered suggestion, yet something impelled me to ask, in a low tone, "Major, has General Rodes been killed?" In an equally low, subdued tone, that gallant officer answered, "Yes, but keep it to yourself; do not let your men know it." "Then who succeeds to the command of the division?" I asked. "General Battle," said he, and rode on to the next brigade. The dreaded news of Major-General Rodes' sudden death, at such a critical moment, distressed and grieved me beyond expression. There was no better officer in the entire army than he; very few as brave, skillful and thoroughly trained. . . . A fragment of shell struck him behind the ear, and in a few hours this brave, skillful and trusted officer yielded up his heroic life as a holocaust to his country's cause.

In March 1862 Private George W. Wills (right) of the 43d North Carolina sent this ambrotype portrait to his sister, Lucy. Promoted to the rank of lieutenant, Wills was advancing with Brigadier General Bryan Grimes' brigade on the right flank of Rodes' division at Winchester when he was killed by the concussion of an exploding shell.

Major General Robert E. Rodes (above) was a VMI graduate who gave up a promising career as a civil engineer to teach at his alma mater. Many considered him the finest division commander in Lee's army, and his death was widely mourned.

CORPORAL CLINTON BECKWITH
121st New York Infantry, Upton's Brigade

General David Russell's division, the last VI Corps division to enter the fight, came into line between Ricketts and Getty but was unable to make any headway against fierce Rebel resistance. As Union losses were mounting, fiery young brigade commander Emory Upton turned the tide of battle when he led three regiments in a charge on Rodes' left flank. Beckwith, who was just 15 years old when he enlisted in 1862, described the decisive attack in his 1921 regimental history.

For a time, things seemed to be going our way, and the enemy had been driven back a considerable distance by both corps. But in advancing, a gap had been opened between the right of our corps and the 19th which Getty's division could not close. Seeing this weak spot and an opening in our line, the enemy massed some troops of Rodes' division and made a gallant and desperate charge upon the left of the 19th Corps. It was at this time that we were sent in, moving by left of regiment at quickstep across the pike and for some distance through a field into a wood. There we were ordered to lie down, General Upton riding out some distance to hurry the broken troops behind our line. . . . We could see the enemy coming up in line of battle, and some of the men said it was our own troops, and others said, "No, they

Though bleeding from a bullet wound in the chest, Brigadier General David A. Russell (left) remained in the saddle at the head of his division. Moments later he was killed by an exploding shell. He was the highest ranking Union soldier to die at Winchester. "He was one of those we cannot afford to lose," a comrade wrote; "straightforward, conscientious, full of good common sense, and always to be relied upon in any emergency."

poured in our volley. . . . We continued firing some until about 4 o'clock, and the 37th, being in the open, kept up a continuous fire. We being screened by small trees and brush, could not see anything to fire at, but we kept a few men in advance a little distance to keep any one from stealing upon us. About 4 o'clock we advanced about a third of a mile to some heavy timber, where the enemy opened a heavy fire upon us. But we charged them on the run, and they did not stop running away from us till they got to the village of Winchester, and we advanced to the railroad. After leaving the last piece of woods they kept us dodging their cannon shots, from two batteries playing upon us as we advanced. It was a splendid sight to see our troops coming up on the right—Crook's and Emory's, I think they were, and the cavalry on the left closing in on them and charging over the open field, with their batteries on the hill back of the town, glistening in the rays of the sun, blazing away at our charging columns.

are Rebs." I remember Wilbur Phillips making several such statements before being convinced. To our right we could see our line advancing and the enemy in retreat both firing, the color sergeants waving their standards to encourage the men. . . . General Upton ordered us to fix bayonets and not to fire until he gave the command, and the word was passed along the line. At last the enemy reached to where there could not be any doubt of their identity, and General Upton gave the order, "Ready, aim, fire," and crash went that volley of lead, and down tumbled those brave fellows. "Forward, charge," rang out Upton's short, incisive command, and away we went. Reaching the point where their line had stood we saw many of them lying there, not all shot however. Some of them had dropped down to escape death and became our prisoners. But those who could get away fled for their lives, not stopping on the order of their going. At once out rushed our companion regiments in fine order. The 2d Connecticut advancing and firing, was compelled to withstand a severe fire from the right as well as front, and suffered severely. We reformed and were immediately moved forward and placed on the left of the 37th Massachusetts to close up a gap. This splendid regiment, armed with Spencer repeating rifles, had charged in on the charging Rebels in the nick of time, and had saved our (Stevens') battery near the road, while we had reached their front and

PRIVATE HENRY R. BERKELEY
AMHERST (VIRGINIA) BATTERY

Lieutenant Colonel William Nelson's three batteries, firing from a position astride the Berryville pike, inflicted heavy losses on the advancing Federal ranks. But the Yankee juggernaut was not to be stopped. In late afternoon Ramseur ordered the guns to fall back to a new line on the outskirts of Winchester, as 24-year-old Berkeley recalled.

At one time today there came a Yankee shell, which struck the middle horse of my limber right between its eyes, and bursting, took off the middle horse's head, cut off the hind legs of the saddle horse in front of him and the front legs of the horse just behind him, cut the pole of the limber in two pieces, passed through the limber box, which fortunately was nearly empty, and knocked Bill

"After the bursting of the shell, Charley was left unhurt . . . but covered from his face to his knees with the brains and blood of the horse."

This drawing by Waud shows the ranks of Wright's VI Corps as the determined Yankees resume their advance to the edge of Winchester. By 4:00 p.m. mounting Union pressure on the Confederate left had compelled Early's weakened right wing to pull back toward the town, where the Rebels girded for a last, desperate stand.

McDaniel down, who was standing just behind the limber box. Bill was acting as Number 6. None of the drivers were hurt and Bill soon picked himself up, being more frightened than hurt. I don't see how Charley Taliaferro, who was the driver of the horse that had its head carried away, could possibly have escaped, but he did most wonderfully. He was holding his horse close up near the bit, when the shell struck it, and, after the bursting of the shell, Charley was left unhurt, holding the reins and bit in his right hand, but covered from his face to his knees with the brains and blood of the horse. I could not help being amused at his appearance, yet it was an awful gruesome place to be amused. But Charles quietly went to the limber, gathered up a handful of cotton, dipped it into the sponge bucket and proceeded to wipe his face and clothes off. Soldiers are never made cooler, or braver, than Charles Taliaferro. It is sad to think that such men are falling around us every day. When will this cruel war be over? It happened on another part of the field today that at my gun, three men, one after the other, were shot down at my right hand: viz., Jim Pleasants, John Graves and James Monroe. Jim Pleasants lost his right foot, by a musket ball burying it-self in his ankle; John Graves was knocked over, but the strap on his belt saved his life. Jim Monroe was wounded in the fleshy part of his right leg and will get well. These three men, with several others at our other guns, were wounded by Yankee shooters who had gotten up into trees and whom we could not bring our guns to bear on. I thought my time would certainly come next. A sharpshooter's ball went through my gaiter and scraped my ankle. Gen. Ramseur came up about this time, and I told him that if he kept us there much longer that every one of my men would be picked off by the Yankee sharpshooters. He then ordered me to retire to the hill just behind where we then were, and which we did very handsomely and without loss of men or horses.

COLONEL AUGUSTUS FORSBERG

BRIGADE COMMANDER, ARMY OF THE VALLEY

A former officer in the Swedish Army, Forsberg commanded a brigade of four Virginia units in Wharton's division. His troops helped stymie Merritt's cavalry northeast of Winchester till the afternoon. When Early ordered his northern flank to concentrate before the town, Forsberg joined this final line.

By degrees the whole line was thrown in confusion and I had no other recourse but to rally the Brigade on higher ground. . . . There we took a stand and for hours successfully repulsed numerous charges by the enemy's cavalry mounted and dismounted. Col. Smith's Brigade and two pieces of Artillery had been sent to my assistance and participated in this spirited engagement. . . .

After many fruitless attempts to dislodge us from the position we occupied the Feds. retired from our front, but the sharp firing on our right, in direction of Berryville, indicated that Gen. Ramseur's Division was hard pressed, and our safety endangered. On the left the firing was not so incessant, but the enemy was gaining ground. Gen. Breckenridge, after examining the situation, ordered me to withdraw quietly and if possible unobserved by the enemy, who was massing on our left. By deploying cavalry in front our move was partly masked, but two of the enemy's batteries followed us some distance, alternately changing their position and firing into our flank. We retreated to within a mile of Winchester and were kept for awhile in reserve. The fighting had been so much in detail that we knew little of what had transpired on other points of the field. The gallant Gen. Rodes had fallen and our losses had been severe, but the punishment inflicted on the enemy was such as to inspire us with the most encouraging hope of a final success. . . . Throughout the day we had noticed the demoralization of the enemy's Infantry, their Officers were seen driving the men up to the constantly wavering lines, and I honestly believe that ten or fifteen minutes longer occupation of the position, in which we were placed about 5 o'clock P.M., with continuous firing, would have routed their Infantry, and secured us a glorious victory. But the superiority and number of their cavalry, upon which now rested their whole dependance, and some minutes inactivity on our part changed our bright prospects into a signal defeat. This Cavalry had been several times repulsed by our Division, which now was lying down to rest and to be less exposed to the flying shots & shells, and considering it imprudent to make further attempts on our Infantry they commenced massing on the extreme left of our line to force our poorly equiped and jaded cavalry, which defended that part of the line. The result of such an attempt could not be very doubtful and aroused me with the liveliest apprehension of the approaching danger.

LIEUTENANT COLONEL JAMES COMLY

23D OHIO INFANTRY, HAYES' BRIGADE

General Crook's VIII Corps was dispatched to the far right of Sheridan's force and made preparations to strike the northern flank of Early's line. At 3:30 p.m. Colonel Isaac Duval's division, supported by artillery fire, advanced southward toward Redbud Run. The stream flowed through a steep ravine, and its swampy banks disordered the Yankee lines as they floundered through the boggy ground. Comly, a former newspaper editor, described his regiment's ordeal.

We reached our position under cover of an almost impenetrable growth of cedar, crossing a swampy stream. Here the Division halted, and was formed. 1st Brigade in front and 2nd (Johnson's) in rear. Throwing out a light line of skirmishers we advanced rapidly to the front, driving the enemy's cavalry. Our cavalry at the same time advanced out of the woods on our right. After advancing in this way over two or three open fields under a scattering fire, we reached the crest of a slight elevation, when the enemy's infantry lines came in view, off diagonally to the left front, and he opened upon us a brisk artillery fire. Moving forward double quick under this fire, we soon reached a thick fringe of underbrush, dashing through which, we came upon a deep slough, twenty or thirty yards wide, and nearly waist deep,—with deep, soft mud at the bottom, and the surface overgrown with a thick bed of moss, nearly strong enough to bear the weight of a man. It seemed impossible to get through it, and the whole line was staggered for a moment. Just then I saw Colonel Hayes plunge in with his horse, and under a shower of bullets and shells, with his horse sometimes down, sometimes up, he rode, waded and dragged his way through, the first man over. I immediately ordered the Regiment by the right flank, and over at the same place. It was a work of almost incredible difficulty to cross the slough, even without opposition. It is not possible to give one an idea of the labor, who has never seen a morass of this description. Men were drowned or suffocated in the slimy mud or tangled in the moss, wounded, and could not be got out. But still the men plunged through. I was the first one over on foot. I had to leave my horse with my orderly on account of the fences we passed, in order to keep with the regiment. After a pause only long enough to partially reform, the line charged forward again, yelling and driving the enemy. Sheridan's old cavalry kept close up on our right, and every time we drove the enemy from cover charged them, captur-

ing large numbers of prisoners. The fire grew hotter and more rapid, and our lines thinner and thinner. as we approached the strong field works—The approach to which was also enfiladed by guns on the Star Fort off to our right on the Heights. A number of the enemy had covered under a stone fence on our right, and poured a most galling enfilading fire into us. The 36th Ohio and 5th W.Va.—glorious Regiments, both,—charged and drove them from cover, when our cavalry charged and captured them, as they ran in confusion. . . . We met several checks crossing the space in front of the works we were making for—the whole front being swept by a cross-fire from the works in front and from the Star Fort in flank. Several times, as we lay at the crest of a slight elevation in right of the enemy it seemed impossible to hold our position. The men had been very much scattered in crossing the morass. The supporting line was mixed up with the first line, until the whole formed an irregular, thin, long and straggling line, which looked almost as if it would break of its own weakness.

Looking toward Hackwood—the Clevenger and Spangler families' estate situated northwest of Winchester beyond—this postwar photograph shows part of the ground over which Crook's divisions launched their decisive assault on Early's northern flank. The imposing mansion, which dated from the late 18th century, was crowded with soldiers wounded from the morning's fight who found themselves caught in the cross fire when the tide of battle swept past the home's bullet-scarred walls.

COLONEL JAMES H. KIDD
6TH MICHIGAN CAVALRY, CUSTER'S BRIGADE

The withdrawal of Breckinridge and Wharton to Winchester freed Merritt's and Averell's cavalry divisions to advance en masse astride the Martinsburg pike. At 5:00 p.m. the Yankee horsemen, including Kidd's and Custer's "Wolverines," thundered forward in one of the largest cavalry onslaughts of the war to date.

T he signs and sounds of a great battle became startlingly distinct. The roar of artillery and the rattle of small arms saluted the ear. Within sight of the fortifications, around that historic town, a duel was raging between the infantry of the two armies. The lines of blue and gray were in plain sight off to the left. Puffs of smoke and an angry roar told where the opposing batteries were planted. Dense masses of smoke enveloped the lines. From the heights to the front and right, cannon belched fire and destruction.

The Union cavalrymen were now all mounted. The Michigan brigade was on the left of the turnpike; to its left, the brigades of Devin and Lowell; on the right, Averell's division of two brigades—five brigades in all—each brigade in line of squadron columns, double ranks. This made a front of more than half a mile, three lines deep, of mounted men. . . . At almost the same moment of time, the entire line emerged from the woods into the sunlight. A more enlivening and imposing spectacle never was seen. Guidons fluttered and sabers glistened. Officers vied with their men in gallantry and in zeal. Even the horses seemed to catch the inspiration of the scene and emulated the martial ardor of their riders. Then a left half wheel began the grand flanking movement which broke Early's left flank and won the battle.

When the Michigan brigade came out of the woods, it found a line of confederate horse behind a stone fence. . . . There were places where the stones had fallen or had been thrown down, making openings through which horses could pass one, or at most two, at a time. The

The regimental colors of the 7th Michigan Cavalry (above) were carried through the fight at Winchester by 24-year-old Sergeant Albert Shotwell (left). After brushing aside the outnumbered Rebel cavalry north of Winchester, the Michiganders joined in the climactic charge on Early's left flank. "One shell hit my horse in the head," Shotwell recalled, "and in falling he threw me, colors and all, quite a number of feet."

Union cavalrymen made for these openings, not halting or hesitating for an instant. The fence was taken and breaking through they put to flight the confederate cavalrymen who did not stop until they found refuge behind their infantry lines.

The union line was broken up too. The country for a mile was full of charging columns—regiments, troops, squads—the pursuit taking them in every direction where a mounted enemy could be seen. The cavalry disposed of, the infantry was next taken in hand. . . .

The portion of the command with which I found myself followed Lee's cavalry for a long distance when, reaching the top of a slope over which they had gone in their retreat, we found ourselves face to face

Flourishing his saber, Major Smith Hastings leads the 5th Michigan Cavalry in a final charge on the collapsing Rebel line. "Officers and men seemed to vie with each other as to who should lead," General Custer reported. "The enemy upon our approach turned and delivered a well-directed volley of musketry, but before a second discharge could be given my command was in their midst, sabering right and left, capturing prisoners more rapidly than they could be disposed of." Custer claimed to have rounded up 700 captives, as well as seven battle flags.

with a strong line of infantry which had changed front to receive us, and gave us a volley that filled the air with a swarm of bullets. This stopped the onset for the time, in that part of the field, and the cavalry fell back behind the crest of the hill to reform and, to tell the truth, to get under cover, for the infantry fire was exceedingly hot. . . .

As my horse swerved to the left, a bullet struck my right thigh and, peeling the skin off that, cut a deep gash through the saddle to the opening in the center. The saddle caused it to deflect upwards, or it would have gone through the other leg. At the moment I supposed it had gone through the right leg. . . . The wound was not serious and I proceeded to assist in rallying as many men of the regiment as possible to report to General Custer who was preparing for what proved to be the final charge of the battle. This was made upon a brigade of infantry which was still gallantly trying to make a stand toward Winchester and in front of a large stone house. The ground descended from Custer's position to that occupied by this infantry. Custer formed his men in line and, at the moment when the enemy began a movement to the rear, charged down upon them with a yell that could be heard above the din of the battle. In a brief time he was in their midst. They threw down their arms and surrendered. Several hundred of them had retreated to the inside of the stone house. The house was surrounded and they were all made prisoners.

Colonel John H. S. Funk (left), commander of the 5th Virginia Infantry, was also leading the remnants of the famed Stonewall Brigade when severely wounded as his men waged a desperate stand behind the cover of a limestone outcropping on the Hackwood farm. A native of Winchester and an 1860 graduate of the town's medical college, the stricken officer was carried to his mother's home. He died there of his injuries two days later.

CAPTAIN PENROSE G. MARK

93D PENNSYLVANIA INFANTRY, WHEATON'S BRIGADE

Mark and his regiment, along with the rest of Getty's division, joined Crook's corps and Torbert's cavalry to break the last-ditch Rebel line at the edge of Winchester. Only 20 years old, Mark rose through the ranks to company command and in 1865 was brevetted for gallantry at Petersburg.

It was three o'clock when we heard heavy firing on our right, and all were ready to advance. The 93rd held to its former position, when Gen. Sheridan was seen coming along the line from our right, the perspiration rolling over his forehead and his black steed "Rienzi" covered with foam. He rode straight up to Gen. Getty, exclaiming: "General, I have put Torbert on the right, and told him to give 'em h——l, and he is doing it. Crook, too, is on the right, and giving it to them. Press them, General; they'll run!" And then using one of those phrases sometimes employed in the army, to give additional force to language, he shouted again: "*Press them, General; I know they'll run!*" and the shout of the men drowned all noise of battle. . . .

. . . We again advanced once more, charged across the undulating plain and gained the ridge at the brick mansion, and kept it, though suffering severely from the fire of a battery on our left, before the ridge was reached, and drove the Rebels towards Winchester. . . . As the Regiment gained the ridge at the brick mansion, there was seen right across the valley one of the grandest sights probably witnessed in the late Rebellion.

Within the valley were thousands of the Rebels, fleeing in all directions towards Winchester, along the turnpike leading down the valley, while along the left flank of them came regiments of Union cavalry, with their sabres drawn and on full charge, cutting down the retreating foe, and crushing some beneath the tramp of their horses, while others scattered in every direction, and although it was the work of but a few moments, yet terrible was the result.

SERGEANT SAMUEL P. COLLIER
2D NORTH CAROLINA INFANTRY, COX'S BRIGADE

Waging a fighting retreat against the advancing VI Corps, Rodes' division—now under Ramseur's command—re-formed behind a line of earthworks just northeast of Winchester. But its stand was of short duration. Averell's and Merritt's cavalry had broken the Confederate left and were sweeping around the open flank and rear of Early's force. Collier, only recently recovered from a bout with dysentery, managed to make his escape when the Rebel defense disintegrated.

We started back to the line which we reached in safety. After being in there a few minutes we heard very heavy firing in our rear. Col Brown of the 1st N.C. Regt but now commander of the Division sharpshooters called for them and carried us at a double-quick to where our cavalry were fighting both Yankee infantry and cavalry. They came pouring down upon us like a thousand bricks which of course we could not stand. We fell back when every thing at this moment began to move, Waggins, Ambulances and every thing, mixed up to-gether. The whole face of the earth was litterally alive with rebels running for their lives. I would run a while and stop and laugh at others and think what fools we were making of ourselves when some shell would come tearing among us and every thing would start off again. I would be among them. I never ran so fast in all my life. To come out and tell the truth I ran from two miles the other side of Winchester to Newtown a distance of ten (10) miles and can assure you I had company from Brig Genls down to privates. But there is one thing that I did not do. That was to throw away my gun and things. I always held on to them let what may happen.

It was equal to the 1st Manassas stampede. I never saw any thing like it before. They never captured any of our weapons or Ambulances. That was the only difference.

While trying to rally his fleeing brigade in a Winchester street, Colonel George S. Patton (above), grandfather of the celebrated World War II commander, was wounded when a shell fragment passed through his shirttail (left) and tore into his right thigh. Carried into a nearby dwelling, Patton refused to permit the amputation of his mangled leg, even after gangrene set in, threatening to shoot any surgeon who attempted the operation. He died on September 25 and was buried beside his brother, who had fallen at Gettysburg.

CAPTAIN GEORGE P. RING

6TH LOUISIANA INFANTRY, YORK'S BRIGADE

Writing to his wife, Ring described the collapse of Gordon's division, which had fought valiantly against great odds. Gordon's brigades were hit on their left by Crook's onslaught and forced to yield their position in the First Woods, retreating in disorder toward Winchester. Mrs. Gordon, who often accompanied her husband on campaign, joined him in a fruitless attempt to rally the demoralized soldiers.

As we came out on the open fields immediately above Winchester, I said that the jig was up with our army unless some extraordinary dispensation of Providence. All over the plain men could be seen flying to the rear, Officers riding to and fro trying to rally and reform the men. It was a mortifying but very exciting scene. Officers would rally their men after strenuous efforts and just as they would have a line formed, some other command would commence giving away and first one and then another would give away until the whole line would be in motion. As our line extended about two miles and as the line would give back I thought that if the Yankees only had the sense to press right forward on us in their compact form that they would get us all. Darling the scene was one of terrible interest and it was worth all the risk and danger to witness it. . . . I never saw as fine a sight in my life as our noble Gen Gordon presented, as he galloped down the line with a stand of colors in his hand, his hat off and his long hair streaming back in the wind. He passed by me when I had the colors of Staffords Brigade with a few men and as he passed sang out to me, Form your men Captain I know they will stand by me—By this time four oclock I supposed it was—our army or some portions of it had become so completely demoralized that they would not stop for anything or any body, but poured into and through Winchester out the Valley Pike and I dont think some of them stopped until they reached this point 22 miles from Winchester. The Ladies of Winchester came into the streets and begged them, crying bitterly to make a stand for their sakes if not for their own honor, but with no avail—the cowards did not have the shame to make a pretence of halting but would push by these noble women, resisting tears, entreatings and reproaches as each was used. Mrs Gen Gordon who was in Winchester seized Division Hd Qrs flag and running into the street called upon any of her husband Division to rally round *her flag* and that she would lead them. She rallied a party of near two hundred and sent them back to the field. The Yankee cavalry made a charge on this mob as they were pouring into town, went right through them and run right over one Brigade of Breckinridge's Division that fortunately were in good order and who gave them one volley, that . . . emptied nearly every saddle—After we had fallen back through and around the town, we managed to get the different commands or the fighting part of them together and formed a new line of battle, but the enemy seemed to be satisfied with having driven us through town and night coming on we were enabled to fall back in pretty good order.

LIEUTENANT JOHN H. WORSHAM

21ST VIRGINIA INFANTRY, TERRY'S BRIGADE

Worsham, promoted to lieutenant and adjutant of his regiment a week before Winchester, was shot in the leg while helping Gordon form his final line on the northern edge of town. Though unable to walk, and faint from loss of blood, Worsham managed to escape the debacle and was taken to a hospital in Charlottesville, where the bullet was extracted from his knee.

By this time I was so sick that I thought my time to die had come. As I looked at my knee, I saw the blood running freely down my pants. . . . Two of my comrades took me by my arms and carried me off the field. After going a short distance I begged to be allowed to lie down, thinking that I would otherwise die. They would not listen to me while the cannons were plowing great gaps in the earth all around us, but they promised that, as soon as we reached a large rock which we were approaching, they would let me lie down under its protection.

We soon reached it, and I lay at full length in hopes of getting some relief. But a cannon shot struck the rock, glanced off, and went up out of sight. In an instant I was taken up by my comrades and carried on until we reached the first house in Winchester, a small, one-story brick building at the corner of an alley. I was allowed to lie down behind this; almost instantly a cannon shot went crashing through it, throwing pieces of brick and mortar on us. They had me going again at once. . . .

. . . Soon afterward we met Ira Blunt, our hospital steward and also an old member of F Company. Running to me, he put a canteen to my lips and told me to take a good pull. I drank some new apple brandy. Its effect was instantaneous; I felt perfectly well. Thanking him, I went on in search of our surgeon. As I turned the corner of the next street, I saw our surgeon, Dr. Malcolm N. Fleming, mounting his horse. I called him, and he rode to meet me. He said that he had sent all his stores to the rear and had just mounted his horse to follow, but that he would get me away if possible. Insofar as he knew, all the ambulances had gone. Just at this moment an ambulance turned the corner into our street and came toward us with the mules in a run. The surgeon ordered the driver to stop. For an answer, the driver whipped his team into a faster gait. Our surgeon mounted his horse and put him into a run. Overtaking the ambulance and catching one of the mules, he stopped the team by main force. I went forward to the ambulance, and my two comrades pitched me into the rear. The surgeon let the mules go, and we were off!

The ambulance was filled with medical chests, and I tried to arrange them so as to make a comfortable seat. But I could not. In the hinder part of the ambulance was a chest. At its end was a bucket, and the handle of the chest came over the bucket in such a manner that the bucket could not move. The other part of the ambulance was filled with chests piled one on top of the other, leaving only the chest in the rear on which to sit. I managed to put the foot of my wounded leg in the bucket, letting my good leg hang out.

By this time the ambulance had caught up with the wagon train, moving two abreast up the Valley pike. The enemy on the right of our line now opened on our wagon train with one piece of artillery. The first shot they fired went over the train a little in front of my ambulance. The next shot went through the top of the wagon just in front of us. Amidst the cracking of whips, yells, and oaths, the wagon train went in a hurry down the pike! In a few minutes they got behind the woods, and the firing from the Yankee gun ceased. Yet my ambulance driver had become demoralized. He wheeled his team to the right, and over a stone wall he went! How it was done I shall never know, but he did it, and through the field his flying mules went! It was an old cornfield, and the reader may know how comfortable I was!

A Rebel field officer, striving for order in the chaos of the retreat, leads a column through Winchester in this drawing by James E. Taylor. Wounded men are borne up the porticoed steps of Taylor's Hotel (right), while an ambulance bearing the body of General Rodes is visible in the background at left.

A Federal burial detail digs a mass grave for fallen soldiers of Keifer's brigade in this sketch by Taylor, which includes an image of himself at work while perched atop a bullet-riddled fence on the Dinkle farm, the scene of heavy combat earlier in the day. "Look into the faces of a hundred men killed in battle and you will find the same general expression," Taylor observed. "It is a look of surprise and fear."

PRIVATE WILBUR FISK

2D VERMONT INFANTRY, WARNER'S BRIGADE

The 25-year-old Fisk, a farmer from Tunbridge, Vermont, writes movingly about the hundreds of Union wounded who were left behind in improvised field hospitals as Sheridan's victorious army prepared to follow the retreating Early up the Valley. Deeply affected by his wartime experiences, Fisk later became a Congregational minister.

Down by the creek where the train stopped, they put up the division hospitals for our corps. Ambulance loads of wounded men were continually coming in, and the surgeons had all they could attend to, and more too. Wounds of every description; some in the head, some in the body, some in the hands, arms, legs or feet were constantly being brought forward for attention. It was impossible to attend to them all at once, and many had to wait and suffer a long time with their savage wounds undressed. Amputations at several tables were being made all the time. As fast as one man was removed from the board another was put on. Many poor fellows had to wait for several hours before their turn came. The surgeons, besmeared with blood, and hardened to their business, looked more like butchers cutting up beef than like professional men, adopting the stern alternative of removing a limb to save the life of a fellow man. A hospital on the battlefield always presents a horrid ghastly sight. Surely our national honor ought to be imperishable, purchased at such a cost.

Among those brought in were several of my own comrades. One man struck in the thigh with a piece of shell, which broke his leg, and bruised it badly, was brought in about noon, and it was not till night that any attention was paid to his wounds, except what we could do ourselves. It was not till night that he had any shelter either, and then it was only a fly overhead—a roof without walls. But it was the best they could do, and it is not always at such times, that they can do as well as that. It was a chilly night, and the men, many of whom had to have their clothing cut from their wounds, leaving them in some instances half naked, had but one blanket for two men. I remember I promised to bring my friend a rubber blanket from the train, but the train moved along, and I could not do as I had promised. Yesterday I suppose he, with the rest of the wounded, were removed to a general hospital. It will be a tedious and painful journey over the rough roads for men with such wounds as his, but I know my friend is a brave man, as indeed they all are, and I know that bodily pain cannot crush his spirit.

Right by the side of the tent where my friend lay was another soldier, mortally wounded, and left there to die. I couldn't help noticing him in particular, though I never had seen him before. Fair looking and intelligent, too young and too tenderly reared, one would think, to endure the hardships of a soldier's life. Alas, he did not have to suffer long. He was wounded in the head, and died that night. I first noticed him a little past noon. He could not speak, but he appeared conscious. A fellow from his company asked him if he knew him. He signified, by a pressure of the hand, that he did. I saw him again at night, he was dying then. Oh what would a brother or sister have given to have been with him then—to have called his name and received back a pressure of recognition? What would his mother give now to drop a tear by his rude grave—a sacred spot that she may never be able to find? And thus have perished thousands since this war began. Verily war is cruel, and none more terribly so than this which the rebellion has forced upon us. God forgive those who started it, they knew not what they did.

On the night of September 19 a Federal cavalry officer reports to Sheridan, who sits on a campstool beside his headquarters campfire with a bayonet serving him as an improvised candleholder (right) in this Waud rendering. One of General Torbert's aides noted that the habitually intense and often irascible army commander "was feeling unusually happy, and well he might, for he had gained a great victory." The next day Sheridan set his troops in motion toward Strasburg and Fisher's Hill, seeking a decisive engagement with Early's reeling army.

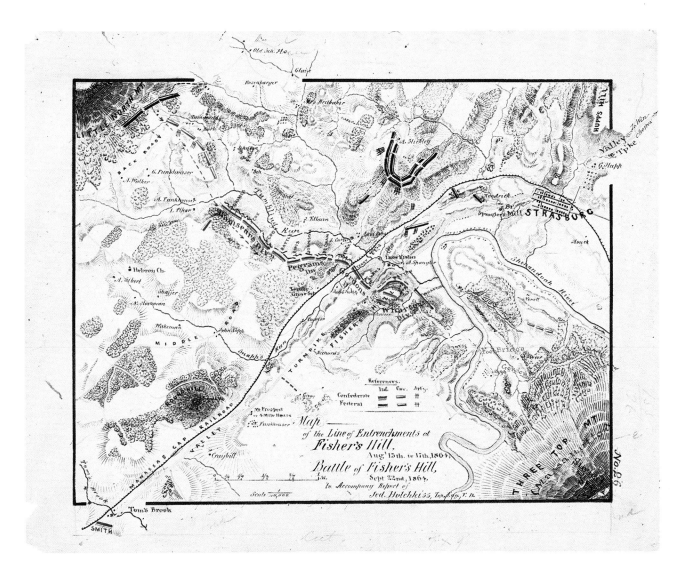

The day after the debacle at Winchester, Early began reassembling his scattered units some 20 miles to the south, directing them to dig in along a commanding elevation called Fisher's Hill. Rather than attack this strong line head-on, Sheridan decided to pin the Rebels in place with the VI and XIX Corps while George Crook led the two divisions of his Army of West Virginia along the slopes of Little North Mountain and struck the vulnerable left of the line. Jedediah Hotchkiss executed this detailed map of the September 22 engagement.

CAPTAIN GEORGE W. BOOTH
STAFF, BRIGADIER GENERAL BRADLEY T. JOHNSON

Although Fisher's Hill was a formidable defensive position, Early lacked sufficient troops to man the entire four-mile front between Little North and Massanutten Mountains. The far left—where Crook's divisions launched their surprise attack— was held by three understrength and poorly armed cavalry brigades commanded by Major General Lunsford L. Lomax. Dismounted and extended in thin skirmish lines, the Rebels were no match for the determined Yankees, as Booth recalled.

We discovered on the slopes of the mountains on our extreme left a line of infantry making their way around our flank, the sunlight flashing on their burnished muskets and bayonets making a glimmering sheen of silver as seen through the openings in the mountain foliage. General Johnson directed me to call the attention of General Lomax to the movement, and when I found him the firing had broken out fiercely on our left and our lines were being driven back. The danger to our led horses at once occurred to me, and at a gallop I rode to the point where they were being held, one man caring for six or eight horses, so anxious had we been to strengthen our line of battle. On the way I met Lieutenant-Colonel Dorsey, with the Maryland cavalry, who was retiring before a body of the enemy, but he immediately halted at my earnest request and held the road, while I was engaged in moving the horses out of the field. The difficulty in handling so large a number of animals amid the excitement and confusion was great, but they finally were put in motion, and all would have gone well had it not been for the break in our lines at this time, which caused our men to give way in a semi-panic, and this started the men leading the horses into a gallop, and soon the whole outfit was in a helpless state of rout; saddles were slipping and turning, horses were breaking away from their holders, baggage and bundles were being spilled all along the road in the utter confusion. It was not within the limit of human ability to stop or stem the mad flying column until we reached the town of Woodstock, where I called on the provost guard to turn back or stop the flight by firing upon the runaways if necessary.

West Point–educated Lunsford Lomax (above) rendered distinguished service in regimental and brigade command. But his tenure as a senior cavalry officer in Early's army was marked by a series of disasters, beginning with Fisher's Hill.

LIEUTENANT COLONEL THOMAS F. WILDES
116TH OHIO INFANTRY, WELLS' BRIGADE

Gaining the slope of Little North Mountain unopposed, Crook deployed his 5,500 troops in two lines—Hayes' division on the right and Thoburn's on the left. By 4:00 p.m. Crook was ready to attack, and though his men began to draw artillery fire, nothing could stem the blue-clad juggernaut. Wildes' regiment fought its way down the line of Rebel breastworks and with little loss scattered the defenders.

About 3 P.M., we got squarely on the enemy's flank, with our left past his entrenchments. Now fronting, we started quietly down the mountain side, our division on the left, and the 2d on the right. The 116th, being in its old position, on the extreme left, and in the front line, could now see, through an occasional open space, that we were going in with our left just inside the rebel works. It gave us a fair prospect for some hard fighting, and every man nerved himself for the shock soon to come. But now we were discovered, and the enemy opened on us with shot and shell. *Too late!* The first shot was the signal to charge, and before they could make any, even the slightest, preparations to meet us, we were upon them with the bayonet. Our movement was a complete surprise to them, and they had now only to get out of our way or surrender. . . .

Thence we went, sweeping down their works like a western cyclone, every man for himself, firing whenever he saw a rebel, and always yelling and cheering to the extent of his ability. Being closest to the works, we were confronted and stopped at several points by small bodies of the enemy, but such stops were only momentary, for as soon as a little sharp firing was heard at any point, the men would, of their own accord, concentrate there, and in a few moments would be rushing on again. At the moment we charged on the flank, the 6th and 19th corps moved on the rebel front, and now, when we had stripped away about a mile of the rebel line, the heavy columns of the 6th corps came on over the works by our side, to the rear and in front of us. Two Ohio regiments with the 6th corps, the 110th and 122d, with which we were once brigaded, came over the works, as the 116th and 123d were running along inside, and partaking at once of our enthusiasm, pressed on with us, after giving the well known "West Virginia yell." The rebel right broke in dire confusion, on the approach of the 19th corps, and, in great disorganization, the enemy fled from all parts of the field towards Woodstock, abandoning artillery, horses, wagons, muskets, knapsacks, canteens and clothing, which the pursuers found covering the roads and fields.

CAPTAIN SAMUEL D. BUCK
13TH VIRGINIA INFANTRY, HOFFMAN'S BRIGADE

After driving off the Rebel cavalry, Crook's troops swept down on the left flank of Ramseur's division as Wright's VI Corps charged them in front. Ramseur's brigades quickly collapsed in succession. When General Bryan Grimes' North Carolinians gave way, the left flank of Pegram's division was exposed and routed. Buck, a former Winchester store clerk, described the vain effort to rally the stampeded units.

Immediately on our left was a North Carolina brigade and one of the men kept starting back and strange to say, his officers said nothing to him. Seeing the effect his conduct was having on the troops about him I ordered the fellow to take his place in the ranks, he looked at me with a "none of your business" expression on his face but took his place but only for a few moments when he jumped up and started on a run. I at once threw myself before him and again ordered him in the ranks and in the absence of my sword which I had left with my sweetheart in Winchester, I picked up a dogwood club and told him

if he left the ranks again "I would break his head." I meant it and he saw it as plainly as my own men did and he at once took his place and kept it. As the firing increased and drew nearer to us, Gen. Pegram rode up to our brigade and told us he wanted us to file out of the works and drive the enemy back on our left. The brigade was moving out and would have saved the day but the North Carolina brigade on our left concluded Gen. Pegram was trying to get his old brigade (ours) out and leave them to be captured, and, without firing a shot, broke and ran over us, carrying us off the field without any organization. While they were breaking into us Gen. Early rode up and ordered our regiment to fire into them if they would not halt. No one obeyed the order. Gen. Pegram made every possible effort to rally the men but words had no effect. I went with the crowd until we got to the Pike where I found men and horses all crowded together trying to escape, all honor gone, their escape only seemed to occupy their attention. What a disgrace! Men who had fought and were victorious when fighting five to one now flying with scarcely an enemy in sight and the entreaties of the officers had no effect.

James E. Taylor portrayed the climactic Union charge at Fisher's Hill from his vantage point on a bluff overlooking Tumbling Run and the Rebel entrenchments beyond. Averell's Federal cavalry gallop forward in support of Ricketts' VI Corps division, while Crook's men overrun the Confederate flank (right background). It was, Taylor wrote, "a wild scene of scurrying horses, crackling muskets, and flashing steel, which, with mingling shouts of victory, rent the air."

MAJOR HENRY KYD DOUGLAS
STAFF, BRIGADIER GENERAL JOHN PEGRAM

With darkness closing in on the beaten Confederate forces retreating southward toward Tom's Brook, Brigadier General William R. Cox formed a line across the Valley pike and attempted to check the Yankee pursuit. In the fight that followed, Jubal Early's adjutant general, Sandie Pendleton, was fatally wounded. The tragic loss of the popular young officer was recalled by his friend Henry Kyd Douglas, who had earlier served with Pendleton on Stonewall Jackson's staff.

*I*n the rear, on the retreat, I was directed to give special attention to the rear guard skirmish line, and remained with it in the dark and distressing march. Sandy Pendleton, General Early's Chief of Staff, came back to enquire into the situation and remained with me a short time. He was riding a white horse, and I warned him against riding such a beast on such a night. He made some light remark about the "deadly white horse," and rode along the skirmish line which was falling back very slowly. My orders were against unnecessary firing, but the enemy were practicing in the dark and at random. We had stopped for a minute, when Pendleton gave a groan and tottered forward on his horse. I dismounted, called a man or two; he fell gently into my arms and was taken from his horse. He tried to walk but could not get far and, just then, the man on the opposite side from me in assisting him was shot and he sank to the ground. Several strong men helped to carry him to the rear as the enemy's fire became more galling. I had sent for an ambulance and when it arrived he was placed in it. He was shot in the groin and through the body. He told me he was mortally wounded. He gave me his watch, pocketbook, prayer book, Bible, and haversack, and some letters from his wife, to be sent to her, and asked me to write and tell her of his death. He was taken to Dr. Murphy's of Woodstock —that home of all Confederates in need—and died the next day in the hands of the enemy.

Stonewall Jackson's favorite aide, Sandie Pendleton—photographed in 1863 wearing a mourning badge for his late commander (above, right)—was five days shy of his 24th birthday when he fell at Fisher's Hill. The son of Brigadier General William N. Pendleton, the Confederate chief of artillery, Sandie was known throughout the army as an energetic officer and a pleasant companion. The dead man's haversack (right) was returned to his wife, Kate, who was expecting their first child.

CAPTAIN SEATON GALES

Staff, Brigadier General William R. Cox

Confederate casualties at Fisher's Hill amounted to fewer than 300 killed or wounded but nearly 1,000 men missing in action. At least half of these latter were taken prisoner by the triumphant Yankees, who also captured 14 Rebel cannons. By contrast, only six of the 356 Federal casualties were listed as missing. Gales was among the crestfallen but defiant Rebel captives who were marched back under guard to Winchester.

This second national pattern Confederate flag was carried at Fisher's Hill by the 44th Georgia, a unit in Cook's brigade of Ramseur's division. Colorbearer John C. Copeland was killed during the fight, and although the banner was saved from capture here it was lost to the Yankees a month later in the Battle of Cedar Creek.

I was at once placed under guard with other prisoners and hurried rapidly forward with the now advancing enemy,—frequently at a double quick,—through the livelong night, reaching Woodstock, where their army halted, just as the first light of dawn began to streak the east.

Once during the night I abortively essayed to escape. We stopped for a few moments by the roadside, under the shelter of a barn. The night was almost impenetrably dark, but, perceiving the barn door to be open, I gently lifted myself into it,—intending, if possible, to grope through to the back part and then out and make for the woods. I found, however, the floor covered with recumbent yankees, (whether sleeping or not I could not tell,) who had crept in for protection from the night air, and so had to retrace my steps and let myself down into my former position. . . .

Sept. 23.—All the prisoners, five or six hundred in number were penned up this morning near Sheridan's headquarters. How shall I attempt to describe my feelings? Jaded and weary; cold, hungry and dirty; without overcoat, blanket, or change of outer or under-clothing; depressed at our disaster; humiliated at being a captive to the insolent and jubilant foe, who were about us as thick as the locusts of Egypt; and sad and sorrowful at the prospect of close confinement and long and bitter separation from my heart's treasures, no words can adequately portray my sensations. They were, without doubt, plainly depicted upon my countenance, for friends (and, though it may savor of the selfish philosophy of Rochefoucault, I thank heaven that there were friends and acquaintances among my fellow-prisoners) would clap me upon the back and tell me to "cheer up,"—which I endeavored as much as possible to do.

After remaining in our new position all day, we were all placed in wagons (a Commissary train going back for supplies,) about sunset, and jolted back to Strasburg, which we reached at midnight. Here I slept—or tried to sleep—until day, without other shelter or mantle than the clear cold sky. It was a raw autumnal night, and I suffered no little.

Sept. 24.—Walked part and rode part of the way back to Winchester—a distance of twenty miles—reaching it just before night. By this time we had partially regained our spirits, and surely there never was a more defiant and impudent set of rebels than those who were paraded through the streets of that town that evening. A yankee band of music preceded us, exultantly playing "Carry me back to old Virginny," while thick files of yankee sentinels marched on either flank of our column. Undaunted by their presence, we cheered long and lustily for "Jeff. Davis," and made the air vocal with the strains of "Dixie," while each one tried to sing at the "top of his bent," while the ladies—God bless them!—alike undaunted, and unmindful, in their unselfish, patriotic sympathies, of the consequences, cheered us with the waving of handkerchiefs and with outspoken words of comfort. Ah! it was a scene which I shall never forget.

General Sheridan (left foreground) doffs his hat in acknowledgment of his cheering soldiers as the Army of the Shenandoah continues the relentless pursuit of Early's forces. Calling Fisher's Hill "a most signal victory," the Union commander expected to soon finish off Early once and for all. But Sheridan's hopes were dashed when Torbert's cavalry failed to move up the Luray Valley and cut off the Rebel line of retreat.

SURGEON GEORGE T. STEVENS

77TH NEW YORK INFANTRY, BIDWELL'S BRIGADE

Although the Rebels had yet to be decisively vanquished, most Yankee soldiers shared Stevens' optimism as they marched southward up the Valley. The zealous young doctor served as chief surgeon of his brigade and eventually as medical director of the VI Corps. In 1866 he published a classic memoir, "Three Years in the Sixth Corps."

We followed the routed army through Mount Jackson, where were large hospitals, occupied by wounded confederates, and attended by confederate surgeons; then pressed on to New Market, keeping up a running fight with the rear-guard of the rebel army.

On the 25th we reached Harrisonburgh, a village more than sixty miles above Winchester.

Our march had been a grand triumphal pursuit of a routed enemy. Never had we marched with such light hearts; and, though each day had found us pursuing rapidly from dawn till dark, the men seemed to endure the fatigue with wonderful patience. Our column, as it swept up the valley, was a spectacle of rare beauty. Never had we, in all our campaigns, seen anything to compare with the appearance of this victorious little army. The smooth, wide turnpike was occupied by the artillery, ambulances and baggage wagons moving in double file. The infantry marched in several parallel columns on either side of the pike, and a line of cavalry, followed by a skirmish line of infantry, led the

"I believe that some punishment was deserved,–but I hardly think we were within the laws of war, and any violation of them opens the door for all sorts of barbarity."

way. Cavalry, too, hung on either flank, and scouted the country. It was intensely exciting to watch the steady progress of the advancing skirmishers. Now, as they reached the base of some sloping eminence, the rebel skirmishers would confront them; then, as they advanced, never halting nor slackening their pace, the confederates would surrender the ground, to appear in our front on the next commanding ground. So we marched up the valley—a grand excursion—skirmishing only enough to maintain a constant state of pleasant excitement.

COLONEL CHARLES R. LOWELL

Brigade Commander, Army of the Shenandoah

An intellectual Harvard graduate, Lowell won praise for his bravery as commander of the cavalry's Reserve Brigade; nine horses were shot from under him in the Valley campaign. Lowell described in a letter to his wife, Effie, the increasingly brutal retaliation inflicted upon Confederate guerrillas and civilians for ambushing Federal officers.

Near Mt. Crawford, Oct. 5, 1864.

I have *reveille* about one hour before daybreak,—am always awake, but never get up now, unless there are Rebs round. Did you see the new moon last night within a quarter of an inch of the evening star, and turning her back on him? They must have been close together an hour before I could see them; for an hour after, they were still less than an inch apart. They looked very strangely calm and peaceful and almost reproachful in the West last night,—with the whole North and East, far and near, lighted up by burning barns and houses. Lieutenant Meigs was shot by a guerrilla, and by order the village of Dayton and everything for several miles around was burned. I am very glad my Brigade had no hand in it. Though if it will help end bushwhacking, I approve it, and I would *cheerfully* assist in making this whole Valley a desert from Staunton northward,—for that would have, I am sure, an important effect on the campaign of the Spring,—but in *partial* burnings I see less justice and less propriety. I was sorry enough the other day that my Brigade should have had a part in the hanging and shooting of some of Mosby's men who were taken,—I believe that some punishment was deserved,—but I hardly think we were within the laws of war, and any violation of them opens the door for all sorts of barbarity,—it was all by order of the Division Commander, however. The war in this part of the country is becoming very unpleasant to an officer's feelings. . . .

I think —— [the mail-carrier] is miserably timid about guerrillas,— he won't come unless he has at least a brigade for escort,—perhaps he is right, however; important despatches from General Grant to Sheridan were taken, day before yesterday, by guerrillas,—provoking enough when we are hoping to hear that Petersburg is taken, or perhaps to get the orders which instruct us how to coöperate in taking it.

I think that we shall move soon. As we are foraging our horses entirely upon the country, we have to move frequently, but lately we have done a little too much of it. This is a very scrubby letter and written before breakfast, too.

I *do* wish this war was over! . . . Never mind. I'm doing all I can to end it. Good-bye.

NEWTON BURKHOLDER
Confederate Guerrilla

As Sheridan's army withdrew northward to a new base of operations, Yankee burning parties systematically destroyed all the crops, barns, and mills that lay in their path. Burkholder, a member of a loosely organized band of mounted convalescent Rebel soldiers and civilians that had been harassing Sheridan's supply trains and lines of communication, recalled the guerrillas' frustration and rage at their powerlessness to check the wanton destruction.

On the morning of the 6th of October, the ever memorable day of the burning [in Rockingham County], our little troop rendesvoused at the wire suspension bridge on the Linvill's Creek road, just south of Broadway. For some unknown reason only about half the band appeared. We decided to ride up the creek road. We could get no news from Harrisonburg. When we reached the Branner place we noticed smoke on southward about Harrisonburg. Turning off to the right we rode to the highest point we could find in the crest of a hill range. The smoke increased. Tongues of flame some declared they saw. A long, white canvass-covered wagon-train was now seen moving along down northward on the Ridge road far across yonder

As smoke from burning farms rises in the background, Rebel troopers like Corporal Pleasant Kiser of the 11th Virginia Cavalry (above), fighting from the tree line in the middle distance, engage dismounted cavalrymen of Sheridan's rear guard on October 8, 1864. Major General Thomas L. Rosser, the newly appointed commander of Early's cavalry, aggressively dogged the heels of the Yankees falling back down the Valley.

wide. On the destroyer comes—spot after spot, belching vast clouds of smoke and flame like Tophet, out there in the Valley beneath us. Some count barns ablaze. I could not count. Some point out the fire fiends darting now here, now there; now riding furiously fast cross-fields to a neighboring barn about to escape by neglect.

Our eyes are riveted on the infernal scene! Now the whole vale is red with fire mile on mile, and enveloped in smoke high overhead, twisting and writhing, disolving. Is the world being set on fire?

Cousins of Abraham Lincoln, Albert C. Lincoln fought as a Rebel guerrilla, and Abigail Lincoln Coffman lost most of her farm to Yankee burnings. Albert Lincoln once quipped, "As long as Cousin Abe keeps sendin' 'em down the Valley, Cousin Al will keep killin' 'em."

COLONEL THOMAS T. MUNFORD
BRIGADE COMMANDER, ARMY OF THE VALLEY

Ordered by Sheridan to "whip the Rebels or get whipped," on October 9 General Torbert turned on Rosser's pursuing cavalry at Tom's Brook. Munford alerted Rosser to the threat but was rebuffed. The Rebels were swept aside by Merritt's and Custer's Federal troopers—"routed," Sheridan reported, "beyond my power to describe."

eastward—it had passed Linville and was moving towards Broadway.

What could this mean? Too many wagons for a foraging party. What was Sheridan doing? A retreating force never left the Valley pike—the great highway and a magnificent road—so no one thought of retreat. We could not grasp it, it was too bad to think. Falling back along all roads and burning as he comes did not suggest itself to one of our little party, till at last, as we sat on our horses there on that lone peak, motionless and horror struck for our country, we saw the awful work come toward us. . . . The blazing buildings everywhere—the blackened sites of once spacious barns—the smoke that all that day obscured the sun and flying cinders of shingle and of straw—the countenances of women, and little children holding them by the hand, looking on! . . . Until this day no such desolation had been witnessed since the war began. What were we coming to? What would all this end in?

Slowly and relentlessly it ate its way. All the way here before us from Edom northward to Broadway and from ridge to mountain lay as fair a land as ever met the eye of man. Awful tragedy! Barn after barn, at first in the distance as by some invisible hand, takes fire. Then horsemen become visible, threading the fields as the tide rolled nearer, far and

At the first dawn I was notified that the enemy was astir. Boots and saddles were sounded, and we were ready to move as soon as it was light. I notified Rosser, and sent several couriers and a staff officer, requesting him to come up to where I was. After repeated couriers had been sent, he came up, and in a vaunting manner asked me "What was the matter?" I replied, the enemy are moving up to attack us, and we can't hold this position against such odds. In the same tone and spirit he replied, "I'll drive them into Strasburg by ten o'clock." I then said they will turn your left—said he, "I'll look out for that." I had been down to the picket and seen what was going on. We rode on during this conversation towards the picket, and I then pointed to the enemy, and we could see their masses in full view. A courier dashed up and said, "Captain Strothers says they are very near him." We had no time for further parley. . . . The enemy, in considerable numbers, dismounted, were moving up to occupy the opposite bank; but the enemy's command—two full divisions—stretched from the Valley Pike, and connected entirely across to our front. As they developed I endeavored to keep my right extending, to prevent being turned. While I was thus engaged on the right, Rosser, superintending the left, became heavily engaged at the ford, and I was skirmishing with their dismounted men in front of me all along on the line of the creek bank. Rosser repulsed the first attack at the creek, which was intended as a feint, and his two guns under the gallant Carter were very active. I could see that we were in imminent danger of capture. The enemy fell back in Rosser's immediate front. Payne had now moved up, and when this body fell back, another column, unobserved by Rosser, passed under and behind a hill to his left, and pushed rapidly in his rear towards our hospital of the evening before, and our camp. The next time the enemy moved up to attack Rosser, it was a heavy column, and their whole line started. They soon overpowered Payne and White, of Rosser's brigade. We could now hear the yell of the column on our left and rear, and on my right we could hear Lomax's guns receding. I saw we had no possible chance

now but to move out, and that, at a run, my left had given away, and it was only by a quick run that we escaped capture. . . .

My men could see the enemy's numbers, and it was clear from the very start that this handful had not a glimmering of a chance in its favor. . . . We fell back under fire until we reached a body of timber, which afforded shelter for our men, after which the enemy retired, and we moved to Columbia Furnace, where the remnant of our division and our artillery, officers and men, had assembled. A more discomfited looking body I have never imagined. We had followed Stonewall Jackson up and down the Valley in his great Valley campaign, and when our toils came to an end, we could go to our wagons and enjoy a clean shirt and some of the little comforts that a weary soldier looks forward to. Now we had not even a clean shirt—wagons and all were gone.

Flamboyantly clad in a black velveteen jacket adorned with gold braid (above), General Custer opened the fight at Tom's Brook by bowing to the Confederate commander, his old West Point friend Tom Rosser; Rosser echoed the salute. "It was like the action of a knight in the lists," one of Custer's officers wrote, "a fair fight and no malice!"

Cedar Creek

Fog hovered along Cedar Creek and the North Fork of the Shenandoah River in the predawn hours of October 19 as Early's Rebels prepared to launch their surprise assault. By 5:00 a.m. five Confederate divisions were in place: Wharton's 1,100 men had reached a point just above Hupp's Hill on the Valley Turnpike. Kershaw's 3,200 were poised east of Cedar Creek, near the point where it formed a lazy loop in its southward course toward the North Fork. East of Kershaw's position stood Gordon's corps, with Ramseur's 2,500 soldiers, Clement Evans' 1,800 in Gordon's old division, and Brigadier General John Pegram's 1,650 in a line of battle facing northwest. As the hour of attack drew near, Early said to Samuel J. C. Moore of his staff, "Colonel, this is the most trying experience of my life. If only I could pray like Stonewall Jackson, what a comfort it would be."

Three entire corps of Union infantry—not dreaming of what was about to befall them—occupied camps north and west of the Confederate jumping-off points. Nearest were the two divisions of Crook's VIII Corps, with Thoburn's 1,700 men camped close to earthworks on high ground overlooking Kershaw's position and Colonel Rutherford B. Hayes' 2,400 east of the Valley pike to Thoburn's left rear. Colonel J. Howard Kitching's recently arrived 1,000-man Provisional Division was camped on Hayes' left. West of the pike, Dwight's and Grover's divisions of Emory's XIX Corps, numbering 2,600 and 6,100 men respectively, occupied works that roughly paralleled Cedar Creek. The three divisions of Wright's VI Corps—Brigadier General Frank Wheaton's

2,000 men, Getty's 2,500, and Ricketts' 6,000 —spread across undulating ground north of the XIX Corps, farthest from the waiting Rebels.

Many in Sheridan's army believed that Early's troops had lost their will to fight. "We do not fear an attack while we remain here," wrote an Ohio soldier. "They do not feel like charging up such bluffs as are to be confronted."

The clatter of musketry ended such illusions. Kershaw's brigades surged toward Thoburn's division, shattering one of its brigades and pressing the other toward the pike. Gordon's command soon weighed in, concentrating on Hayes' and Kitching's divisions, the bulk of which managed only brief resistance before fleeing. From Hupp's Hill Rebel artillery divided its fire between the retreating Federals and the line of XIX Corps' works. Wharton's command, the last Confederate division to enter the fray, edged toward Federal units guarding the bridge that carried the pike across Cedar Creek.

First alerted by musketry, the men of the XIX Corps next saw fugitives from the VIII Corps streaming through their ranks. "It was apparent that our left . . . was helplessly broken," wrote one of Emory's soldiers. "Hundreds of men rushed past just as they had sprung from their blankets."

As fragments of VIII Corps units fought a delaying action, Emory moved his lines to meet the impending threat. He recalled the units at the bridge over Cedar Creek—and allowing Wharton's Rebels to advance across the stream —and shifted some of his troops to positions fronting the pike. Colonel Stephen Thomas led a brigade from Dwight's division eastward across the pike, where it fought hero-

ically against elements of Evans' and Ramseur's commands. The brigade's 8th Vermont lost 110 of 164 men in less than an hour.

Momentum and the weight of numbers eventually carried the Confederates across the pike. An hour into the attack the Rebels had driven the XIX Corps northward across fields near the Belle Grove house.

The burden of stemming the Confederate tide then passed to Ricketts' VI Corps. Getty's and Wheaton's divisions initially had advanced across Meadow Brook, a stream that traverses the battlefield. When it became clear that Crook and Emory could not stop the enemy, Getty withdrew across Meadow Brook. Wheaton's division quickly followed, extending Ricketts' left flank, while elements from the XIX Corps rallied to anchor the right.

Kershaw, Evans, and Ramseur mounted new assaults from the southwest and south. In a brief spell of fierce combat, they pushed Wheaton's defenders to the northwest, after which Getty's brigades and Emory's units also abandoned the line. The mass of Federals conducted a sometimes chaotic withdrawal to wooded ground northwest of Middletown.

It was now just midmorning. In less than three hours Early's little army had swept from the field all the Federal VIII and XIX Corps and two divisions of the VI Corps, inflicting more than 4,000 casualties and capturing 24 cannons. One Union division remained intact— Getty's three brigades from the VI Corps, which stood on Cemetery Hill west of Middletown. For almost an hour Getty's soldiers, formed in a horseshoe-shaped line with cavalry extending their flanks, beat back repeated attacks.

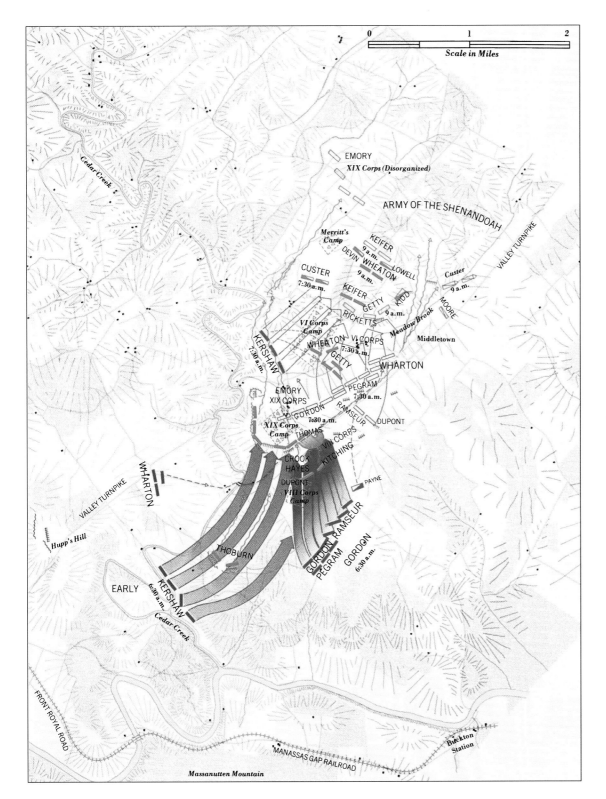

0   1   2

Scale in Miles

EMORY
XIX Corps (Disorganized)

ARMY OF THE SHENANDOAH

Merritt's Camp   KEIFER 9 a.m.   LOWELL

DEVIN WHEATON 9 a.m.

CUSTER 7:30 a.m.

KEIFER

Custer 9 a.m.

GETTY 9 a.m.

KIDD

RICKETTS

MOORE

Cedar Creek

Meadow Brook

Middletown

KERSHAW 7:30 a.m.

VI Corps Camp

WHEATON   VI CORPS 7:30 a.m.

GETTY

WHARTON

EMORY XIX CORPS

PEGRAM 7:30 a.m.

XIX Corps Camp

GORDON 7:30 a.m.   RAMSEUR   DUPONT

THOMAS

CROOK HAYES   VI CORPS   KITCHING

DUPONT

PAYNE

VIII Corps Camp

WHARTON

VALLEY TURNPIKE

Hupp's Hill

THOBURN

GORDON RAMSEUR PEGRAM   GORDON 6:30 a.m.

EARLY

KERSHAW 6:30 a.m.

Cedar Creek

FRONT ROYAL ROAD

Buckton Station

MANASSAS GAP RAILROAD

Massanutten Mountain

VALLEY TURNPIKE

After another defeat, at Fisher's Hill on September 22, Early's army fell back to Waynesboro, where it was again reinforced with Kershaw's division plus artillery and cavalry. The Rebels slipped back down the Valley and, on October 19, launched a massive surprise attack on the Federal camp at Cedar Creek. Gordon's three Confederate divisions tore through the camps of Crook's VIII Corps, and Kershaw's division swept away Thoburn's two brigades, before both commands smashed into Emory's XIX Corps. The Rebel surge began to slow, however, as hungry soldiers left the line to plunder Yankee tents and Wright's Federal VI Corps, though pushed back, stubbornly resisted. The absent Sheridan returned in midmorning and rallied his scattered troops.

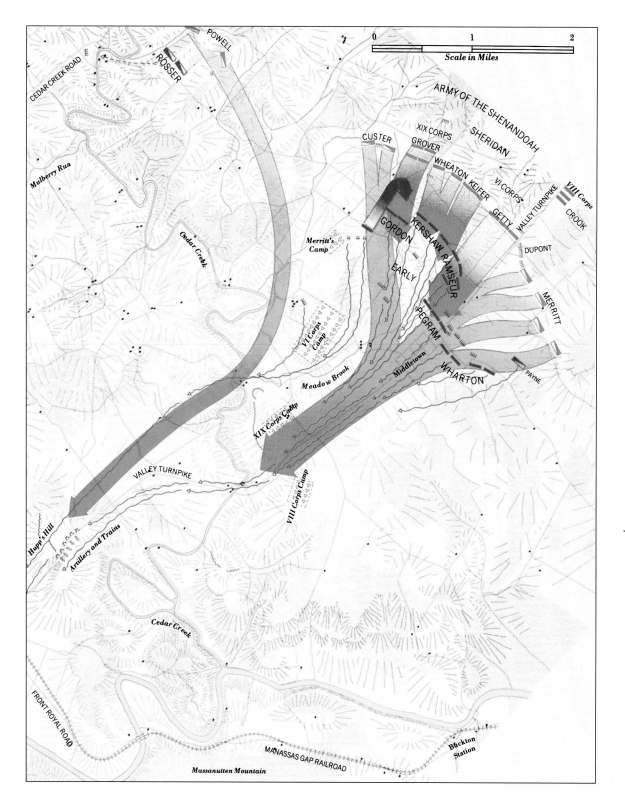

By midday the retreating Yankees at
Cedar Creek had formed a defensive
line north of Middletown. Early, concerned about his spent forces and the
enemy's strength, called a halt to the
flagging Rebel advance. During the lull
Sheridan formed the VI and the XIX
Corps, along with his cavalry, for a
counterattack, which pushed off about
4:00 p.m. After resisting briefly, the
Rebels were flanked on the left, and
their line rapidly crumbled, despite
heroic fighting by Ramseur's division in
the center. Federal cavalry under Custer
and Merritt turned the retreat into a
rout. By nightfall Early's shattered
army had fallen back to New Market
and was finished as a fighting force.

Confederate artillery tipped the balance against Getty at this point. More than two dozen guns massed near the pike south of Middletown by Colonel Thomas H. Carter opened up on Cemetery Hill. Three of Ramseur's brigades then hit the Federal right, which rested in a patch of woods. "The enemy gave way," wrote Colonel Edwin L. Hobson of the 5th Alabama, "and rapidly, in confusion, withdrew from the woods." Finally Getty ordered a retreat from Cemetery Hill. His division withdrew to the northeast, covering the Valley pike.

By 10:00 the Confederates had moved through Middletown and formed a line that extended from Middle Marsh Run on the left to a point well beyond the Valley pike. A critical moment had arrived: Many Confederates expected orders for another attack against their badly mauled enemy. General Early, however, decided not to renew the offensive. He would, he wrote later, "try and hold what had been gained" by carrying off "the captured and abandoned artillery, small arms, and wagons."

This decision led to criticism at the time and later, but Early felt he had good reasons for deciding against further attacks. Thousands of Union cavalrymen hovered opposite the Confederate right flank, east of the pike. Early's men, who had marched all night and fought for the better part of five hours, were exhausted. Moreover, they had been short of food and other supplies for weeks, and the lure of plunder caused many to leave their units and go ransacking through the abandoned Federal camps. One of Ramseur's soldiers observed that in many units "fully one-third [of] their strength quit the lines and resorted to plundering."

By the time Early could have gathered his troops for another full-scale attack, it is likely the Federals would have been able to repulse them. But given the remaining enemy strength in front of him, the decision not to resume the offensive should probably have been followed by a withdrawal to a more defensible position.

About 1:00 p.m. Gordon moved his three divisions forward roughly half a mile, establishing the final Confederate line. For the next hour or so Brigadier General Thomas L. Rosser, whose cavalry operated on Early's far left, reported that the Federals were massing in front of Gordon's lines. Confederate signalmen on Massanutten Mountain also warned of a Yankee build-up. By 3:30 a sense of profound concern had replaced the feeling of triumph in Early's army.

Union commander Phil Sheridan was making preparations to see to it that the Confederates' concerns were realized. Sheridan had spent the night before the battle in Winchester, en route to his army from a meeting in Washington. He learned at 7:00 the next morning that artillery fire could be heard from the south, farther up the Valley pike. Leaving Winchester about 9:00 a.m., he and two staff officers rode rapidly up the pike. As they neared the battlefield about 10:30, they found, as Sheridan later described it, a "stricken army—hundreds of slightly wounded men, throngs of others unhurt but utterly demoralized, and baggage wagons by the score, all pressing to the rear in hopeless confusion, telling only too plainly that a disaster had occurred at the front."

Sheridan's soldiers responded almost instantly to his presence. "The men sprang to their feet and cheered as only men under such circumstances can," stated one Federal. "Now we all burned to attack the enemy, to drive him back, to retrieve our honor and sleep in our old camp that night."

Commanding the army in Sheridan's absence, Horatio Wright had stabilized the Federal line by the time his chief arrived, and Sheridan turned his attention to a counterattack. By 3:30 he had organized a massive striking force. Wright's corps was on the left, its eastern flank touching the Valley pike; Emory's two divisions were on the right. Crook was in reserve east of the pike and slightly behind Wright's left. Custer's and Merritt's divisions of cavalry massed beyond the infantry's right and left flanks respectively.

Skirmishing erupted as four o'clock approached, followed quickly by a series of heavy Federal assaults. Merritt's cavalry suffered a temporary setback against Wharton's division, but the Rebel left was soon in trouble. Outflanked by Custer's cavalry and under punishing fire from Emory's infantry, Evans' division broke. With the Confederate left thus uncovered, Kershaw's men also retreated, followed in turn by most of Ramseur's division. Ramseur rallied fragments of his and other commands, creating a pocket of resistance amid the general collapse. He soon fell wounded, however, and his makeshift line disintegrated.

Within an hour of the counterattack Early's army was on the run. Stalwart service by Carter's artillery slowed but could not stop Sheridan's juggernaut. One Union captain described the Confederates as "a great, rushing, turbulent, retreating army, without line or apparent organization, hurrying and crowding on in mad retreat." The Federals chased them past Fisher's Hill, gathering prisoners, reclaiming lost artillery, and taking two dozen enemy guns.

The Confederates lost roughly 1,860 killed and wounded, and more than 1,000 captured in their assault and the counterblow. Federal losses were 644 killed, 3,430 wounded, and 1,591 missing or captured. Begun by the Rebels as a brilliantly executed surprise attack against a much larger foe, the Battle of Cedar Creek ended by providing an ignominious coda to Confederate operations in the Shenandoah Valley.

BRIGADIER GENERAL CLEMENT A. EVANS
DIVISION COMMANDER, ARMY OF THE VALLEY

On October 17 Early instructed three of his most capable subordinates to scale Massanutten Mountain and plot the layout of Sheridan's camps north of Cedar Creek. Evans—only recently recovered from a wound suffered at Monocacy and now commanding Gordon's old division—accompanied his corps commander, Gordon, and topographical engineer Jedediah Hotchkiss on the grueling ascent. They saw that the Yankee position was vulnerable to attack, as Evans recounted in a letter to his wife.

My dearest Allie

Yesterday I made a reconnaissance with my brigade in the direction of Cedar Creek beyond which the enemy were found to be entrenched on the hills, and encamped behind their entrenchments. I returned to camp about two o'clock p.m. with the brigade, and hastily eating dinner set out to go to the top of the mountain on our right where we have a signal station. I rode as far as possible, but found that I had to leave my horse and literally climb on foot about three fourths of a mile to reach the top and then to walk nearly a mile along the crest to get to the signal station. It was so steep that I had to travel on all fours, pulling along by the rocks and bushes. The face of the mountain is covered with occasional bushes of mountain growth, and small stunted trees. In many places for hundreds of yards it was all rocks, piled one against the other of various sizes, and over these I had to clamber like a coon. My strength was nearly exhausted when I reached the top, although I had rested frequently, but after another short rest I pushed on along the narrow ridge until I arrived at the Signal Station, or "look out" which was the extreme northern end of the mountain where a tremendous pile of overhanging rock makes a precipice down which you may jump half a mile with perfect ease but not with much safety. What a splendid sight was before me. You can form some idea of it, from the view you obtain by reaching the top of Clark's mountain. But it was far superior to that. Strasburg, Middletown, Newtown & Winchester were in sight visible to the naked eye. The vision was limited by the Blue ridge on the right, the Alleghenies on the left, and before you it melted far off into a hazy horizon—Like a narrow

ditch filled with water the Shenandoah wound its way through the plain at the foot of the mountain toward the Blue ridge, while Cedar Creek like a placid rill showing here and there between the occasional patches of wood, finally buried itself below Strasburg in the bosom of the Shenandoah. So elevated is the position that the valley presented the appearance of a vast level, the highest hills scarcely undertaking its surface. The Valley pike like a white ribbon lay along the center, the country roads looked like foot-paths, the woods like little parks, and the fields like little gardens with nice little fences dividing. But the whole view presented a magnificent natural picture.

The interest of the scene was of course heightened by the full view presented of the enemy's camp. Nearly every tent was visible. We were able to locate precisely his cavalry, his artillery, his infantry and his wagon train. We could see precisely where he had run his line of entrenchments and where they stopped. Even the house where Sheridan made Hd. Qrs. was pointed out. There all was, with the roads leading to it, the place where he could be best attacked, and how the lines could move, how far to go, and what to do—just like a large map.

Accompanied by a group of civilian refugees—most likely religious pacifists and Union sympathizers—a column of Federal supply wagons moves through the sprawling encampment of Sheridan's army in this Waud sketch. The spread of wagons and tents extended across nearly six miles of rolling farmland northeast of Cedar Creek. Enjoying relative tranquillity after the rough campaigning of the previous weeks, the Union soldiers supplemented their standard rations with wagonloads of provisions foraged from the surrounding countryside.

I believe that we can utterly rout them, if we attack their left flank. I think we are going to attack but Gen. Early favors the attack on their right flank. To night we will probably move—Tomorrow in all probability we will have a great battle and I trust a brilliant victory.

CORPORAL CLINTON BECKWITH

121ST NEW YORK INFANTRY, HAMBLIN'S BRIGADE

Half a mile northwest of Sheridan's headquarters at Belle Grove, October 19 began quietly for Beckwith as he fell out for guard duty. While Sheridan was attending a strategy session at the War Department, VI Corps commander Horatio Wright had moved into Belle Grove upon taking temporary command of the Federal forces.

At 5 o'clock on the morning of the 19th I was called to stand my trick. The entertainment of the night before, had robbed me of some needed sleep, and I was reluctant and slow about turning out. Finally I got out, rubbed my eyes and shook myself, looking round to get my bearings. Everything was quiet, except the snoring of the men in the tents. I walked to the fire and crouched around it to get warm letting the corporal I was to relieve, growl for my not hurrying up. The rest of the relief by this time were up and ready, so we marched around and posted them and the relieved guard turned in. I asked where the officer of the day, and the officer of the guard were, and think that I was told that they were at the headquarters of the colonel of the 65th New York. I filled and lit my pipe and sat down by the fire, thinking I would take a walk over there as soon as I got warm and see what was going on. I had been smoking a few minutes by the fire and was getting sleepy. "This won't do," I thought, and got up and stretched myself and took a look about. Looking towards the Belle Grove House, General Wright's headquarters and extending my gaze to the right over the line of camps, I noticed they were hid in a bank of fog, and that the moon had gone

"All was as peaceful and quiet as though no sign of war would ever be seen in that peaceful valley again."

down or was obscured. The time could not have been over half past five, and all was as peaceful and quiet as though no sign of war would ever be seen in that peaceful valley again. Sheridan's army lay in quiet upon the beautiful fields, oblivious of the fact that a Rebel host in battle array was close upon it, and in an hour one of the most remarkable battles in the annals of war would be in progress.

Looking east, this 1885 photograph shows the ground over which Kershaw's division began its advance, spearheading the Confederate surprise attack at Cedar Creek. After fording the stream, Kershaw's men deployed astride the road and passed the C. F. Hite farm at left. Concealed by thick fog, the gray-clad ranks quickly overran the startled Union pickets, then surged uphill to the earthworks and encampments of Thoburn's division—positioned along the ridge on the horizon.

LIEUTENANT COLONEL THOMAS F. WILDES
BRIGADE COMMANDER, VIII CORPS

Although a number of Yankee pickets reported suspicious activity in their front, and occasional shots were fired in the darkness, most Federal officers made nothing of these random alarms. When the attack came, it took the VIII Corps by surprise. One of the first commands engaged, Wildes' brigade lost 408 men, the majority of them taken prisoner in the collapse of Thoburn's division.

Word was sent to General Crook from Kitching's division that his pickets had heard the rustling of underbrush and the tramp of men in their front about 2 o'clock in the morning. Captain John F. Welch, who was then on Thoburn's staff, heard musket firing at 3 o'clock in the morning, and awakening Thoburn told him what he had heard. Both listened for some time, but heard no more. Captain Welch heard firing again between 4 and 5, immediately followed by a volley and by artillery in their front. This last firing was the opening of the rebel advance upon the first division of Crook's corps. Our brigade was aroused by our camp guard, which we never failed to keep, about 4 o'clock, as the rebel columns struck our pickets in our front, when there occurred enough firing to give the alarm. But the 5th New York heavy artillery battalion was captured almost entire on the picket line in our front, only one officer and twelve men escaping. The pickets were not fired upon, and the rush made upon them was so sudden that their fire was only very scattering. The moment the alarm was given our teams were hitched up, wagons loaded and our headquarters stuff, and much of our camp equipage sent to the rear. Skirmishers were sent out in our front, which soon met the enemy silently advancing through the woods. I at once dispatched Captain Karr to division headquarters. With Lieutenant Dissoway, of my staff, I rode to the brigade on our right, which we found in their beds. Some good, vigorous efforts were made to arouse them. There stood guns of the battery with only a sentinel over them, and only a man now and then of the infantry or artillery could be roused up enough to ask "What's up?" or "Who the he——l are you?" Seeing we could do nothing with these sleepy fellows, we rode rapidly back to our brigade, which we had scarcely reached before the storm burst in front and on both flanks. The mist and fog was so heavy that you could hardly see the length of a regiment. The enemy came over the works on both flanks unopposed, but we met the rebel advance with so hot a fire that it fell back in our front, which gave us opportunity to move out unmolested.

CAPTAIN D. AUGUSTUS DICKERT
3D SOUTH CAROLINA INFANTRY, CONNER'S BRIGADE

Its ranks thinned by earlier battles, Conner's brigade moved forward in Kershaw's assault, commanded by one of its few remaining field officers, Major James M. Goggin. The brigade's five South Carolina regiments were briefly checked by rough terrain and enemy fire but were able to resume their advance when other Rebel units flanked Thoburn's entrenchments. Dickert recalled the thrilling scene as the South Carolinians poured through the abandoned enemy camp.

Whether the order was given or not, the troops with one impulse sprang forward. When in a small swale or depression in the ground, near the center of the field, the abattis was discovered in front of the works. Seeing the impossibility to make their way through it under such a fire, the troops halted and returned the fire. Those behind the works would raise their bare heads above the trenches, fire away, regardless of aim or direction, then fall to the bottom to reload. This did not continue long, for all down the line from our extreme right the line gave way, and was pushed back to the rear and towards our left, our troops mounting their works and following them as they fled in wild disorder. "Over the works, cross over," was the command now given, and we closed in with a dash to the abattis—over it and down in the trenches—before the enemy realized their position. Such a sight as met our eyes as we mounted their works was not often seen. For a mile or more in every direction towards the rear was a vast plain or broken plateau, with not a tree or shrub in sight. Tents whitened the field from one end to the other for a hundred paces in rear of the line, while the country behind was one living sea of men and horses—all fleeing for life and safety. Men, shoeless and hatless, went flying like mad to the rear, some with and some without their guns. Here was a deserted battery, the horses unhitched from the guns; the caissons were going like the wind, the drivers laying the lash all the while. Cannoneers mounted the unhitched horses barebacked, and were straining every nerve to keep apace with caissons in front. Here and there loose horses galloped at will, some bridleless, others with traces whipping their flanks to a foam. Such confusion, such a panic, was never witnessed before by the troops. Our cannoneers got their guns in position, and enlivened the scene by throwing shell, grape, and cannister into the flying fugitives. Some of the captured guns were turned and opened upon the former owners. Down to our left we could see men leaving the trenches, while others huddled close up to the side of the wall, displaying a white flag. Our ranks soon became almost as much disorganized as those of the enemy. The smoking breakfast, just ready for the table, stood temptingly inviting, while the opened tents displayed a scene almost enchanting to the eyes of the Southern soldier, in the way of costly blankets, overcoats, dress uniforms, hats, caps, boots, and shoes all thrown in wild confusion over the face of the earth. Now and then a suttler's tent displayed all the luxuries and dainties a soldier's heart could wish for. All this fabulous wealth of provisions and clothing looked to the half-fed, half-clothed Confederates like the wealth of the Indies. The soldiers broke over all order and discipline for a moment or two and helped themselves. But their wants were few, or at least that of which they could carry, so they grab a slice of bacon, a piece of bread, a blanket, or an overcoat, and were soon in line again following up the enemy. There was no attempt of alignment until we had left the breastworks, then, a partial line of battle was formed and

Jacob E. Shoffner, photographed here with his wife, Mary Frances, left his farm to enlist in the 42d North Carolina Infantry. Suffering from chronic lung disease, Shoffner was discharged in October 1862 but later reenlisted in the 57th North Carolina—which fought in the Battle of Cedar Creek with Pegram's division. Shoffner was severely wounded during the battle; he died on November 20, his 31st birthday.

After overrunning Thoburn's division, Kershaw wheeled left, joining Evans, and the two forces fought their way across the Valley pike into the rear of Emory's XIX Corps. Emory's men, alerted by the heavy firing, had formed up and were preparing to defend the earthworks fronting Cedar Creek when the Rebels suddenly appeared behind them, "coming across the pike in masses," as one New Yorker recalled. In Waud's sketch, startled XIX Corps troops scramble over their earthworks, seeking cover from the Confederates pouring into the camp behind.

the pursuit taken up. . . . Before long the enemy was on the run again, our troops pouring volley after volley into them as they fled over stone fences, hedges, around farm houses, trying in every conceivable way to shun the bullets of the "dreaded gray-backs." I looked in the rear. What a sight! Here came stragglers, who looked like half the army, laden with every imaginable kind of plunder—some with an eye to comfort, had loaded themselves with new tent cloths, nice blankets, overcoats, or pants, while others, who looked more to actual gain in dollars and cents, had invaded the suttler's tents and were fairly laden down with such articles as they could find readiest sale for. I saw one man with a stack of wool hats on his head, one pressed in the other, until it reached more than an arm's length above his head. Frying-pans were enviable utensils in the army, and tin cups—these articles would be picked up by the first who came along, to be thrown aside when other goods more tempting would meet their sight.

CAPTAIN JOHN W. DE FOREST

12TH CONNECTICUT INFANTRY, McMILLAN'S BRIGADE

Temporarily detailed from his regiment to General Grover's divisional staff, De Forest carried word of the Rebel assault to XIX Corps commander William H. Emory. With Crook's corps in flight, Emory recognized the vulnerability of his own flank and ordered De Forest to apprise General Wright of the danger.

I was at General Grover's quarters (hungry and glad to breakfast with him) at the moment when the battle opened. The "awful rose of dawn," veiled and softened by thick morning mist, had just begun to bloom over an eastern crest of hill, when, a mile away on our left front, a shrill prolonged wail of musketry broke forth, followed by scream on scream of the Rebel yell. The unexpected and astounding clamor revealed to us that Early had assaulted Thoburn's isolated position. General Grover and I silently exchanged a glance of surprise and

comprehension. Then, in his usual gentle, monotonous voice, he said to his aide, "Tell the brigade commanders to move their men into the trenches"; while I tumbled into my saddle and galloped off to inform my chief of the situation.

I found him just up, coatless and hatless and uncombed, shouting for his horse and his orderlies. He was more excited and alarmed than would have seemed necessary to an ignoramus in warlike matters. As an old and trained officer he understood perfectly what a frightful mess we would be in if Early should fall upon the unfortified rear of our poorly connected echelon. Without waiting to hear my report through he answered, "Go to the commanding general with my compliments and state that the enemy have assaulted General Crook's left in force."

As I rode away I heard him grumbling, "I said so; I knew that if we were attacked, it would be there."

I found General Wright, surrounded by his staff, preparing to mount. He knew what I had to tell him, but he listened to my brief message patiently and replied with the formal courtesy of the regular army, "Give my compliments to General Emory and say that I will be with him shortly. But have you any knowledge, Captain, as to how the assault succeeded?"

I told him that I thought it had failed, because the musketry had outlasted the yelling, the latter being probably the Rebels' noise, and the former ours.

"I think so, too," he replied; but we were both mistaken.

Described by a subordinate as "unassuming and modest, never given to pyrotechnics," Horatio G. Wright (left) spent two decades in the Army Corps of Engineers before being promoted to command of a brigade and eventually to corps command. He displayed conspicuous bravery in shoring up the battered Federal defense at Cedar Creek and was cut across the chin by a Rebel bullet.

CAPTAIN MOSES MCFARLAND

8TH VERMONT INFANTRY, THOMAS' BRIGADE

Colonel Stephen Thomas led his brigade across the Valley pike in a desperate attempt to stem Gordon's onslaught but was flanked and driven back. Though weakened by chronic diarrhea, McFarland fought his unit clear of the trap. Thomas praised the 43-year-old officer as "possessing in an extraordinary degree great energy and daring bravery."

No sooner were we in position than our work began. So hot came the shot that we were ordered to lie down, loading and firing as best we could. The fugitives from Crook's corps were streaming through our lines. To check their panic-stricken flight was as impossible as to repeal the onslaught of the enemy. Close on the heels of the fugitives came the enemy, howling and yelling. Many of the rebels wore blue overcoats which they had plundered from the camp they had just left, making it very difficult to tell when we had only the enemy in front. Here Lieut. Cooper, deceived by our overcoats worn by the enemy, lost his life. He was lying a little at my left, where he could see some distance ahead down a wood road. Seeing men approaching, dressed in blue, he rose and said to me, "Captain, we are firing on our own men." I replied, "I think not." Just at that moment he fell, exclaiming, "I am shot by our own men!" Surgeon Ross, who helped bury Lieut. Cooper, said that he was hit by six bullets inside a five inch circle. Sergt. Seth C. Hill saw one rebel who shot Lieut. Cooper as he

Desperate defence of the flags of 8th Vermont.

An illustration from the history of the 8th Vermont depicts the desperate melee around the regiment's color guard. Private Herbert Hill stated that "men seemed more like demons than human beings, as they struck fiercely at each other with clubbed muskets and bayonets." Almost completely surrounded by Evans' Virginia and Louisiana brigades, the Vermonters, before they fell back across the pike, lost 110 of 164 men engaged, including all but three of their 16 officers.

Captain Edward Hall (above) of the 8th Vermont had been captured during the regiment's service in Louisiana but was exchanged and returned to command his company in the Valley campaign. During the desperate stand at Cedar Creek, Hall was fatally wounded in the stomach while exhorting his men to hold their ground.

stepped from behind a tree, and sent a ball through him before he had time to regain his cover.

In a very short time this line became untenable and a change of position, always difficult under fire, was well executed, and a new one taken in a ravine at the edge of the woods. Word was brought at this time that Maj. Mead and Capt. Hall were wounded, leaving me the senior officer in command.

Shortly after taking this new position a posse of rebels from the woods in our front confronted the flags and demanded their surrender. The reply went back, "Never!" and then followed one of the most desperate hand to hand encounters around the flags of which there is any record. . . .

A rebel of powerful build attempted to bayonet Corp. Worden of the color guard. Worden, a tall, sinewy man, having no bayonet on his gun, parried the thrust while some one shot the rebel dead. Another of the enemy then leveled his gun and shot Corp. Petre, who had the colors, in the thigh, making a terrible wound from which he died that night.

As he fell he cried, "Boys, leave me and take care of yourselves and the flag!" but not even in that vortex of hell was it necessary to remind men to look after the flag. As Petre crawled away to die the colors were seized and carried aloft by Corp. Perham and at once demanded by a rebel who attempted to grasp them, but Sergt. Shores placed his musket at the rebel's breast, fired and killed him. Another flash and a cruel bullet from the dead rebel's companion laid Corp. Perham low, and the colors again fell to the earth, and again, amid terrific yells, they were raised by Corp. Blanchard. A rebel discharged his musket within a foot of Corp. Bemis of the color guard, wounding him, but in turn was shot by one of our men. So the fight went on.

A little later Sergt. Shores and Lemuel Simpson were standing together by the flag when three of the enemy attacked them and ordered them to surrender, but, as the rebels had already discharged their pieces, they were not in good condition for either offensive or defensive warfare. Simpson fired, killing one of the three, and Shores bayoneted another. Sergt. Moran, whose devotion to the flag was intensified by forty-three days of heroic service which the regiment gave at Port Hudson, marvelously escaped death, holding as he did the United States flag all through the hottest of the fight, and also assisting now and then in protecting the colors. . . .

Shortly after the hand to hand conflict around the colors, and while we were doing our utmost to beat back the howling mass of demons in our front, Adjt. Shattuck said to me, "Captain, look to the left." Looking, I saw a new line of the enemy advancing on our flank, and but a few rods away. What was to be done? The rebel colors are in our rear and the brigade has given way on our right. Shall the "old Eighth" run? Yes, and at once; every man for himself and to his utmost, if he does not want to take his chances of testing the hospitality of some Southern prison. So the order was given in two words, "Run, boys," and in an undertone, lest the enemy, so close were they upon us, should be apprised of our intended movement. No order of Gen. Thomas' to shorten step, as on a former occasion, would then have been obeyed. Every man took his own course and way out of the corner in which we now found ourselves, happy indeed if he succeeded in getting out at all. We crossed the pike, whence we had come in the early morning, amid a veritable shower of bullets, and took our position a little in rear of the camp we had but recently left. The "old Eighth" had turned its back upon the enemy for the first time, but not until the regiment was surrounded on three sides and crushed by the fierce attack of an overwhelming force.

LIEUTENANT COLONEL EDWIN L. HOBSON
5TH ALABAMA INFANTRY, BATTLE'S BRIGADE

Moving forward on the far right of Ramseur's division, Battle's men pursued the fleeing Yankees of Thoburn's and Kitching's divisions across the Valley pike, then joined with Pegram's troops in an attack on the Federal VI Corps. Hobson—a zealous young officer who had twice been wounded in earlier engagements—wrote proudly of routing large enemy formations after assuming command of the brigade.

While driving the enemy before them Genl. Battle was wounded—about sunrise—Genl. Ramseur rode up to me and told me to take command of the brigade & hold it on the turnpike until further orders. While resting there the enemy shelled us heavily killing and wounding several of my men. I soon got permission to attack the battery that was playing upon us—Upon giving the order to the brigade to storm and take the battery the men bounded forward with a yell and in a few moments they were in the midst of the Artillery calling upon the Yankees to surrender and when failing to do so cutting them down with their swords or shooting them down—We then captured five pieces of artillery and one stand of colors—enclosed I send you one of the stars from this flag—The artillery we captured belonged to the Sixth Maine Artillery—I captured it with Battle's brigade—Just

An Alabama lawyer who fervently advocated Southern rights, Brigadier General Cullen A. Battle (left) was a skilled orator whose speaking abilities led one listener to write of "the witchery of his eloquence." At Cedar Creek his brigade met little opposition until gaining the Valley pike, where Battle was shot in the left knee. The injury knocked him out of active duty and kept him on crutches for the next two years.

in rear of this artillery the enemy were formed in a square and in the center of this square was a white flag—This I recognized as the Hd Quarter flag of some Genl. and immediately attacked it. The square was formed of at least three times as many men as I had but my brave men attacked it so vigorously that we drove it back and scattered it in every direction killing & captured many who were in the square. . . . after we had driven the square back some distance broken & routed it I had to move back the brigade and assist in driving back the troops that were immediately on my right & who had stubbornly & firmly resisted Genl. Wharton. I directed my movements on their, the enemy's, right flank and in less than ten minutes we routed them as completely as troops ever were. We advanced some four or five hundred yds then halted to reform the lines. While halted Genl. Ramseur dashed up to me & in a loud voice said "Col Hobson, old fellow, you are still in the front," and then pulling off his hat said "hurrah for you"—Genl. Early soon rode up to the place I had the brigade & expressing himself to Genl. R as very much delighted with what he had done, Genl. Ramseur turned to Battle's brigade & pointing to them said "Genl. these are the men who have done all this."

PRIVATE ALFRED S. ROE
9TH NEW YORK HEAVY ARTILLERY, BALL'S BRIGADE

Bolstered by Terry's brigade of Gordon's division, Kershaw fought his way northward, driving back the battered XIX Corps. But the veteran Federal VI Corps was not so easily defeated, holding its ground with grim determination. Despite the presence of 400 inexperienced recruits in its ranks, Roe's unit displayed remarkable discipline and bravery. Its 208 casualties—including 64 men killed or mortally wounded—was the greatest regimental loss in the battle.

We fall back to a knoll, and again halt and pour in our fire. Here our color-bearer, Thomas Paden, of Company M, was shot and killed. Our colors fell to the ground stained by the blood of the brave color-bearer, but they hardly touched the ground before they were caught up by one of our Company F, and waved triumphantly in the face of the foe. Here my tent-mate, Wilmer Stout, was wounded. Firing three rounds after he was hit, he refused help to go to the rear, and hobbled off from the field alone; such is the material the 6th Corps is composed of; God bless them. Again the rebel flanks us on the left; again we are compelled to fall back slowly, fighting at every step, contesting every inch of ground. The enemy has got range of us now, and pours in such a hail of canister, shot and shell, the air is boiling and seething with bullets; solid shot tear through our ranks, and make fearful vacancies, which are quickly and steadily filled up. The men move as steadily as if they were on drill or parade, their comrades falling on every side; they heed it not, but stubbornly fight and repeatedly ask to charge the rebels. They do not know what defeat is; they do not know how to retreat. Here one of our boys, Anthony Riley, was shot and killed; his father was by his side; the blood and brains of his son covered the face and hands of the father. I never saw a more affecting sight than this; the poor old man kneels over the body of his dead son; his tears mingle with his son's blood. O God! what a sight; he can stop but a moment, for the rebels are pressing us; he must leave his dying boy in the hands of the devilish foe; he bends over him, kisses his cheek, and with tearful eyes rushes to the fight, determined on revenge for his son. We continue to fall back slowly, fighting at every inch; the musketry fire now slackens, and we rectify our alignment and fall back in splendid order.

MAJOR GENERAL JOHN B. GORDON
Corps Commander, Army of the Valley

By midmorning, Sheridan's army was a shambles. The VIII Corps was hopelessly scattered, the XIX Corps in nearly the same condition, and two of the three divisions of the VI Corps in retreat northward past the village of Middletown. The only unbroken formation—Getty's VI Corps division—held a position on a ridge just west of the town. Gordon was preparing to assault this last strongpoint when Early called off the attack.

At little after sunrise we had captured nearly all of the Union artillery; we had scattered in veriest rout two thirds of the Union army; while less than one third of the Confederate forces had been under fire, and that third intact and jubilant. Only the Sixth Corps of Sheridan's entire force held its ground. . . . It was at that hour largely outnumbered, and I had directed every Confederate command then subject to my orders to assail it in front and upon both flanks simultaneously. At the same time I had directed the brilliant chief of artillery, Colonel Thomas H. Carter of Virginia, who had no superior in ability and fighting qualities in that arm of the service in either army, to gallop along the broad highway with all his batteries and with every piece of captured artillery available, and to pour an incessant stream

Clad in distinctive Zouave uniforms, the 95th Pennsylvania Infantry—a regiment in Colonel Joseph E. Hamblin's brigade of the VI Corps—was among the Federal units driven from the ridge west of Meadow Brook by Ramseur's and Pegram's charge. Sergeant John B. Cooke, who wore this Zouave jacket in the last year of war, survived the battle unharmed; Corporal Joseph Ginther (top) was killed.

"That is the Sixth Corps, general. It will not go unless we drive it from the field."

MAJOR GEORGE A. FORSYTH
STAFF, MAJOR GENERAL PHILIP SHERIDAN

One of Sheridan's most trusted aides, Forsyth accompanied the general on his famous ride from Winchester to the battlefield of Cedar Creek. Forsyth's humor, energy, and swashbuckling style made him popular throughout the army, and his bravery in dozens of engagements brought him the brevet rank of brigadier general.

of shot and shell upon this solitary remaining corps, explaining to him at the same time the movements I had ordered the infantry to make. As Colonel Carter surveyed the position of Sheridan's Sixth Corps (it could not have been better placed for our purposes), he exclaimed: "General, you will need no infantry. With enfilade fire from my batteries I will destroy that corps in twenty minutes."

At this moment General Early came upon the field, and said:

"Well, Gordon, this is glory enough for one day. This is the 19th. Precisely one month ago to-day we were going in the opposite direction."

His allusion was to our flight from Winchester on the 19th of September. I replied: "It is very well so far, general; but we have one more blow to strike, and then there will not be left an organized company of infantry in Sheridan's army."

I pointed to the Sixth Corps and explained the movements I had ordered, which I felt sure would compass the capture of that corps— certainly its destruction. When I had finished, he said: "No use in that; they will all go directly."

"That is the Sixth Corps, general. It will not go unless we drive it from the field."

"Yes, it will go too, directly."

My heart went into my boots. Visions of the fatal halt on the first day at Gettysburg, and of the whole day's hesitation to permit an assault on Grant's exposed flank on the 6th of May in the Wilderness, rose before me. And so it came to pass that the fatal halting, the hesitation, the spasmodic firing, and the isolated movements in the face of the sullen, slow, and orderly retreat of this superb Federal corps, lost us the great opportunity, and converted the brilliant victory of the morning into disastrous defeat in the evening.

We could occasionally hear the far-away sound of heavy guns, and as we moved out with our escort behind us I thought that the general was becoming anxious. He leaned forward and listened intently, and once he dismounted and placed his ear near the ground, seeming somewhat disconcerted as he rose again and remounted. We had not gone far, probably not more than a mile, when, at the crest of a little hill on the road, we found the pike obstructed by some supply-trains which had started on their way to the army. They were now halted, and seemingly in great confusion. Part of the wagons faced one way, part the other; others were half turned round, in position to swing either way, but were huddled together, completely blocking the road.

Turning to me, the general said, "Ride forward quickly and find out the trouble here, and report promptly." I rode rapidly to the head of the train and asked for the quartermaster in charge, and was told he had gone up the road a short distance.

On reaching him, I found him conversing with a quartermaster-sergeant. They informed me that an officer had come from the front and told them to go back at once, as our army had been attacked at daylight, defeated, and was being driven down the valley. The officer, they said, had gone back towards the front after warning them to come no further.

Galloping back, I made my report. . . . Turning to his chief of staff, Colonel J. W. Forsyth, the general said something regarding certain instructions he had evidently been giving him, and then said to me,

"You and Captain O'Keeffe will go with me"; and nodding good-bye to the other gentlemen of our party, with whom he had probably been conferring while I was making up the cavalry detail, he turned his horse's head southward, tightening the reins of his bridle, and with a slight touch of the spur he dashed up the turnpike and was off. A yard in rear, and side by side, Captain O'Keeffe and myself swept after him, while the escort, breaking from a trot to a gallop, came thundering on behind. . . .

Within a mile we met more supply-trains that had turned back, and the general stopped long enough to order the officer in charge to halt, park his trains just where he was, and await further instructions. Then on we dashed again, only to meet, within a few moments, more supply-trains hurrying to the rear. . . .

. . . About a mile in advance of us the road was filled and the fields dotted with wagons and men belonging to the various brigade, division, and corps headquarters, and in among them officers' servants with led horses, and here and there a broken ambulance, sutlers' supply-trains, a battery forge or two, horses and mules hastily packed with officers' mess kits, led by their cooks, and now and then a group of soldiers, evidently detailed enlisted men attached to the headquarters trains. In fact, this was the first driftwood of a flood just beyond and soon to come sweeping down the road. Passing this accumulation of debris with a rush by leaving the pike and galloping over the open fields on the side of the road, we pushed rapidly on; but not so quickly but that we caught an echoing cheer from the enlisted men and servants, who recognized the general, and shouted and swung their hats in glee. . . .

. . . Soon we began to see small bodies of soldiers in the fields with stacked arms, evidently cooking breakfast. As we debouched into the fields and passed around the wagons and through these groups, the general would wave his hat to the men and point to the front, never lessening his speed as he pressed forward. It was enough; one glance at the eager face and familiar black horse and they knew him, and starting

Sheridan inde
Battle of Cedar Creek oct 19 64

Shown in this Waud sketch spurring his black horse Rienzi onto the battlefield at the conclusion of his celebrated gallop from Winchester, General Sheridan exhorts the retreating Federal troops to re-form and counterattack the Rebels. All along the route soldiers had reacted spontaneously to his inspirational blend of enthusiasm, combativeness, and profanity, and most turned to follow him back into battle.

As the sun sets, the Vermont Brigade mounts a furious charge against Ramseur's line north of Middletown. This panorama of the Federal counterattack was painted in 1874 by Julian Scott, a Vermonter. Scott incorporated dozens of individual portraits in his 10-by-20-foot canvas, including Brigadier General Lewis A. Grant, who led the brigade until taking over divisional command that morning, on horseback beside the Rebel prisoners in the left foreground; wounded Lieutenant Colonel Amasa Tracy, who replaced Grant at the head of the brigade, next to the white horse; and Lieutenant Colonel Charles Hunsdon, leading the 11th Vermont at center.

to their feet, they swung their caps around their heads and broke into cheers as he passed beyond them; and then, gathering up their belongings and shouldering their arms, they started after him for the front, shouting to the comrades further out in the fields, "Sheridan! Sheridan!" waving their hats, and pointing after him as he dashed onward; and they too comprehended instantly, for they took up the cheer and turned back for the battle-field.

. . . From the time we met the first stragglers who had drifted back from the army, his appearance and his cheery shout of "Turn back, men! turn back! Face the other way!" as he waved his hat towards the front, had but one result: a wild cheer of recognition, an answering wave of the cap. In no case, as I glanced back, did I fail to see the men shoulder their arms and follow us. I think it is no exaggeration to say that as he dashed on to the field of battle, for miles back the turnpike was lined with men pressing forward after him to the front.

MAJOR ALDACE F. WALKER

11TH VERMONT INFANTRY, GRANT'S BRIGADE

Counterattacking in the center of Getty's division, Grant's Vermont troops clashed with Ramseur's force near the home of farmer David Miller. After driving the Rebels from their position behind a stone wall, the Vermonters re-formed and continued their advance. Walker was brevetted for "distinguished gallantry" in the campaign.

*D*irectly in front of our position were a house, mill, and other outbuildings, swarming with the enemy, our only approach to which was along a narrow road by the side of a little mill-pond formed by a dam across our old annoyance, Meadow Run. . . .

. . . Our Brigade poured over the wall which had covered it, and rushed promiscuously into the *cul de sac* by the mill-pond. The attack was successful, and the group of buildings from which the enemy fled

in confusion to a wall which protected their second line, was as good a protection for us as it had been for the rebels. The troops of our Brigade were now scattered about the grounds and out-buildings just mentioned, some of them being behind and upon two large hay-stacks, and fully one third of the command being advanced quite a distance further, to the cover of a broken garden wall and among several large trees. . . . Officers sent over the hill to reconnoitre found a rebel line of battle and a section of their artillery nearly on the prolongation of our line, and it was considered that we should be doing extremely well if we were able to hold our then position. . . .

Therefore we kept concealed as much as was consistent with expending the full fifty rounds of ammunition consumed in the next half hour, the rebel fire meanwhile being so hot that we could not carry off our wounded or send for more cartridges. At last however the excellence of Sheridan's plan was proved; a movement became apparent on the right, . . . and with a cheer we made a final charge against the walls before us. The enemy faced our advance but for a moment and then fled in confusion; we pursued faster and faster, only stopping to hastily fill our cartridge-boxes with captured ammunition; the retreat became a stampede, the pursuit became a reckless chase, and with tumultuous cheers and throbbing hearts we crowded the motley mob before us, on and on over the miles of hill and plain to the banks of Cedar Creek. Our formation was entirely lost but we had the organization and enthusiasm of recognized success; every man felt that it would not do to allow the enemy to rally on this side of the stream; the front was presently occupied by flags alone, as the more heavily loaded troops became unable to keep up with the energetic color-sergeants; the strong cavalry force on our distant right were seen charging down the field; the rebels obliqued confusedly and in uncontrollable dismay towards the turnpike and the bridge; a final attempt was made to organize a last resistance on the hills that crowned the Creek, but after a feeble volley the line melted away; a last battery faced us with a round of canister, but in vain; we saw the flag that followed Sheridan, a white star on the red above a red star on the white, flashing in the front and centre of the army, literally leading it to victory; the regimental standard bearers vied with each other in an eager strife to be first in the works of the morning, every brigade in the army afterwards claiming the distinction, our own brigade certainly not with the least ground of any; and so at last we manned the entrenchments of the Nineteenth Corps, while the foe toiled up the other bank of Cedar Creek and hastily formed a battle-line outside our musket range.

ANONYMOUS
CHARLOTTESVILLE (VIRGINIA) ARTILLERY, CUTSHAW'S BATTALION

Shortly before the Federal counterattack, Early dispatched some artillery to shore up the left of his line. But, as this unknown Confederate gunner recalled in a letter home, his battery was scarcely in place before it was forced to flee by Sheridan's onslaught.

About three P.M. . . . our battery, accompanied by two pieces of Second Howitzers, was sent about one and one half miles to the left of Middletown, on the extreme left of our lines. To our left, there was only a line of skirmishers across the field, stretched, I suppose, fifteen or twenty yards apart extending three quarters of a mile, connecting with our cavalry that was guarding our left flank. On our immediate right was a large body of woods, and in the wood stretched for a quarter of a mile, was a weak line, formed by a portion of General Gordon's old Brigade. We had just unlimbered and taken position, when the enemy advanced a line of skirmishers in our front, and a line of battle or heavy line of skirmishers in front of Gordon's old Brigade. Fighting commenced at once on our right, and we had orders to load and fire in the line in our front. We could not see what was going on on our right, but the musketry was not very rapid and we thought it allright, but before we could fire General Gordon rode up to Major Cutshaw, and told him to get out directly, and try to save his guns. We limbered up and moved towards the rear. I did not yet know what was out. One of our pieces was left to fire a few shots while the others retreated. My piece had gone on my curiousity lead me to remain behind, and walk slowly off the field; but just before I got to a piece of woods in the rear, I found that Gordon's men had behaved most shamefully and cowardly, had broken in confusion, and let the enemy in between our guns and the rest of our lines and were scattered all over the field in the rear of the woods. I looked to the left, and saw all of our skirmishers running for dear life in the position we had just left. I saw advancing towards me the old Stars and Stripes. The infantry had just left me on the left, and I assure you that I did get up and dust out of there—expected every minute for a Yankee to halt me, ran about half a mile and overtook the battery, found General Gordon there, trying to rally his men. . . . The Yankees came on in line, and Gordons men broke again in greater confusion than ever. Before getting in firing distance our guns on our right held their position until the enemy was right on them in front, and had flanked right and left. Just then our whole lines broke, I never saw such a sight.

Major Wilfred E. Cutshaw (right), who commanded the artillery battalion positioned precariously on the Rebel left, managed to extricate his batteries from the collapsing line and fall back to Hupp's Hill, a mile south of Cedar Creek. When the Yankee pursuit continued, he again limbered up and retreated. Cutshaw's guns were cut off and captured when he was caught on the Valley pike in a jam of wagons and fugitives.

MAJOR A. BAYARD NETTLETON
2D OHIO CAVALRY, PENNINGTON'S BRIGADE

Because their camps lay some distance from the Federal infantry, Torbert's cavalry was largely unaffected by the initial Confederate assaults. Custer guarded the right flank and Merritt the left while the army re-formed north of Middletown, and when Sheridan counterattacked, the horsemen thundered down on the Rebel line of retreat.

The long line of cavalry and infantry moved steadily forward across the open plain, under a heavy fire, towards the rebel position, with a coolness and order I never saw surpassed during four years of service. To one who had seen the rout and panic and loss of the morning, it seemed impossible that this was the same army. The enemy was evidently astonished at our taking the offensive, but met our attack with confident coolness, and then with determined fury. As soon as the Confederate infantry was fully engaged with ours in the centre, the order was given for the cavalry divisions to charge both flanks of the enemy's line. The bugles sounded, the horses caught the spirit of the hour, and pressed forward with steady but resistless speed; seven thousand troopers, with drawn sabres, sent up a battle yell wild enough to wake the slain over whom we galloped, and we were in the midst of that grandest of martial movements,—a genuine cavalry charge.

The effect was magical. The enemy's mounted troops first made a stout resistance, then scattered like sheep to the hills, and his infantry line, having both flanks turned back upon itself by our cavalry, and its centre crushed by a final magnificent charge of our infantry, broke in confusion, and started southward in confused retreat. Panic seized every part of the rebel force; infantry vied with artillery, and both with the wagon-trains, in a harum-scarum race from the Cedar Creek Ford, and, as the sun went down, the army which at daybreak had gained one of the most dramatic and overwhelming victories of the war was a frantic rabble, decimated in numbers, and flying before the same army it had twelve hours before so completely surprised and routed. Our cavalry pressed the pursuit with a vehemence and success that astonished even the much-expecting Sheridan. Merritt on the left of the pike, and Custer on the right, met with no opposition from the scared and fugitive mob of mingled "horse, foot, and dragoons." The pike was blockaded for miles with cannon, caissons, ambulances, and baggage-wagons, which our troopers easily captured and turned backward towards our lines. The chase continued, with constant captures of prisoners and war material, until, near the foot of Fisher's Hill, the dense darkness enforced a truce between pursuers and pursued. Both infantry and cavalry returned to sleep in their camps of the night before, hungry and half dead with fatigue, but happy, and having about them, as trophies of the day's work, forty-five pieces of captured and recaptured artillery, and a field full of wagons, ambulances, and prisoners of war. This ended the career of Early's army. As an army it never fought another battle,—its commander never again attempted to redeem the Shenandoah Valley, nor to invade the North.

Troopers of Custer's division—sporting red neckties in emulation of their flamboyant commander—cut their way through the fleeing Confederates at Hupp's Hill. In the foreground Quartermaster Sergeant David S. Scofield of the 5th New York Cavalry captures the battle flag of the 13th Virginia, a deed that earned him the Medal of Honor. Though severely wounded, the Rebel colorbearer managed to elude capture and made his way to Fisher's Hill under cover of darkness.

This battle flag of the 18th Georgia was seized by Private Ulric Crocker of the 6th Michigan Cavalry when Colonel James H. Kidd's brigade cut across the Rebel line of retreat. Kidd later wrote, "Darkness alone saved Early's army from capture."

PRIVATE GEORGE Q. PEYTON

13TH VIRGINIA INFANTRY, HOFFMAN'S BRIGADE

Peyton and his comrades in Pegram's division were posted as the rear guard of Early's retreating army. For a time they managed an orderly withdrawal and maintained a heavy fire on the advancing Yankees. But when Pegram's soldiers reached the banks of Cedar Creek, most broke formation and joined the mad scramble across the stream. Peyton recounted Pegram's efforts to rally his men along the road to Hupp's Hill as Custer's cavalry harassed their flight.

We started back in good order but soon became a regular mob. I fired just before I got to a rock fence. I had poured the powder in my gun and in climbing over the fence I poured it out and when I tried to shoot, the cap just bursted. I poured some powder in the tube, and twisted a cap in it and the ball blew out and then I could shoot. A ball went through a new blanket that I had picked up and another one

went through my left pants and burned my leg a little. After getting over the creek, Gen. Pegram halted the brigade until the stragglers got by and then formed our regiment as a rear guard. We stopped on top of a small rise in the road and a squadron of Yankee cavalry charged us. We killed some of them and started on. Our men took off through the woods but I followed Gen. Pegram as he said he was going to have the brigade to support us. I got to a place where the house had a picket fence on the pike. I tried to get into the yard where a picket was off but my knapsack hung and I could not get through and the Yankee cavalry got by me. One poked his pistol in my face and told me to surrender. "All right" said I and got up with my gun in my hands. "Throw down your gun" which I did and then I was a prisoner of war. The road was full of the cavalry charging and I saw Custer with his long curls hanging down his back. For a few minutes I thought that I was the only one captured, but I had not gone far before I saw a lot who were captured before I was. . . . The man who captured me took me back to Sheridan's Headquarters and by next morning there were 945 of us there.

A 24-year-old farmer, Francis H. Bolen (above) served as a sergeant in the 49th Virginia Infantry of Pegram's division. Lamed by a leg wound he had received in the Chancellorsville campaign, Bolen was unable to keep up with his retreating comrades and was captured while filling his canteen in Cedar Creek.

PRIVATE DEWITT C. GALLAHER

STAFF, BRIGADIER GENERAL THOMAS L. ROSSER

When the fleeing Rebels reached the bridge over Tumbling Run south of Strasburg, they found it blocked by dead horses and over-turned artillery limbers. Hundreds of men were overtaken and cap-tured by the Yankee cavalry, as Gallaher recalled. Gallaher—whose shell jacket is shown at right—had left college to enlist in the Confederate cavalry and served as a courier on Rosser's staff.

They captured hundreds, recaptured all their artillery which we had captured in the forenoon and nearly all of Early's artillery besides. There is a narrow roadway on the Pike along there and a bridge and there being a jam and stoppage of wagons and artillery there, the capture was easily made of all our artillery (nearly) and a big wagon train.

Early fell back to Fisher's Hill that night about 4 miles from the early morning fighting.

About 9:00 p.m. General Rosser sent me over to General Early's on the Pike to learn the situation and to ask for orders. It was some miles away and about midnight I found him and his staff asleep near the Pike on Fisher's Hill. He was awakened and sent word to Rosser fully as to his plans. Meanwhile, I delivered Rosser's request to General Early to have one of Rosser's Regiments called in which was picketing on our extreme right—on detached duty, as our cavalry's main body was on Early's left flank. General Early said he had no one to send and that I would have to call the Regiment in as he would fall back at daylight. So I had to go. It was a rather, ticklish business. The Regiment was some three or four miles away and the night very dark and I knew absolutely nothing of the roads. I was told they were along Cedar Creek. So off I started, riding with ears open and my pistol in my right hand ready for

trouble. Finally passing through some very dark woods, I was challanged by a picket. Not knowing if I had run into a Yankee or not, I wheeled my horse around ready to escape, if I had struck the enemy. I inquired of the picket "what Regiment is yours?" He replied and then, knowing who was in command of it that day, I asked him who was in command and he answering correctly; I advanced and told him to get out of there at once. So about daylight we reached the Pike where we found the army had left and only a rear guard just moving off.

Had we been a half hour later we would have been captured. By this time, I was about "all in," and so was my horse for I had ridden on him the night before and all day and all night just gone, and had nothing to eat for either man or beast except a few crackers and some oats and corn gathered from the Yankee Camp.

CAPTAIN GEORGE B. SANFORD
STAFF, MAJOR GENERAL ALFRED A. TORBERT

A freshman at Yale University when the war began, Sanford obtained a commission in the 1st U.S. Cavalry and made the army a lifelong career. As aide-de-camp to Generals Merritt and Torbert he played an active part in the Valley campaign and won the brevet of major for his performance at Cedar Creek. In his postwar memoirs Sanford recalled his mingled sense of exultation and exhaustion on the night following the battle.

When Gen. Sheridan decided to suspend the general pursuit, he proceeded with his staff to his former Headquarters at the Belle Grove house, and as usual Gen. Torbert and his staff accompanied him. Of course we were without tents or baggage or anything else, except what we had on our backs, but I knew where our hay stack had stood in the morning, and judging that some of it at least would still be there, I made up my mind to crawl in under the hay, and had no doubt as to my ability to sleep well. Before attempting this, however, I walked over, with one or two of our own staff, to a big fire which some of Sheridan's aides had started near the house. Everyone was excited and delighted with the day's work of course, and when somebody came up from the wagon train with a supply of bacon and hard bread, we soon had a welcome feast.

Not a man at Headquarters was aware at this time of what had been accomplished on the other side of Cedar Creek by the Cavalry, but as we were sitting laughing and talking an aide de camp of Gen. Merritt's, Lt. Trimble of the 1st Cavalry, rode up with despatches for Gen. Torbert. I think Forsyth carried the despatches into the house, where Torbert and Sheridan were together while Trimble stood telling the news. In a moment Gen. Sheridan himself came out evidently very much excited by the despatches, and commenced questioning Trimble with great rapidity. He broke off in a moment to send orders to Gen. Emory to hurry a division of the 19th corps across, and then gave other directions. The news spread rapidly and the excitement was intense.

For some purpose which I have now forgotten the General directed me to go into the Belle Grove house, where his quarters were. The surgeons had taken a part of the house for a hospital and in one room I saw a very distinguished looking officer, Major General Stephen D. Ramseur of the Confederate Army, dying of wounds received that day. Ramseur had graduated at West Point only four years before, but had resigned his commission to join the Southern army. Custer, who had been three years at the Academy with him, came into the room while I was there and greeted Ramseur in his bluff, hearty manner, but he scarcely responded. His aide de camp soon came in under a flag of truce, and next morning returned with Gen. Ramseur's remains to the Rebel lines. . . .

. . . After talking the battle over with my friends on our own and Sheridan's staff until quite late, I concluded to hunt my "haystack" bed, and accordingly started off with Lieut. Wallace of the Michigan Cavalry, one of our aides. It was very dark and we had to walk carefully to keep from stumbling over sleeping soldiers; but we managed to find some vacant spots in the hay, and as each of us had an overcoat for a pillow we were soon all right. I slept like a top until daylight and was suddenly awakened by my hand coming into contact with an icy cold face of a man. I started up in a moment, and looking closely at my neighbor, I saw that certainly he would never awaken again until the last reveille. He was a Confederate private, and stone dead. Near him lay an officer of the same army, of the grade of Captain, and scattered about were numerous others. The sight was decidedly eerie, and I had no inclination to turn over and try another nap. I remember that the Captain, poor fellow, had evidently tried to take a last smoke before he died. His tobacco bag lay beside him, half open, and in his hand was his brier root pipe,—filled but apparently never lighted. Either his strength failed him or possibly another shot struck him and ended his career and his smoke together.

A Troubled Aftermath

After the Battle of Cedar Creek, Jubal Early's beaten army paused at Fisher's Hill, then retreated up the Valley to New Market. The Federals pursued briefly but soon returned to their camps at Cedar Creek. In his report to Robert E. Lee, Early rather ungallantly evaded the blame for the defeat: "I found it impossible to rally the troops, they would not listen to entreaties, threats, or appeals of any kind. A terror of the enemy's cavalry had seized them. The rout was as thorough and disgraceful as ever happened to our army." Although he insisted sourly that it was his men who had failed, not he, in the same breath Early offered to pay the price for what he called his "reverses." Lee declined to relieve Early then, but it scarcely mattered. The nearly 3,000 casualties the Army of the Valley had suffered, combined with the dreadful toll taken on its morale by this de-

feat, meant that it was finished as a fighting force. Neither the lost men nor the lost spirit could be replaced. Sheridan had sustained nearly double Early's casualties, but new men were available to him in plenty. The conquering Yankee army, now in control of the Shenandoah, enjoyed soaring morale.

Beginning in November the two armies were gradually dismantled. Early's command first lost Kershaw's division and then the entire Second Corps, both to bolster Lee's hard-pressed defenses around Petersburg. Sheridan's army went into winter quarters around Winchester. During December his VI and VIII Corps departed the Valley, and the XIX Corps and two cavalry divisions assumed garrison duty.

Early's army, now down to a single depleted division with some cavalry and artillery, spent a bitter winter near Staunton, the men suffering from a lack of food and supplies. In February 1865 Sheridan led one last advance up the Valley. Early made a defiant stand in front of Waynesboro on March 2, but the Federals swept up the weakened and dispirited Confederates. Only Early and a handful of his men managed to escape, ingloriously closing the final chapter of the Valley campaign.

Fresh from the Battle of Cedar Creek, soldiers representing regiments that had captured Rebel colors proudly presented the flags in Washington. The men posed with General Custer in front of the War Department for this sketch by Alfred Waud.

SURGEON GEORGE T. STEVENS

77TH NEW YORK INFANTRY, FRENCH'S BRIGADE

During the opening phase of Sheridan's counterattack, the 77th New York and the rest of French's brigade advanced on the far left as the pivot point of the turning Federal line. Moving forward slowly, they encountered "a withering fire" from Ramseur's Confederates posted behind a stone wall and backed by sharpshooters hidden in a brick mill. That evening Stevens came across some of the fallen when he walked the battlefield.

The moon shining brightly over the battle-field revealed the camps of the living side by side with the resting places of the dead. All the way from Middletown to Cedar creek the debris of battle was scattered over the fields. Here and there were seen the remains of our comrades of the morning, their lifeless bodies stripped by vandal rebels of almost every garment. They lay like specters in the pale moonlight; here, still in death, under a cluster of bushes, was stretched a group; there, by the side of a wall, a row of inanimate bodies marked a spot where brave men had fallen at their posts; in the ravine where the little creek wound its way, and beneath the boughs of the chestnut trees of the grove, many slept their last sleep. Among our camps, the spades of the pioneers were heard as they hollowed out the shallow graves; and as we threw ourselves upon the ground to rest, we mourned for our comrades, and we rejoiced for our victory.

Sad, sad it was to think of the noble ones who had left us. Never again were we to see the form of the great-hearted Bidwell at the head of his brigade. We remembered his heroic bravery in all the terrible fights of those bloody days, from the Rapidan to Petersburgh; we thought of him when, at Winchester and Fisher Hill, he directed the movements of his brigade with such consummate coolness and skill; we remembered his cordial smile and friendly words, and then we

After the Rebels shot down two of the 77th's colorbearers in rapid succession, Gilbert F. Thomas (above, right) seized and carried the banners until he, too, was brought down by enemy fire. A blacksmith by trade, Thomas had risen through the ranks and was serving as the regimental adjutant when he was killed. Captain Martin Lennon (right) of the 77th, a native of Saratoga, fell mortally wounded during the action and died 12 days later.

thought of his heroism in the morning, and our hearts were heavy to think that he was gone.

Adjutant Thomas, too, had left us; our noble, beautiful boy. Could he have died a grander death had he been spared longer? Could his last words have been better chosen had he expired in the embrace of loved ones at home? "Forward, men; forward!" Were they not grand dying words? Rest, brother; thy death was as grand as thy life was lovely.

Lennon's bright eye must soon close forever. We should never again hear his hearty laugh or listen to his sparkling wit. He had fallen as a hero falls, and his life had been the life of a hero and patriot. Belding and Tabor, too, brave captains of brave men, each had fallen in advance of his friends.

A prominent citizen of Buffalo, Brigadier General Daniel D. Bidwell was mortally wounded during the midmorning stand of Getty's VI Corps division in Middletown's cemetery. Bidwell had just ridden forward to rally his brigade when a Confederate shell exploded overhead, tearing away his shoulder and puncturing a lung.

MAJOR ROBERT R. HUTCHINSON
STAFF, MAJOR GENERAL STEPHEN D. RAMSEUR

A native of Charlottesville, Hutchinson graduated from the University of Virginia in 1859 and then moved to St. Louis to practice law. With the outbreak of war he joined a Confederate Missouri unit but soon transferred to the staff of General John S. Bowen, where he served until his capture at Vicksburg in 1863. After being exchanged, Hutchinson came east, serving under Rodes and then Ramseur, to whose wife he wrote this letter following the general's death.

Near Strasburg, Va., October 20, 1864.

Mrs. S. D. Ramseur, Milton, N.C.:

Dear Madam: I do not know how to write to you; how to express my deep sympathy in your grievous affliction; but the Christian soldier who has gone before us to that other world has asked me to do it, and I must not shrink from the performance of this duty, however painful. I am writing by the side of him whose last thought was of you and his God, his country and his duty. He died this day at twenty-seven minutes past 10 o'clock A.M., and had at least the consolation of having by his side some who wore the same uniform and served in the same holy cause as himself. His last moments were peaceful; his wounds were painful, but his hope in Christ led him to endure *all* patiently. He received his mortal wound yesterday afternoon (October 19th) between the hours of 5 and 6 P.M. at the post of honor and of danger, where he always was. Our troops had fallen back a short distance but had reformed, and were stubbornly contesting a position on a hill which the enemy attacked from three sides. He exposed himself to every shot, cheering and encouraging all. I was not far from him when I saw his horse shot; he procured another, which was shot also, and immediately after he received his fatal wound (the second), all in the space of a very few minutes. I ran over to him, got some men, and bore him to the rear, your brother joining us on the way. I then went off after an ambulance, found it, but saw on returning with it that he had been left, as I thought, in the enemy's lines. This fear was soon after dissipated, however, by seeing him on Captain Randolph's horse, the captain running along side and supporting him. We got him then to the ambulance I had brought up. I thought he was safe then, not knowing how dangerous was his wound, and remained with the rear guard. When I was subsequently captured by the enemy's cavalry, I was carried to General Sheridan's headquarters, and learning that General Ramseur had been captured, asked and obtained permission to remain with him. The road had been blocked up by wagons, causing a delay, that gave the enemy time to get up and take him prisoner, just south of Strasburg. Many of his former friends (West Pointers) called to see him yesterday and to-day, and offered every assistance in their power, General Sheridan among the number. He was taken to General Sheridan's headquarters and made as comfortable as circumstances would permit. Dr. James Gillespie (Cutshaw's battalion of artillery), a Confederate surgeon, assisted by the enemy's surgeons, attended to him and did all that could be done under the circumstances. He suffered a good deal from his wound, the ball having entered his right side, penetrating the right and

left lung, and lodging near the left side. But the end was peaceful and quiet. He spoke continually of you, and sent very many messages to his family, but above all, to his wife. He told the ambulance driver to tell General Hoke that he "died a Christian and had done his duty." He told me to "give his love and send some of his hair to his darling wife"; and often wished he could "see his wife and little child before he died." He told me to tell you he had a "firm hope in Christ, and hoped to meet you hereafter." He died as became a Confederate soldier and a firm believer.

I inclose the lock of hair he desired sent you.

After the grievously wounded Ramseur was captured by Federal cavalry, he was brought to Belle Grove, the bluestone manor house that was serving as Sheridan's headquarters. In this James Taylor sketch Ramseur is shown lying on his deathbed in the mansion's library, attended by Confederate surgeon James Gillespie and Major Hutchinson. Before he died, leaving behind a newborn he would never see, the 27-year-old Ramseur was visited by several friends from his West Point days, among them General Custer.

LIEUTENANT GENERAL JUBAL A. EARLY
COMMANDER, ARMY OF THE VALLEY

Early scathingly blamed what he termed the poor discipline of his officers and men as the main reason for the defeat at Cedar Creek, a conviction he made abundantly clear in this message to his troops three days after the battle. Although some soldiers shared his opinion, this letter provoked, in the words of Clement Evans, "the deepest resentment" among most of his men, who believed that inept leadership on Early's part had played an equally prominent role in the rout.

Head Quarters Valley District
October 22d, 1864.
Soldiers of the Army of the Valley:
I had hoped to have congratulated you on the splendid victory won by you on the morning of the 19th at Bell Grove, on Cedar Creek, when you surprised and routed two corps of Sheridan's Army and drove back several miles the remaining Corps, capturing 18 pieces of Artillery, 1500 prisoners, a number of colours, a large quantity of small arms and many wagons and ambulances, with the entire camps of the two routed Corps; but I have the mortification of announcing to you, that, by your subsequent misconduct, all the benefits of that victory were lost and a serious disaster incurred. Had you remained steadfast to your duty and your colours, the victory would have been one of the most brilliant and decisive of the war,—you would have gloriously retrieved the reverses at Winchester and Fisher's Hill and entitled yourselves to the admiration and gratitude of your country. But many of you, including some commissioned officers, yielded to a disgraceful propensity for plunder, deserted your colours to appropriate to yourselves the abandoned property of the enemy and subsequently those who had previously remained at their post, seeing their ranks thinned by the absence

Sergeant Peter B. Boarts (above, left) of the 22d Iowa, part of Colonel Edward L. Molineux's brigade of the XIX Corps, was slightly wounded in the right leg at Cedar Creek. Two days later, he wrote a letter (first page shown at left) to his parents describing the battle. Near the end of the letter, Boarts colorfully summed up the Federal counterattack, saying, "When we got the rebs started we made them travel." But he also admitted that among hard battles, Cedar Creek "beats them all." Boarts, who also fought at Port Gibson and Vicksburg, mustered out in July 1865.

of the plunderers, when the enemy, late in the afternoon, with his shattered columns made but a feeble effort to retrieve the fortunes of the day, yielded to a needless panic and fled the field in confusion, thereby converting a splendid victory into a disaster. Had any respectable number of you listened to the appeals made to you and made a stand even at the last moment, the disaster would have been averted and the substantial fruits of victory secured,—but under the insane dread of being flanked and a panic stricken terror of the enemy's cavalry, you would listen to no appeal, threat or order, and allowed a small body of cavalry to penetrate to our train and carry off a number of pieces of Artillery and wagons which your disorder left unprotected. You have thus obscured that glorious fame won in conjunction with the gallant men of the Army of Northern Virginia who still remain proudly defiant in the trenches around Richmond and Petersburg.—Before you can again claim them as comrades you will have to erase from your escutcheons the blemishes which now obscure them, and this you can do if you will but be true to your former reputation, your country and your homes. You who have fought at Manassa, Richmond, Sharpsburg, Fredericksburg, Chancellorsville, Gettysburg, and from the Wilderness to the Banks of James River, and especially you who were with the immortal Jackson in all his triumphs are capable of better things. Arouse yourselves then to a sense of your manhood and an appreciation of the sacred cause in which you are engaged. Yield to the mandates of discipline—resolve to stand by your colours in future at all hazards and you can yet retrieve your reputation and strike effective blows for your country and its causes. Let every man spurn from him the vile plunder gathered on the field of the 19th, and let no man whatever his rank, whether combatant or non-combatant, dare exhibit his spoils of that day. They will be the badges of his dishonor, the insignia of his disgrace. The officer who pauses in the career of victory to place a guard over a sutler's wagon for his private use is as bad as the soldier who halts to secure for himself the abandoned clothing or money of flying foe, and they both sell the honour of the Army and the blood of their country for a paltry price. He who follows his colours into the ranks of the enemy in pursuit of victory, disclaiming the miserable passion for gathering booty, comes out of the battle with his honour untarnished and, though barefooted and ragged, is far more to be envied than he that is laden with rich spoils gathered in the trail of his victorious comrades.

There were some exceptions to the general misconduct on the afternoon of the 19th, but it would be difficult to specify them all. Let those who did their duty be satisfied with the consciousness of having done it, and mourn that their efforts were paralized by the misbehaviour of others. Let them be consoled to some extent by the reflection that the enemy has nothing to boast on his part. The Artillery and wagons taken were not won by his valour. His camps were destroyed, his army terribly shattered and demoralized, his losses far heavier than ours even in proportion to the relative strength of the armies, his plans materially impeded and he was unable to pursue by reason of his crippled condition. Soldiers of the Army of the Valley! I do not speak to you in anger. I wish to speak in kindness though in sorrow—my purpose is to show you the causes of our late misfortune and point out the way to avoid similar ones in the future and ensure success to our arms. Success can only be secured by the enforcement and observance of the most rigid discipline—officers, whatever their rank, must not only give orders but set the example by obeying them and the men must follow that example.

Fellow Soldiers: I am ready to lead you again in defence of our common cause, and I appeal to you by the remembrance of the glorious career in which you have formerly participated, by the woes of your bleeding country, the ruined homes and devastated fields you see around you, the cries of anguish which come up from the widows and orphans of your dead comrades, the horrors which await you and all that is yours in the future if your country is subjugated, and your hopes of freedom for yourselves and your posterity, to render a cheerful and willing obedience to the rules of discipline, and to shoulder your muskets again with the determination never more to turn your backs on the foe, but to do battle like men and soldiers until the last vestiges of the footsteps of our barbarous and cruel enemies is erased from the soil they desecrate and the independence of our country is firmly established. If you will do this and rely upon the protecting care of a just and merciful God all will be well, you will again be what you once were, and I will be proud to lead you once more to battle.

J. A. Early, Lt. Gen'l.

CAPTAIN JESSE C. WRIGHT
17TH MISSISSIPPI INFANTRY, MOODY'S BRIGADE

Moody's Mississippians suffered heavily at Cedar Creek, losing 184 out of 500 men taken into battle that morning. Wright was wounded in the left leg during the fighting at Spotsylvania in May 1864 and had only returned to his unit in August. A few days after Cedar Creek he wrote this letter to the father of one of his men killed in the battle. Wright was captured at Sayler's Creek the following April and held at the Johnson's Island prison camp until June.

"I have chosen this hour for the purpose of informing you of the death of your son A. J. Byers."

Camp 17th Miss. Regt.
New Market, Va., Oct 24th, 1864
Col. Amzi Byers,

I have chosen this hour for the purpose of informing you of the death of your son A. J. Byers, who was killed in battle on the 19th inst., near Strawsburg, Va. He was shot through the heart and died instantly. I don't suppose he ever spoke after he was shot. There was no one of the company near him at the time but found him in a short time afterwards. We got his pocket book and what money he had besides other articles of clothing and will send everything with Gilbert as soon as an opportunity presents itself.

His loss is very much felt by every member of his company. He was a friend that I highly prized. He had never gave me any trouble, allways being at his post of duty, and I humbly trust he has found a home in heaven. He had been quite a moral man. I don't think he ever swore any at all and think he had become very much devoted to Christ. I trust God will comfort the hearts of you and your berieved family and friends. "Oh" this is a cruel war and I feel that we should all consecrate our hearts to God for we are liable to be cut down by his will . . . by our enemys . . . at any time.

Almuth has allways acted very gallantly on every field and has shown to the world that his whole soul was in the cause. When we first attacked the enemy they were completely surprised and routed. We drove them six miles, captured their encampment with everything. They had eighteen pieces of artillery among the rest, but late in the afternoon the federals attacked our lines and the Divisions on our left and right gave way and fell back in confusion. And of course our Division followed but my Brigade rallied behind a rock fence and checked the whole army, and I did hope that we would retrieve the fortunes of the day, but soon the enemy flanked us and we left the whole of the ground in the hands of the enemy with the loss of 12 pieces of artillery, a few wagons and some

prisoners. Our loss was very light. We captured twelve thousand prisoners and brought them off safe.

There is something due Almuth by the Government which I will collect if you will forward me the power of Attorney. My kind regards to your family. If I can do anything for you I will be happy to serve you.

Private John Alemeth Byers enlisted in Company H, the "Panola Vindicators," of the 17th Mississippi in 1861. Sick with measles and jaundice, he recovered in time to be wounded at Second Manassas. Wounded again and captured at Gettysburg, Byers returned to his unit in the summer of 1864 only to fall at Cedar Creek.

"I verily believe they were stampeded by a vastly inferior force."

LIEUTENANT JOHN T. GAY
4TH GEORGIA INFANTRY, COOK'S BRIGADE

In this October 25 letter to his wife, Gay echoed Early's harsh opinion of the Army of the Valley's performance and was probably not alone in finding fault with "every other brigade" but his own. Wounded and captured at Antietam, Gay was hospitalized for much of the war. He fell ill in March 1865 and died a month later in Richmond.

$\mathcal{I}$ have thought for the last three days that I ought to write to you, but have been just in that state of perplexity and indescission which has rendered me perfectly inadequate to the task. The fact is, the recent disaster which has befallen our army was in itself so disgraceful & mortifying that I have scarcely done anything since but think and O, what thoughts! enough to run any mind half crazy. Just to think that this, the 2d Corps of Lee's army, once the pride & admiration of the confederacy, could have degenerated in so short a time as to merit the scorn & contempt of the whole world; and yet it is only just, that it should be so stigmatized, for such *dastardly cowardice* was never displayed on any battle field, as this corps exhibited on the afternoon of the 19th inst. I never believed that Southern troops could so degrade themselves. Had they been beaten and forced back by overwhelming numbers, the stampede could have been looked upon with some degree of leniency, but such was not the case, for I verily believe they were stampeded by a vastly inferior force, in point of numbers, and

a force too that had been badly whiped & put to flight by them in the morning. The people and the press may say and write all sort of slanderous things about Genl Early, but they are unmerited, for I cannot conceive that he or his Generals were atall to blame for the disaster unless it was for being too lenient. . . . Never was a battle better planned or fought than that of which I write, and had the troops acted with one spark of gallantry or patriotism, there would have been recorded, even now, in our favor, one of the grandest victories of the war.

It is not for my individual act of my own, or for any member of my co, that I blush, for no stain rests upon the character of any one of us, nor is our brigade atall responsible for the misfortune of that day. Tis true, had we retained our organization and have come off the field in good order, the more honor would have been ours, but how were we to keep up any organization when every over brigade was running helter skelter? Such a thing would have been impossible.

PRIVATE ABEL CRAWFORD
61ST ALABAMA INFANTRY, BATTLE'S BRIGADE

Organized in 1863, Crawford's regiment served along the gulf coast until joining Lee's army in time for the opening of the 1864 Virginia campaigns. In this letter written a month after Cedar Creek, Crawford expresses feelings shared by many of his weary but still unbeaten fellow Confederates. Crawford survived the last grim months of the war, returned to his wife Dora in Cotton Valley, Alabama, and fathered 10 children. He died in 1923 at the age of 79.

$\mathcal{C}$amp Near New Market Va Nov. 16—1864
Dear Dora—
Though it Seems that I am never going to hear from you again, still I have hopes enough to continue writing—I have not received a letter from you since the last of September—The last one that I received came by Mr. Jackson I have been daily looking for a letter for the last month, but I am still daily disappointed—I know not the cause but am Satisfied you have written often but they have not reached me— . . . I have written to you so often without any answer that I scarcely Know what to write—I have no news at all—We are expecting to move back up the Valley towards Staunton—It is also rumored in Camp that one Division of our Corps is going to Mobile—You can give it its due credit—I dont give it much though it is believed that we are going back toward Staunton for the purpose of going into winter quarters—I hope

it is so—I think it is full time we were getting into winter quarters— The weather is getting very cold and the Soldiers generally are thinly clad, though I believe I have a plenty with the exception of an over- coat. . . . Lincoln is elected and has called for one million Volunteers and of course he intends to carry on the war by calling out that many men therefore it seems that we will have to endure the hardships of another four years war if any of us should survive that long, but I am in hopes that something will turn up so as to prevent any more fighting, for I am really tired of it, but if the war goes on there will be no alterna- tive but to fight it out, but God grant that another gun may never be fired but that just and honorable peace may be restored to our country and that we all may Soon arrive at home in Safety.

Not long after Cedar Creek, one of the last tragic episodes of the campaign was played out. In early November the Rebel partisan commander Mosby ordered the execution of seven captured Federal cavalrymen in retaliation for the execution of seven of his men carried out earlier by Sheridan's cavalry. In this Taylor drawing, prisoners from the Michigan Brigade draw lots to see who will be among the unlucky seven. One survivor recalled, "Along that line I saw bowed heads and lips moving in silent prayer." In the end, Mosby's men botched the execution, and only three Yankees were hanged. Two were shot but survived, and two others escaped.

ACKNOWLEDGMENTS

The editors wish to thank the following for their valuable assistance in the preparation of this volume:

Deborah Basham, West Virginia State Archives, Charleston; James Baughman, U.S. Army Military History Institute (USAMHI), Carlisle Barracks, Pa.; Marvin Berg, Middleburg, Va.; Beth Bilderbach, South Caroliniana Library, University of South Carolina, Columbia; Barbara Blakey, Virginia Military Institute Museum, Lexington; Thomas C. Bradshaw, Virginia Military Institute Museum, Lexington; Scott Burgard, York, Pa.; Ellen Callahan, New Jersey State Archives, Trenton; Eric Campbell, Gettysburg National Military Park, Gettysburg, Pa.; Kerry Chartkoff, Michigan State Capitol Building, Lansing; Pam Cheney, USAMHI, Carlisle Barracks, Pa.; Ann Christiansen, Minnesota Historical Society, St. Paul; Tom DuClos, New York Division of Military and Naval Affairs, Albany; Gary L. Ecel-barger, Sterling, Va.; Tom Fife; Harrisonburg, Va.; Keith Gibson, Virginia Military Institute Museum, Lexington; Cyndy Gilley, Do You Graphics, Woodbine, Md.; Gil Gonzalez, Rutherford B. Hayes Presidential Center, Fremont, Ohio; Randy W. Hacken-burg, USAMHI, Carlisle Barracks, Pa.; Barbara Hall, Hagley Museum and Library, Wilmington, Del.; Travis Haymaker, Win-chester, Va.; Kevin Hershberger, Gloucester Point, Va.; Earl M. Hess, USAMHI, Carlisle Barracks, Pa.; Terri Hudgins, Museum of the Confederacy, Richmond; Mary Ison and Staff, Library of Congress, Washington, D.C.; Diane Jacob, Virginia Military Institute Archives, Lexington; Audrey Johnson, Library of Virginia, Richmond; Roger Keller, Hagerstown, Md.; David Keough, USAMHI, Carlisle Barracks, Pa.; Robert E. L. Krick, Richmond; Bill LaFevor, Bill LaFevor Photography, Nashville; Paul Loane, Cherry Hill, N.J.; Mike McAfee, Newburgh, N.Y.; Steve Massen-gill, North Carolina Division of Archives and History, Raleigh; Sue Miller, *Civil War Times Illustrated,* Harrisburg, Pa.; Charles Morris, West Virginia Division of Culture and History, Charleston; Judy Morrison, California State Capitol Museum, Sacramento; Louis Netherland, Rogersville, Tenn.; Dorothy Olsen, Georgia State Capitol Museum, Atlanta; Nicholas P. Picer-no, Springfield, Vt.; Ann Marie Price, Virginia Historical Society, Richmond; Jennie Rathbun, Harvard University, Cambridge, Mass.; Ben Ritter, Winchester, Va.; Ann Sindelar, Western Reserve Historical Society, Cleveland; Dr. Richard Sommers, USAMHI, Carlisle Barracks, Pa.; Larry M. Strayer, Dayton; Allan L. Tischler, Winchester, Va.; William Turner, La Plata, Md.; Lee Vivrette, Library of Virginia, Richmond; Pamela Webster, Histori-cal Society of Pennsylvania, Philadelphia; Michael J. Winey, USAMHI, Carlisle Barracks, Pa.; Frank Wood, Alexandria, Va.

PICTURE CREDITS

The sources for the illustrations are listed below. Credits from left to right are separated by semicolons, from top to bottom by dashes.

Dust jacket: front, National Archives, Neg. No. III-B-497; rear, Roger D. Hunt Collection at the U.S. Army Military History Insti-tute (USAMHI), copied by A. Pierce Bounds.

All calligraphy by Mary O'Brian/Inkwell, Inc.

6, 7: Map by Paul Salmon. 8: Virginia Military Institute Ar-chives, Lexington. 11: Map by R. R. Donnelley & Co., Carto-graphic Services, overlay by Time-Life Books. 16: Painting by E. F. Andrews, Kentucky Museum, Western Kentucky University, Bowling Green, photographed by Bill LaFevor—New Market Battlefield State Historical Park, Hall of Valor Museum, New Market, Va., photographed by Larry Sherer. 18: National Archives, Neg. No. III-B-6144; from *The End of an Era*, by John Sergeant Wise, Thomas Yoseloff, New York, 1965. 19: Virginia Military Institute Archives, Lexington. 21: Map by R. R. Donnelley & Co., Cartographic Services. 22: Firelands Gallery Collection, copied by M. L. Burr—from *The New Market Campaign*, by Edmund Ray-mond Turner, Whittet & Shepperson, Richmond, 1912. 23: New Market Battlefield State Historical Park, Hall of Valor Museum, New Market, Va., photographed by Larry Sherer. 25: Massachu-setts Military Order of the Loyal Legion and the U.S. Army Mili-tary History Institute (MASS-MOLLUS/USAMHI), copied by A. Pierce Bounds. 26: From *The Battle of New Market*, by William C. Davis, Doubleday & Co., Garden City, N.Y., 1975—Virginia Military Institute Museum, Lexington. 27: MASS-MOLLUS/ USAMHI, copied by A. Pierce Bounds—courtesy John L. Heat-wole. 28: Virginia Military Institute Museum, Lexington; New Market Battlefield State Historical Park. 29: Virginia Military Institute Archives, Lexington; New Market Battlefield State His-torical Park—Nicholas Picerno Collection. 30: Gil Barrett Collec-tion at the USAMHI, copied by A. Pierce Bounds. 31: Library of Congress, Neg. No. LC-B8172-1820. 32: Roger D. Hunt Collec-tion at the USAMHI, copied by A. Pierce Bounds—Society of Port Republic Preservationists, Port Republic, Va., photographed by Larry Sherer. 33: William A. Turner Collection; courtesy *Civil War Times Illustrated.* 34: Courtesy Bob Walter; courtesy *Civil War Times Illustrated.* 35: Gil Barrett Collection at the USAMHI, copied by A. Pierce Bounds. 36: Massachusetts Historical Society, Boston—L. M. Strayer Collection. 37: From *Confederate Military History*, edited by Clement A. Evans, Confederate Publishing Company, Atlanta, 1899. 39: Museum of the Confederacy, Rich-mond, photographed by Larry Sherer—New York Division of Military and Naval Affairs, Albany, photographed by Randall Perry. 41: Washington & Lee University, University Library, Spe-cial Collections, Ellinor Gadsden Papers; MASS-MOLLUS/ USAMHI, copied by A. Pierce Bounds. 43: Virginia Military Insti-tute Archives, Lexington; Virginia Military Institute Museum, Lexington, photographed by Larry Sherer. 44: Courtesy Hagley Museum and Library, Wilmington, Del. 45: West Virginia Divi-sion of Culture and History, Charleston. 46: Library of Congress, Maps Division, photographed by Larry Sherer. 47: William A. Turner Collection. 48: Roger D. Hunt Collection at the USAMHI, copied by A. Pierce Bounds; L. M. Strayer Collection, copied by Bill Patterson. 50, 51: Library of Congress, Manuscript Division, Jubal Early Papers, container 18 (2)—Mary Baldwin Col-lege, Staunton, Va. 52: Courtesy Rachel Covington Hassett, pho-tographed by David Plank. 53: L. M. Strayer Collection, pho-tographed by Bill Patterson. 54: Museum of the Confederacy, Richmond, copied by Katherine Wetzel. 55: Library of Congress, Manuscripts Division. 57: Map by William L. Hezlep. 58: Library of Congress, Neg. No. LC-BH82-3804. 59: William A. Turner Collection—from the collections of the Monmouth County His-torical Association Library and Archives, Freehold, N.J. 60: National Archives, Neg. No. III-B-1789; courtesy Russell W. Hicks Jr., photographed by Henry Mintz. 61: USAMHI, copied by A. Pierce Bounds. 63: Painting by Milner Benedict, Georgia State Capitol, Office of Secretary of State Lewis Massey, Atlanta, photographed by Michael W. Thomas. 64: Frank and Marie-Thérèse Wood Print Collections, Alexandria, Va. 65: Courtesy John Carter Bradley, photographed by Henry Mintz. 66: Library of Congress; from *The Defenses of Washington*, by William V. Cox, printed for the officers and members of the Fort Stevens-Lincoln Military Park Association, 1910. 67: Courtesy Erick Davis. 68: Courtesy C. Paul Loane, photographed by Robert J. Laramie— L. M. Strayer Collection, copied by Bill Patterson. 69: Museum of the Confederacy, Richmond; from *Biographies of Representative Women of The South, 1861–1863*, Vol. 2, Margaret Wooten Collier, privately published, 1923. 70: West Virginia Division of Culture and History, Charleston. 71: L. M. Strayer Collection, copied by Bill Patterson. 72: Alabama Department of Archives and History, Montgomery. 73: Historical Society of Pennsylvania, Philadel-phia. 74: Courtesy Erick Davis. 75: National Archives, Neg. No. III-B-4691; courtesy Erick Davis, copied by Jeremy Ross. 76: Dave Zullo Collection at the USAMHI, copied by A. Pierce Bounds. 82: Courtesy Brian Pohanka; Library of Congress. 83:

Houghton Library, Harvard University, Cambridge, Mass.—from *Mosby's Rangers*, by James J. Williamson, Ralph B. Kenyon, New York, 1896, courtesy Dave Zullo. 84, 85: From *Mosby's Rangers*, by James J. Williamson, Ralph B. Kenyon, New York, 1896, courtesy Dave Zullo (2); Maryland Historical Society, Baltimore, courtesy Winchester-Frederick County Historical Society, Winchester, Va. 86: Houghton Library, Harvard University, Cambridge, Mass. 87: Western Reserve Historical Society, Cleveland; collection of Michael McAfee, photographed by Larry Sherer. 88: From the Moore Papers, #4618, Southern Historical Collection, Library of the University of North Carolina at Chapel Hill. 89: L. M. Strayer Collection, photographed by Bill Patterson; Library of Congress, Maps Division, photographed by Larry Sherer. 90: Courtesy North Carolina Division of Archives and History, Raleigh. 91: Western Reserve Historical Society, Cleveland. 93: Map by Walter W. Roberts. 94: From *Under the Old Flag*, by James Harrison Wilson, D. Appleton, New York, 1912; Roger D. Hunt Collection at the USAMHI, copied by A. Pierce Bounds. 95: Courtesy North Carolina Division of Archives and History, Raleigh; courtesy Mrs. Mary Wingfield Harris. 97: Library of Congress, Waud #423. 98: Museum of the Confederacy, Richmond. 99: Courtesy Vann Martin, photographed by Henry Mintz. 100: Library of Congress, Waud #753—James Hennessey Collection at the USAMHI, copied by A. Pierce Bounds. 101: James Hennessey Collection at the USAMHI, copied by A. Pierce Bounds. 102: Roger D. Hunt Collection at the USAMHI, copied by A. Pierce Bounds. 103: New Jersey State Archives, Department of State, Trenton. 104: Library of Congress, Waud #293. 105: Museum of the Confederacy, Richmond; courtesy Larry Williford, copied by Henry Mintz. 106: National Archives, Neg. No. 111-B-5277; Virginia Historical Society, Richmond. 107: Library of Congress, Waud #736. 108: From *Foreigners in the Confederacy*, by Ella Lonn, University of North Carolina Press, 1940. 109: MASS-MOLLUS/USAMHI, copied by A. Pierce Bounds. 110: Michigan Capitol Committee, photographed by Peter Glendinning; courtesy Roger D. Hunt— from *Personal and Historical Sketches and Facial History of and by Members of the Seventh Regiment Michigan Volunteer Cavalry,*

1862-1865, compiled by William O. Lee, published by 7th Michigan Cavalry Association, Detroit, facsimile reprint by Detroit Book Press, 1990. 111: Library of Congress, Waud #236. 112: From *Red, White, and Blue Badge*, by Penrose G. Mark, Aughinbaugh Press, Harrisburg, Pa., 1911, reprinted by Butternut and Blue, Baltimore, 1993—courtesy Ben Ritter. 113: Virginia Military Institute Museum, Lexington, photographed by Larry Sherer. 114: From *One of Jackson's Foot Cavalry*, by John H. Worsham, Neale, 1912. 115: Western Reserve Historical Society, Cleveland. 116: Western Reserve Historical Society, Cleveland—from *Hard Marching Every Day*, edited by Emil and Ruth Rosenblatt, University Press of Kansas, Lawrence, 1983. 117: Library of Congress, Waud #394. 118: Library of Congress, Maps Division, photographed by Larry Sherer. 119: MASS-MOLLUS/USAMHI, copied by A. Pierce Bounds. 120: Western Reserve Historical Society, Cleveland. 121: Courtesy Doug Bast/Boonsboro Museum of History, photographed by Larry Sherer—Virginia Military Institute Museum, Lexington, photographed by Larry Sherer. 122: Georgia Capitol Museum of the Georgia Office of Secretary of State. 123: Library of Congress, Waud #158—Edward A. Dowling III Collection at the USAMHI, copied by A. Pierce Bounds. 124: From *Life and Letters of Charles Russell Lowell*, by Edward W. Emerson, Houghton Mifflin, Boston, 1907. 125: Courtesy Jeffrey and Beverly Evans—Library of Congress, Waud #213. 126: Courtesy Carmelita P. Kammann (great-granddaughter); Estate of John W. Wayland, courtesy John L. Heatwole; Cook Collection, Valentine Museum, Richmond. 127: Library of Congress, Waud #214; Custer Battlefield Historical and Museum Association, Crow Agency, Mont., photographed by Dennis Sanders. 129, 130: Maps by Walter W. Roberts and William L. Hezlep. 132, 133: Library of Congress, Waud #730; from *History of the 121st New York State Infantry*, by Isaac O. Best, James H. Smith, Chicago, 1921, copied by Philip Brandt George. 134: L. M. Strayer Collection, photographed by Bill Patterson—MASS-MOLLUS/USAMHI, copied by A. Pierce Bounds. 136: Library of Congress; courtesy Anne Vestal-Miller, copied by Henry Mintz. 137: From *A Volunteer's Adventures*, by John William De Forest, edited by James H.

Croushore, Louisiana State University Press, Baton Rouge, 1996; National Archives, Neg. No. 111-B-4198. 138: USAMHI, copied by A. Pierce Bounds—from *History of the Eighth Regiment Vermont Volunteers, 1861-1865*, by George N. Carpenter, Press of DeLand and Barta, Boston, 1886. 139: Wendell W. Lang Jr. Collection at the USAMHI, copied by A. Pierce Bounds. 140: MASS-MOLLUS/USAMHI, copied by A. Pierce Bounds. 141: Courtesy C. Paul Loane, photographed by Robert J. Laramie—Fredericksburg and Spotsylvania National Military Park, photographed by Andy Franck and Karen Jones of High Impact Photography. 142: Roger D. Hunt Collection at the USAMHI, copied by A. Pierce Bounds. 143: Library of Congress, Waud #445. 144, 145: Painting by Julian Scott, Vermont State House, Montpelier, photographed by Henry Groskinsky. 146: Nicholas Picerno Collection. 147: From *The Long Arm of Lee*, Vol. II, by Crooper Wise, J. P. Bell, Lynchburg, Va., 1915, courtesy Kirk Denkler—MASS-MOLLUS/USAMHI, copied by A. Pierce Bounds. 148: Western Reserve Historical Society, Cleveland. 149: Georgia Capitol Museum of the Georgia Office of Secretary of State—from *History of the Forty-Ninth Virginia Infantry C.S.A.*, by Laura Virginia Hale and Stanley S. Phillips, S. S. Phillips, Lanham, Md., 1981. 150: William A. Turner Collection, photographed by Larry Sherer. 151: From *Fighting Rebels and Redskins: Experiences in Army Life of Colonel George B. Sanford, 1861-1892*, edited by E. R. Hagemann, University of Oklahoma Press, Norman, 1969. 152: Library of Congress, Waud #203. 154: Michael J. McAfee Collection—Division of Military and Naval Affairs, New York State Adjutant General Office, Albany, N.Y. and USAMHI, copied by A. Pierce Bounds. 155: MASS-MOLLUS/USAMHI, copied by A. Pierce Bounds. 156: Western Reserve Historical Society, Cleveland. 157: USAMHI, copied by A. Pierce Bounds—Manuscript Archives, USAMHI, copied by A. Pierce Bounds. 159: Courtesy Gettysburg National Military Park, copied by Lawrence K. Kinneman. 160: From *History of the Doles-Cook Brigade, Army of Northern Virginia, C.S.A.*, by Henry W. Thomas, Atlanta, 1903, copied by Philip Brandt George. 161: Western Reserve Historical Society, Cleveland.

BIBLIOGRAPHY

BOOKS

Beach, William Harrison:
  The First New York (Lincoln) Cavalry: From April 19, 1861, to July 7, 1865. New York: Lincoln Cavalry Association, 1902.
  "Some Reminiscences of the First New York (Lincoln) Cavalry." In *War Papers Being Read before the Commandery of the State of Wisconsin Military Order of the Loyal Legion of the*

United States. Vol. 2. Wilmington, N.C.: Broadfoot, 1993.
Beecher, Harris H. *Record of the 114th Regiment, N. Y. S. V.: Where It Went, What It Saw, and What It Did.* Norwich, N.Y.: J. F. Hubbard Jr., 1866.
Berkeley, Henry Robinson. *Four Years in the Confederate Artillery.* Ed. by William H. Runge. Chapel Hill: University of North Carolina Press, 1961.

Best, Isaac O. *History of the 121st New York State Infantry.* Chicago: James H. Smith, 1921.
Booth, George W. *Personal Reminiscences of a Maryland Soldier in the War between the States, 1861-1865.* Baltimore: Press of Fleet, McGinley and Co., 1898.
Buck, Samuel D. *With the Old Confeds.* Baltimore: H. E. Houck, 1925.

Carpenter, George. *The History of the 8th Vermont Volunteers.* Boston: Press of DeLand and Barta, 1886.

Cox, William R. "Major-General Stephen D. Ramseur: His Life and Character." In *Southern Historical Society Papers,* Vol. 18. Wilmington, N.C.: Broadfoot, 1990.

Cramer, John Henry. *Lincoln under Enemy Fire.* Baton Rouge: Louisiana State University Press, 1948.

De Forest, John William. *A Volunteer's Adventures.* Ed. by James H. Croushore. Baton Rouge: Louisiana State University Press, 1996.

Dickert, D. Augustus. *History of Kershaw's Brigade.* Wilmington, N.C.: Broadfoot, 1990 (reprint of 1899 edition).

Douglas, Henry Kyd. *I Rode with Stonewall.* Chapel Hill: University of North Carolina Press, 1968.

Evans, Clement Anselm. *Intrepid Warrior.* Comp. and ed. by Robert Grier Stephens Jr. Dayton: Morningside, 1992.

Fisk, Wilbur. *Hard Marching Every Day.* Ed. by Emil and Ruth Rosenblatt. Lawrence: University Press of Kansas, 1992.

Fitzsimons, Charles. "The Hunter Raid." In *Military Essays and Recollections: Papers Read before the Commandery of the State of Illinois, Military Order of the Loyal Legion of the United States.* Vol. 4. Wilmington, N.C.: Broadfoot, 1992 (reprint of 1907 edition).

Forsyth, George A. *Thrilling Days in Army Life.* New York: Harper & Brothers, 1900.

Gallaher, DeWitt Clinton. *A Diary Depicting the Experiences of DeWitt Clinton Gallaher in the War between the States while Serving in the Confederate Army.* Charleston, W.Va.: n.p., 1945.

Goodhart, Briscoe. *History of the Independent Loudoun Virginia Rangers.* Gaithersburg, Md.: Butternut Press, 1985 (reprint of 1896 edition).

Gordon, John B. *Reminiscences of the Civil War.* Dayton: Morningside, 1985 (reprint of 1903 edition).

Hewitt, William. *The History of the 12th West Virginia Volunteer Infantry.* N.p.: private printing, 1892.

Imboden, J. D. "Fire, Sword, and the Halter." In *Annals of the War: Written by Leading Participants North and South.* Dayton: Morningside, 1988.

Keyes, Charles M., ed. *The Military History of the 123d Regiment Ohio Volunteer Infantry.* Sandusky, Ohio: Register Steam Press, 1874.

Kidd, J. H. *Personal Recollections of a Cavalryman.* Grand Rapids: Black Letter Press, 1969.

Lee, William O., comp. *Personal and Historical Sketches and Facial History of and by Members of the Seventh Regiment Michigan Volunteer Cavalry, 1862–1865.* Detroit: Detroit Book Press, 1990.

Lincoln, Levi, comp. *A Memorial of William Sever Lincoln.* Worcester, Mass.: N.p., 1889.

Lowell, Charles Russell. *Life and Letters of Charles Russell Low-ell.* Boston: Houghton Mifflin, 1907.

McFarland, Moses. *The Eighth Vermont in the Battle of Cedar Creek.* Hyde Park, Vt.: Lamoille, 1897.

Mark, Penrose G. *Red, White, and Blue Badge.* Baltimore: Butternut and Blue, 1993 (reprint of 1911 edition).

Martin, David G., ed. *The Monocacy Regiment.* Highstown, N.J.: Longstreet House, 1987.

Michie, Peter Smith. *The Life and Letters of Emory Upton.* New York: D. Appleton, 1885.

Munford, T. T. "Reminiscences of Cavalry Operations: Operations under Rosser." In *Southern Historical Society Papers,* Vol. 13. Wilmington, N.C.: Broadfoot, 1990.

Nettleton, A. Bayard. "How the Day Was Saved at the Battle of Cedar Creek." In *Glimpses of the Nation's Struggle: Papers Read before the Minnesota Commandery of the Military Order of the Loyal Legion of the United States, 1887.* Vol. 1. Wilmington, N.C.: Broadfoot, 1992 (reprint of 1874 edition).

Nichols, G. W. *A Soldier's Story of His Regiment (61st Georgia).* Kennesaw, Ga.: Continental, 1961.

O'Ferrall, Charles T. *Forty Years of Active Service.* New York: Neale, 1904.

O'Reilly, Miles. *Baked Meats of the Funeral.* New York: Carleton, 1866.

Park, Robert E. "Diary of Captain Robert E. Park of the Twelfth Alabama Regiment." In *Southern Historical Society Papers,* Vol. 2. Wilmington, N.C.: Broadfoot, 1990.

Roe, Alfred Seelye. *The Ninth New York Heavy Artillery.* Worcester, Mass.: private printing, 1899.

Sanford, George B. *Fighting Rebels and Redskins.* Ed. by E. R. Hagemann. Norman: University of Oklahoma Press, 1969.

Stevens, George T. *Three Years in the Sixth Corps.* Albany, N.Y.: S. R. Gray, 1866.

Strother, David Hunter. *A Virginia Yankee in the Civil War.* Ed. by Cecil D. Eby Jr. Chapel Hill: University of North Carolina Press, 1961.

Thoburn, Joseph. "Hunters Raid, 1864." In *The Diary of Colonel Joseph Thoburn.* N.p.: Thomas Beer, 1914.

United States War Department:
The War of the Rebellion: A Compilation of the Official Records of the Union and Confederate Armies. Series 1, Vol. 37, 2 parts. Washington, D.C.: Government Printing Office, 1891.
The War of the Rebellion: A Compilation of the Official Records of the Union and Confederate Armies. Series 1, Vol. 43, 2 parts. Washington, D.C.: Government Printing Office, 1893.

Walker, Aldace F. *The Vermont Brigade in the Shenandoah Valley, 1864.* Burlington, Vt.: Free Press Association, 1869.

Wallace, Lewis. *Lew Wallace: An Autobiography,* 2 vols. New York: Harper & Brothers Publishers, 1906.

Wildes, Thos. F. *Record of the One Hundred and Sixteenth Regiment Ohio Infantry Volunteers in the War of the Rebellion.* San-dusky, Ohio: I. F. Mack & Bro., 1884.

Williamson, James J. *Mosby's Rangers: A Record of the Operations of the Forty-Third Battalion Virginia Cavalry.* New York: Ralph B. Kenyon, 1896.

Wilson, James Harrison. *Under the Old Flag.* Vol. 1. New York: D. Appleton, 1912.

Wise, John Sergeant. *The End of an Era.* Ed. by Curtis Carroll Davis. New York: Thomas Yoseloff, 1965.

Worsham, John H. *One of Jackson's Foot Cavalry.* Ed. by James I. Robertson Jr. Wilmington, N.C.: Broadfoot, 1987 (reprint of 1912 edition).

PERIODICALS

Anonymous. Article by a member of the 5th West Virginia Infantry. *Ironton* (W.Va) *Register,* September 29, 1864.

Berkeley, Carter F. "Augusta's Battle." *Staunton Vindicator* (Stauton, Va.), July 1864.

Bradwell, I. G.:
"The Battle of Fishers Hill." *Confederate Veteran,* September 1920.
"Early's Valley Campaign, 1864." *Confederate Veteran,* June 1920.
"First of Valley Campaign by General Early." *Confederate Veteran,* May 1911.

Burkholder, Newton. "The Barnburners." *Richmond Dispatch,* July 22, 1900.

Byers, John Alemeth. "The Whole World Was Full of Smoke . . .": The Civil War Letters of Private John Alemeth Byers, 17th Mississippi Infantry. *Military Images,* May-June 1988.

Crim, Mrs. E. C. "Tender Memories of the V.M.I. Cadets." *Confederate Veteran,* June 1926.

Evans, Thomas J. "Capture the Flag." *The Kepi,* December 1983-January 1984.

Freeman, Daniel B. "A Day's Skirmish." *National Tribune,* March 18, 1897.

Gales, Seaton. "Experiences with the Army in Virginia—Campaign of 1864." *Our Living and Our Dead* (Newbern, N.C.), February 25, 1874.

Gatch, Thomas B. "Recollections of New Market." *Confederate Veteran,* June 1926.

Henry, J. L. "First Tennessee Cavalry at Piedmont." *Confederate Veteran,* September 1914.

Howard, John Clarke. "Recollections of New Market." *Confederate Veteran,* February 1926.

McGarity, Abner Embry. "Letters of a Confederate Surgeon: Dr. Abner Embry McGarity, 1862-1865, part 3." *Georgia Historical Quarterly,* December 1945.

Mauzy, Richard. "Vandalism by General Hunter, 1864." *Augusta* (Va.) *History Bulletin,* Spring 1978.

Neilson, T. H. "The Sixty-Second Virginia—New Market." *Confederate Veteran,* February 1908.

Plecker, A. H. "Who Saved Lynchburg from Hunter's Raid?" *Confederate Veteran*, October 1922.

Setchell, George Case. "A Sergeant's View of the Battle of Piedmont." *Civil War Times Illustrated,* May 1963.

Shackleford, Fountain G. "My Recollections of the War." *Nicholas Chronicle* (Nicholas County, W.Va.), July 27, 1895.

OTHER SOURCES

Anonymous. Manuscript, #158, Box #22, Civil War Materials. Charlottesville: University of Virginia Library.

Boarts, Peter B. Papers. Earl M. Hess Collection. Carlisle Barracks, Pa.: U.S. Army Military History Institute.

Collier, Samuel P. Papers. Raleigh: North Carolina State Archives.

Comly, James. Diary. Columbus: Ohio Historical Society.

Cowart, Enoch L. Letter, n.d. Freehold, N.J.: Freehold Historical Society.

Crawford, Abel. Letter, September 22, 1864. Confederate Collection, Box 8f.35. Nashville: Tennessee State Library and Archives, Manuscript Division.

Forsberg, Augustus. Diary. Lexington, Va.: Washington and Lee University, Leyburn Library.

Gay, John T. Letter, October 25, 1864. Mary Barnard Nix Collection, ms. #20. Athens: University of Georgia, Special Collections.

Grimes, Bryan. Letter, June 18, 1864. Chapel Hill: University of North Carolina, Southern Historical Collection.

Hobson, Edwin Lafayette. Letter, October 23, 1864. Hobson Family Papers. Richmond: Virginia Historical Society.

Lee, Mary Greenhow. Diary. Winchester, Va.: Frederick County Historical Society, Handley Library.

Lewis, William Gaston. Letter, June 27, 1864. Chapel Hill: University of North Carolina, Southern Historical Collection.

McIlhenny, William A. "Disaster at New Market." Unpublished manuscript. *Civil War Times Illustrated* collection. Carlisle Barracks, Pa.: U.S. Army Military History Institute.

Moore, Samuel J. C. Papers, 1847-1937. Chapel Hill: University of North Carolina, Southern Historical Collection.

Ocker, Henry. Letter, June 25, 1864. Columbus: Ohio Historical Society.

Palmer, Jewett. Journal. Scott-Palmer Family Papers. Morgantown: West Virginia University.

Peyton, George Q., comp. "A Civil War Record for 1864-1865." Unpublished manuscript, 1929. Manassas, Va.: Bull Run Regional Library.

Ramseur, Stephen Dodson. Papers. Chapel Hill: University of North Carolina, Southern Historical Collection.

Ring, George P. Letter, July 27, 1864. New Orleans: Tulane University Library, Louisiana Historical Association Collection.

Root, Willie. Papers. Carlisle Barracks, Pa.: U.S. Army Military History Institute.

Watkins, Thomas J. Unpublished manuscript. William Alexander Papers. Durham, N.C.: Duke University, William R. Perkins Library.

Wells, George D. Letter, May 14, 1864. Greenville, S.C.: East Carolina University, Joyner Library.

Wright, Rebecca. Document from the Sheridan Papers. Washington, D.C.: Library of Congress, Manuscript Division.

INDEX

Numerals in italics indicate an illustration of the subject.

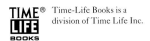

TIME® Time-Life Books is a
division of Time Life Inc.

TIME LIFE INC.
PRESIDENT and CEO: George Artandi

TIME-LIFE BOOKS
PRESIDENT: Stephen R. Frary
PUBLISHER/MANAGING EDITOR: Neil Kagan

VOICES OF THE CIVIL WAR

DIRECTOR OF MARKETING: Pamela R. Farrell

SHENANDOAH 1864

EDITOR: Paul Mathless
Deputy Editors: Kirk Denkler (principal), Harris J. Andrews,
Philip Brandt George
Art Directors: Ellen L. Pattisall (principal),
Barbara M. Sheppard
Associate Editor/Research and Writing: Annette Scarpitta
Senior Copyeditors: Judith Klein (principal),
Mary Beth Oelkers-Keegan
Picture Coordinator: Lisa Groseclose
Editorial Assistant: Christine Higgins

Initial Series Design: Studio A

Special Contributors: Gary W. Gallagher, Scott C. Patchan,
Brian C. Pohanka, Henry Woodhead (text); Charles F.
Cooney, John Heatwole, Robert Lee Hodge, Susan V. Kelly,
Beth Levin, Henry Mintz, Dana B. Shoaf, Kimberly D.
Timmerman (research); Roy Nanovic (index).

Correspondent: Christina Lieberman (New York).

Director of Finance: Christopher Hearing
Directors of Book Production: Marjann Caldwell,
Patricia Pascale
Director of Publishing Technology: Betsi McGrath
Director of Photography and Research: John Conrad Weiser
Director of Editorial Administration: Barbara Levitt
Production Manager: Marlene Zack
Quality Assurance Manager: James King
Chief Librarian: Louise D. Forstall

Consultants

Gary W. Gallagher is a member of the Department of History
at Pennsylvania State University. He has written or edited 17
books on the Civil War, most recently *The Confederate War,
The Wilderness Campaign,* and the forthcoming *Lee and His
Generals at War and in Memory.* He currently is completing a
biography of Jubal A. Early. A founder and first president of
the Association for the Preservation of Civil War Sites, he has
also been active in the field of historic preservation.

Scott C. Patchan is the author of *The Forgotten Fury: The Battle of Piedmont.* He has written dozens of articles and reviews
for *Civil War Magazine* and other periodicals and conducted
numerous battlefield tours in the Shenandoah Valley and
Northern Virginia. He currently is at work on a history of
Sheridan's Valley campaign. He is a past president of the
Bull Run Civil War Round Table and has also been active
in battlefield preservation.

J. Tracy Power is a historian at the South Carolina Department of Archives and History and the author of *Lee's
Miserables: Life in the Army of Northern Virginia from the
Wilderness to Appomattox,* to be published in 1998. His other
publications include articles in *Civil War History* and *Civil
War Times Illustrated* and contributions to the *Encyclopedia
of the Confederacy.*

First printing. Printed in U.S.A.
School and library distribution by Time-Life Education,
P.O. Box 85026, Richmond, Virginia 23285-5026.

TIME-LIFE is a trademark of Time Warner Inc. U.S.A.

Library of Congress Cataloging-in-Publication Data
Shenandoah 1864 / by the editors of Time-Life Books.
    p.   cm.—(Voices of the Civil War)
    Includes bibliographical references (p.   ) and index.
    ISBN 0-7835-4717-x
    1. Shenandoah Valley Campaign, 1864 (May-August).
    2. Shenandoah Valley Campaign, 1864 (August-November)
    I. Time-Life Books. II. Series.
E476.66.S54   1998
973.7'37—dc21   97-43711
                                                CIP